VIOLENCE IN THE FAMILY

GARLAND REFERENCE LIBRARY
OF SOCIAL SCIENCE
(VOL. 182)

VIOLENCE IN THE FAMILY
An Annotated Bibliography

Elizabeth Kemmer

GARLAND PUBLISHING, INC. • **NEW YORK & LONDON**
1984

Library of Congress Cataloging in Publication Data

Kemmer, Elizabeth Jane.
  Violence in the family.

  (Garland reference library of social science ; v. 182)
  Includes indexes.
  1. Family violence—Bibliography. I. Title.
II. Series.
Z5703.4.F35K45 1984   016.3628′2   83-48198
[HQ809]
ISBN 0-8240-9090-X (alk. paper)

Cover design by Laurence Walczak

Printed on acid-free, 250-year-life paper
Manufactured in the United States of America

To my parents, who always provided a loving home

Contents

Acknowledgments ix

Introduction xi

Annotated Bibliography 1

Author Index 177

Subject Index 187

Acknowledgments

Many people have contributed to this work. I am particularly indebted to Marie Ellen Larcada, Editor at Garland, for her guidance, patience and understanding throughout this project. I would also like to thank Pam Chergotis and Phyllis Korper, also of Garland, for their editorial and production assistance. Special thanks to Una McGinnis and Typesetting, Etc., in San Antonio, Texas, for the use of equipment and facilities to complete the production of the book. And to all of the people who provided support, encouragement and love over the long months of research and writing — Thank You, Gracias.

Introduction

Families have traditionally existed in worlds of their own. Laws and customs which governed behavior among the general population did not usually apply to the family as a unit and marriage and the family, especially among the middle class, have been essentially peaceful and sacred institutions. Until recently, this delicate balance has remained theoretically intact.

In the early 1970s, the problem of abuse within the family unit began to surface on a large scale, particularly among the lower class. Society acknowledged the existence of the problem, but tended to file it away with other problems of poorer communities. Interpersonal violence was considered a typically lower class phenomenon, and violence in the family was merely another reflection of this.

1975 was a significant year for the recognition of intrafamilial violence. The media began to treat the issue as a phenomenon which extended beyond class and race barriers. No longer was violence depicted as an essentially lower class characteristic, and incidents of intrafamilial violence, particularly wife and child abuse, were being reported from the suburbs as well as from the inner city.

Significant literature on family violence began to emerge during this period, although the scientific community was reluctant to recognize the problem as prevalent enough for study. Consequently, most of the literature appeared in the form of articles in popular magazines. It was not long, however, before family violence began to move out of the home. Previously viewed as a problem to be dealt with in the family unit itself, violence in the home was finally recognized as a social problem. This recognition provided the impetus for more concern and investigation of the issue. As a result, literature on marital violence emerged from all facets of society.

Most of the significant work in the area is descriptive as opposed to analytical, and there are few cross cultural and longitudinal studies available. These voids in the literature may be attributed to difficulties in obtaining data for study. Society's reluctance to acknowledge the prevalence of the problem may account for this. Also, the fact that violence in the family is often considered to be a private affair, stigma is attached to any public declaration of its occurrence. Thus, solutions and assistance must come from society as a whole if constructive work in the area of family violence is to be fruitful and progress.

This bibliography contains information published in English from 1960-1982. It is arranged alphabetically by author, or by the first significant word in the title if no author is given. A concise subject index and an author index follow the bibliography itself. Please note that the reference numbers in the indexes refer to entry numbers and not page numbers.

1. Abrams, Susan. "The Battered Husband Bandwagon." **Seven Days**, 2:20, September 29, 1981.

   Discusses the husband as the victim of marital violence.

2. "Abused Child." **Today's Education**, 63:40–43, January–February 1974.

   This general discussion of child abuse emphasizes the role of the school in prevention and outlines steps a school can take to aid in child abuse management.

3. Ackley, Dana C. "A Brief Overview of Child Abuse." **Social Casework**, 58:21–24, January 1977.

   Explores the reasons why some parents are abusive and points out the necessity of helping abusing parents.

4. Acton, William D., Jr. "Who Policies Child Abuse and Neglect on Military Enclaves Over Which the Federal Government Exercises Exclusive Juristiction?" **North Carolina Central Law Journal**, 8:261–67, Spring 1977.

   Discusses the Army Child Avocacy Program, developed by the United Army, which was designed to manage and prevent child abuse in military families. In addition, this program is examined in light of the North Carolina Child Abuse Reporting Law, which requires the reporting of all cases of child abuse and neglect to the local Department of Social Services. The applicability of the North Carolina law to a military base exclusively under federal juristiction is also explored.

5. Adelson, Lester. "The Battering Child." **The Journal of the American Medical Association**, 222(2):159–61, 1972.

   This study examines five cases of infants, all under one year old, who were killed by children eight years of age or younger. The victims did not show any signs of having been battered by adults. The author states that a child who perceives a person as a threat to this security, either within the family or outside, is capable of intense rage which may culminate in homicide.

6. _____. "Slaughter of the Innocents." **New England Journal of Medicine**, 264:1345–49, June 29, 1961.

   Upon examining forty-six homicide cases in which the victims were children, it was discovered that thirty-seven had been killed by a parent or other family member. The most common precipitating factors are discussed, and the perpetrators' reactions to the incidents are explored.

7. Adler, Lorraine. "Child Victims: Are They Also Victims of an Adversarial and Hierarchial Court System?" **Pepperdine Law Review**, 5:717–39, 1978.

1

Examines the court system's handling of child abuse cases. The significance of adjustments made within the system for the coordination of, and communication among, professional agencies which deal with child abuse is emphasized as focusing on the needs of the children involved.

8. Ahrens, Lois. "Battered Women's Refuges." **Fight Back!: Feminist Resistance to Male Violence**. Edited by Frederique Delacoste and Felice Newman. Minneapolis, Minnesota: Cleis Press, 1981, pp. 104–09.

Outlines the development of a shelter for battered women — the formative stages, the administration and staff choices, changes needed after opening, and the disintegration of the original center structure. The authors trace the center's transition from a collective to a hierarchical structure of a "professionalized" social service institution divorced from the community it was set up to service.

9. "Aid to Abused and Neglected Children." **Intellect**, 102:415, April 1974.

Describes a project developed in Los Angeles to assess the effects of readily available medical, legal and social services to abused children and their parents.

10. Alexander, Helen. "Long-Term Treatment." **The Battered Child**. Edited by C. Henry Kempe and Ray E. Helfer. Chicago: University of Chicago Press, 1980, pp. 288–96.

States that long-term treatment is essential to any adequate treatment program for child abuse and neglect, and that without on-going care, crisis intervention will have little effect on the situation. Describes some long-term plans such as crisis nurseries, lay therapists, parents groups and child day care, discussing also the difficulties involved in such programs. Examples from actual cases are used to illustrate factors involved in treatment, and subsequent results.

11. _____. "The Social Worker and the Family." **Helping the Battered Child and His Family**. Edited by C. Henry Kempe and Ray E. Helfer. Philadelphia: J.B. Lippincott Company, 1972, pp. 22–40.

Discusses the relationship between the social worker and the family in therapy. Ways in which parents seek help, establishing the therapist-patient relationship, the importance of trust, marital patterns and problems, parental ties between abusing parents and their own parents, and parent-child relationships are among the topics explored.

12. Alexander, Helen and others. "Residential Family Therapy." **The Abused Child: A Multidisciplinary Approach to Developmental Issues and Treatment**. Edited by Harold P. Martin. Cambridge, Massachusetts: Ballinger Publishing Company, 1976, pp. 235–50.

Discusses the treatment of abused children, their siblings, and their parents, focusing on the residential treatment process.

13. Alexander, Jerry. "Protecting the Children of Life-Threatening Parents." **Journal of Clinical Child Psychology**, 3:53-4, Summer 1974.

A statistical overview of child abuse is presented and recommendations are made for its prevention.

14. Allen, Letitia J. "Child Abuse: A Critical Review of the Research and the Theory." **Violence in the Family**. Edited by J.P. Martin. New York: John Wiley and Sons, 1978, pp. 43-79.

Focuses on the difficulties associated with defining child abuse, the quality of research in the area, and the role of existing theories in understanding abusive behavior.

15. Allen, Marilyn. "Child Maltreatment in Military Communities." **Juvenile Justice**, 26:11-20, May 1975.

Examines the problem of child abuse in military communities, outlining an effective program for its management on military installations.

16. Allott, Roger. "The District Attorney." **Helping the Battered Child and His Family**. Edited by C. Henry Kempe and Ray E. Helfer. Philadelphia: J.B. Lippincott Company, 1972, pp. 256-67.

States that ensuring the child's safety and welfare is the first priority of the District Attorney's office, and is also the standard on which that office bases all of its actions. The importance of maintaining continuous coordination between the various agencies involved in child abuse cases is emphasized, and basic procedures for the investigation of suspected child abuse cases are outlined.

17. Alvy, Kerby T. "On Child Abuse: Values and Analytic Approaches." **Journal of Clinical Child Psychology**, 4:36-7, Spring 1975.

The necessity of an expanded definition of child abuse which would include sociocultural forms of abuse is outlined.

18. _____. "Preventing Child Abuse." **American Psychologist**, 30:921-28, September 1975.

Explores the physical abuse of children, emphasizing the relationship between theoretical formulations of causes and prevention programs. The successful reinforcement of these programs as a step in raising public consciousness concerning abuse is also discussed.

19. American Humane Association. "Guidelines for Schools — Teachers, Nurses, Counselors, Administrators — to Help Protect Neglected and Abused Children." **The Battered Child**. Compiled by Jerome E. Leavitt. Morristown, New Jersey: General Learning Press, 1974, pp. 221-23.

that the responsibility of a teacher is to be alert to signs of child abuse and neglect, and emphasizes the importance of early case finding for management and future prevention. Details indicators of a child's need for protection, including the child's behavior, his appearance, and his attitude toward his parents. The role of child protective services is also discussed.

20. Andell, Eric G. "A Minor Has an Absolute Right to Sue His Parents for a Negligent Tort." **Houston Law Review**, 8(1):183–89, September 1970.

Focuses on the case of *Peterson v. City and County of Honolulu*, 462 P.2d 1007 (Hawaii 1970). The ruling in this case by the Hawaii Supreme Court states that a child who is injured by the negligence of his parent has the absolute right to bring suit.

21. Anderson, George M. "Child Abuse." **America**, 136:478–82, May 28, 1977.

Discusses child abuse as a consequence of traditional attitudes toward the roles of parents and children in the family. Foster homes are examined and their effectiveness as a solution is criticized. Examples of successful treatment programs are outlined.

22. _____. "Wives, Mothers and Victims." **America**, 137:46–50, July 30–August 6, 1977.

Discusses violence in American society as being rooted primarily in the family institution. Battering in general, the establishment of shelters in England, the role of the police intervention in family disputes, alcohol as a factor in family violence, and current and proposed legislation are among topics explored.

23. Anderson, William R. and R. Page Hudson. "Self-Inflicted Bite Marks in Battered Child Syndrome." **Forensic Science**, 7(1):71–74, 1976.

Upon examining the bite marks on a child abuse victim, it was revealed that the bite had been made by the victim himself. The significance of this phenomenon is discussed.

24. Anthony, E. James and Norman Kreitman. "Murderous Obsessions in Mothers Toward Their Children." **Parenthood: Its Psychology and Psychopathology**. Edited by E. James Anthony and Therese Benedek. Boston: Little, Brown and Company, 1970, pp. 479–98.

Examines information gained from a therapeutic study of forty women who had exhibited "murderous obsessions" toward their children. Symptoms and diagnostic types are discussed, and the women's histories and relationships with their families and husbands are explored. The psychodynamics of the murderous relationship and the treatment method for these patients are detailed. A bibliography of pertinent works is included.

25. Appleton, Peter L. "Ethological Methods for Studying the Behavior and Development of Young Children from Abusing Families." **The Abused Child: A Multidisciplinary Approach to Developmental Issues and Treatment**. Edited by Harold P. Martin. Cambridge, Massachusetts: Ballinger Publishing Company, 1976, pp. 129-37.

Examines the ethological method of study with particular reference to children from abusing families.

26. Areen, Judith. "Intervention Between Parent and Child: A Reappraisal of the State's Role in Child Neglect and Abuse Cases." **Georgetown Law Journal**, 63:887-937, March 1975.

Explores the role of the states in cases of child abuse and neglect. Current neglect standards are presented with an analysis, and an approach to reform is discussed from an historical perspective. A model neglect statute is examined, and commentary is offered on each provision.

27. Armstrong, Louise. "Blowing the Whistle on Child Abusers." **Woman's Day**, June 15, 1982, pp. 75 & 146-49.

Emphasizes the importance of people reporting suspected child abuse to the proper authorities. Guidelines to assist in deciding when to take action to protect a possible victim are outlined, and procedures for reporting abuse and neglect are provided.

28. Arnold, George L. and Jeanne L. Hurd. "Child Protection: A Suggested Role for Members of the Wyoming State Bar." **Land and Water Law Review**, 9:187-208, 1974.

Discusses the role of the legal profession in the solution of the problem of child abuse. A multidisciplinary approach to the management and prevention of abuse and neglect is suggested.

29. Arnold, Mildred. "Children in Limbo." **Public Welfare**, 25(3):221-28, July 1967.

Limbo is defined as a state of stagnation and isolation in which nothing is happening in a child's psychological growth and development, and nothing is being done to meet his needs. Cases of child abuse and neglect are among the various types examined. Factors contributing to children being in this state are discussed, and ways of bringing children out of limbo are outlined.

30. Arvanian, Ann L. "Dynamics of Separation and Placement." **Child Abuse: Intervention and Treatment**. Edited by Nancy B. Ebeling and Deborah A. Hill. Acton, Massachusetts: Publishing Sciences Group, Inc., 1975, pp. 117-22.

Explores the factors involved in decisions to place children in foster homes and possible results of this placement for the child and the family.

31. Asch, Stuart S. "Crib Deaths: Their Possible Relationship to Post-Partum Depression and Infanticide." **Journal of the Mount Sinai Hospital**, 35:214–20, 1968.

    Infanticide is discussed as a dangerous consequence of post-partum depression. It is theorized that a large proportion of crib deaths of unknown cause may actually be cases of covert infanticide due to post-partum depression in the infant's mother. The development of post-partum depression and psychosis in women, and the depressed mother's responses to her child are explored.

32. "Authorities Face Up to the Child Abuse Problem." **U.S. News and World Report**, 80:83–84, May 3, 1976.

    Efforts by various groups and agencies to reduce the incidence of child abuse are explored. Methods of treatment for abusers, damage suffered by victims, and new state legislation are among the issues discussed. It is suggested that new laws and approaches to the problem may reverse the upward trend of child abuse and neglect within the next few years.

33. Avery, Nancy C. "Viewing Child Abuse and Neglect as Symptoms of Family Dysfunctioning." **Child Abuse: Intervention and Treatment**. Edited by Nancy B. Ebeling and Deborah A. Hill. Acton, Massachusetts: Publishing Sciences Group, Inc., 1975, pp. 87–91.

    Discusses intervention and treatment in terms of two levels of dysfunction within the family: the individual interpersonal level and the family dynamic level.

34. Ayoub, Catherine and Donald R. Pfeifer. "An Approach to Primary Prevention: the 'At-Risk' Program." **Children Today**, 6:14–17, May–June 1977.

    Describes the functions and operations of a hospital's "at-risk" program for the detection and prevention of child abuse.

35. Badinter, Elisabeth. **Mother Love: Myth and Reality**. New York: Macmillan, 1981. 306 pp.

    Provides a detailed exploration of mother love, emphasizing the idea of the "maternal instinct" as persisting in today's society. Discussions of child abuse and neglect are included.

36. Baher, Edwina and others. **At Risk: An Account of the Work of the Battered Child Research Department, NSPCC**. London: Routledge and Kegan Paul, 1976. 246 pp.

    Discusses a study conducted by the National Society for the Prevention of Cruelty to Children. The subjects were families in which a child under four years of age was suspected of being a victim of non-accidental injury. Topics explored include injuries and problems of diagnosis, management of cases, protection of children, psychological characteristics of abusive parents and abused children, and an evaluation of progress in families toward a resolution of the problem. Recommendations for further study and ways to meet the needs of victims, their parents and the family unit are presented.

37. Bain, Katherine. "The Physically Abused Child." **The Battered Child.** Compiled by Jerome E. Leavitt. Morristown, New Jersey: General Learning Press, 1974.

Provides a general discussion of the medical aspects of child abuse with emphasis on reporting laws for physicians.

38. Bakan, David. **Slaughter of the Innocents.** San Francisco: Jossey-Bass Publishers, 1976. 128 pp.

Hypothesizes that child abuse is an "evolutionary mechanism" which controls population growth, and that when man understands what is "natural," he is able to modify the condition and thus manage it. The incidence of child abuse, the reasons why the public is reluctant to face the problem, an historical exploration of child abuse, and the significance of child abuse for population control are among the topics discussed within the framework of Bakan's hypothesis.

39. Baldwin, J.A. and J.E. Oliver. "Epidemiology and Family Characteristics of Severely Abused Children." **British Journal of Preventive and Social Medicine**, 29:205–21, December 1975.

Discusses the results of a study of severely abused children in Wiltshire, England. It was found that many of the children were born with some type of abnormality, be it a congenital birth defect, a premature birth, or illegitimacy. Specific characteristics of the childrens' families are presented and the most common types of injuries sustained by the children are mentioned.

40. Ball, Margaret. "Issues of Violence in Family Casework." **Social Casework**, 58:3–12, January 1977.

Discusses the work of the Family Service of Detroit and Wayne County caseworkers with child abuse. Case material is summarized, highlighting issues of violence and how they are dealt with by caseworkers.

41. Ball, Patricia G. and Elizabeth Wyman. "Battered Wives and Powerlessness: What Can Counselors Do?" **Victimology: An International Journal**, 2:545–52, 1977–78.

Techniques of feminist counseling for battered wives are reviewed. Female socialization, assumptions of feminist therapy, battered wives

Seligman's theory of learned helplessness, and the emotional and behavioral problems of victims are among the issues discussed.

42. Bamford, Frank N. "Medical Diagnosis in Non-Accidental Injury of Children." **Violence in the Family**. Edited by Marie Borland. Atlantic Highlands, New Jersey: Humanities Press, 1976, pp. 50–60.

    Focuses on the duties of the medical profession in the diagnosis of child abuse.

43. Banagale, Raul C. and Matilda S. McIntire. "Child Abuse and Neglect: A Study of Cases Reported to the Douglas County Child Protective Service from 1967–1973." **Nebraska Medical Journal**, 60:353-441, September 1975.

    Statistics concerning reported cases of child abuse in Omaha, Nebraska are presented. Factors contributing to child abuse were found to include the immaturity of parents, unemployment, alcohol and drug abuse, and financial and marital problems. The reluctance of physicians to report suspected child abuse and neglect is also explored.

44. Bard, E. Ronald. "Connecticut's Child Abuse Law." **Connecticut Bar Journal**, 48:260–78, September 1974.

    Following discussions of the incidence of child abuse, the theory and purpose of reporting laws, and social planning to meet the needs of the child, an analysis of Connecticut's Child Abuse Law is presented. In addition, recommendations are made for further legislative action in the area of child abuse.

45. _____. "To Heal the Wounded Family." **Human Ecology Forum**, 7(1):6–8, Summer 1976.

    Focuses on the shortage of child protective service workers in New York State, and the effect that this has on services. Various service options are discussed, and the difficulties of each are examined. Current and proposed legislation in the area of child abuse and family law is summarized, and the significance of the New York State Assembly working in conjunction with service professionals to find solutions to the problems of the family is stressed.

46. Bard, Morton. "Family Crisis Intervention: From Concept to Implementation." **Battered Women: A Psychosociological Study of Domestic Violence**. Edited by Marie Roy. New York: Van Nostrand Reinhold Company, 1977, pp. 172–92.

    Explains the concepts underlying the training of police for crisis intervention and discusses guidelines and problems involved in organizing such a program.

47. _____. "Family Intervention Police Teams as a Community

Health Resource." **Journal of Criminal Law, Criminology and Police Science** , 60(2):247-50, 1969.

Describes a program in which a local police department and an academic institution united to form a program of family crisis intervention. The advantages of a program of realistic police services for the community, and the psychological aspects for the police department's performance are reviewed, and the wider applications of such resources for other programs are examined.

48. _____. **The Function of the Police in Crisis Intervention and Conflict Management: A Training Manual**. Washington, D.C.: U.S. Department of Justice, Law Enforcement Assistance Administration, 1975.

Discusses crisis intervention and its implementation by the police. Methods for organizing field training programs, developing procedures, and actual cases are detailed.

49. _____. "The Study and Modification of Intra-Familial Violence." **The Control of Agression and Violence: Cognitive and Physiological Factors**. Edited by Jerome L. Singer. New York: Academic Press, 1971, pp. 149-64.

Presents statistics on intrafamily violence in New York City in 1965 and briefly summarizes a number of approaches to human aggression from various disciplines. States that violence is a "family affair" and to understand the origins of violence and agression, one must study the basic family unit. A program of police family crisis intervention in Harlem is described, emphasizing the need for effective change and innovation in existing social institutions to meet the unique needs of the community they serve.

50. Bard, Morton and Joseph Zacker. "Assaultiveness and Alcohol Use in Family Disputes: Police Perceptions." **Criminology**, 12:281-92, November 1974.

Discusses police intervention in family disputes which may develop into violent encounters, and examines the use of alcohol as a precipitating factor in assaultive behavior.

51. _____. "The Prevention of Family Violence: Dilemmas of Community Intervention." **Journal of Marriage and the Family**, 33:677-82, 1974.

Explores the problems involved in community intervention programs designed to prevent family violence. A program which was developed in one city to train police to deal with specific problems involved in the management of intrafamilial violence is described.

52. Barnes, Geoffrey B. and others. "Team Treatment for Abusive

Families." **Social Casework**, 55:600–11, December 1974.

Examines the team treatment approach to the problem of child abuse as it is employed by a Baltimore, Maryland hospital.

53. Barnett, Ellen R. and Leslie Landis. **Handbook for Abused Women**. Rockville, Maryland: National Clearinghouse for Domestic Violence, May 1981. 18 pp.

Provides a guide for the abused woman in order to understand what is happening to her, how it affects her and her family, and what alternatives are available for ending the abuse.

54. Barocas, Harvey A. "Urban Policemen: Crisis Mediators or Crisis Creators?" **American Journal of Orthopsychiatry**, 43(4):623–39, 1973.

Discusses police intervention in a crisis situation as intensifying rather than reducing the conflict. Ways of preventing this situation through psychological training are presented.

55. Bass, David and Janet Rice. "Agency Responses to the Abused Wife." **Social Casework**, 60:338–42, June 1979.

Discusses a study which hypothesized that agencies would view wife abuse as symptomatic of other family problems and not as a problem of importance in its own right. Results showed that most counselors tried to treat wife abuse as they treated other family problems, and that they did not know which specialized resources were available to deal with the problem. It is suggested that there must be integration among services in order to deal effectively with wife abuse.

56. "The Battered Baby Syndrome: Some Practical Aspects." **Medical Journal of Australia**, 2:231–32, August 17, 1974.

Explores the possibility of establishing a nationwide child abuse prevention system in Australia.

57. "Battered Child." **Good Housekeeping**, 178:18 + , May 1974.

Presents one woman's account of her efforts to help the abused child next door.

58. "Battered Families: A Growing Nightmare." **U.S. News and World Report**, 86:60–61, January 15, 1979.

Quotes statistics on violence in the home, including parental abuse of children, violence between siblings, spouse abuse, and abuse of parents by children. Programs for the prevention and treatment of family violence, along with specific problems involved, are discussed.

59. "The Battered Husbands." **Time**, 111:69, March 20, 1978.

Explores the incidence of husband battering and the characteristics of wives who are victims. Aid available to the victim is outlined.

60. "Battered Wives: Now They're Fighting Back." **U.S. News and World Report**, 81:47–48, September 20, 1976.

   Discusses the problem of wifebeating and efforts being made to combat it.

61. "Battered Women Conference." **Off Our Backs**, 6:4–5, December 1976.

   Discusses proceedings of a conference on battered women. Topics explored include why women are victims of battering and rape by men, factors which condone assaults on women in this society, and reasons why domestic violence is of low priority within the legal system.

62. Bean, Shirley L. "The Parent's Center Project: A Multi-Service Approach to the Prevention of Child Abuse." **The Battered Child**. Compiled by Jerome E. Leavitt. Morristown, New Jersey: General Learning Press, 1974, pp. 56–61.

   Describes the conception and operation of a group therapy program designed to aid parents in families where patterns of child abuse were developing. Treating parents through group therapy is discussed, and problems of operation are examined.

63. _____. "The Use of Specialized Day Care in Preventing Child Abuse." **Child Abuse: Intervention and Treatment**. Edited by Nancy B. Ebeling and Deborah A. Hill. Acton, Massachusetts: Publishing Sciences Group, Inc., 1975, pp. 137–42.

   Discusses the conception, purposes and operation of the day care center of the Parents' and Children's Service Program for Study and Prevention of Child Abuse.

64. "Beating Up Hubby: Husbands are Battered as Often as Wives; Overall Violence Index." **Human Behavior**, 7:60, November 1978.

   A study of the extent of violence employed by spouses during family fights showed that husband and wife came within one-half a point of each other on the researchers' overall violence index, and that wives were somewhat more persistently and "severely" violent.

65. Bechtold, Mary Lee. "Silent Partner to a Parent's Brutality." **School and Community**, 52(3):33, November 1965.

   Relates the history of an abused child and makes suggestions as to how professionals who come into contact with battered children can protect them from further abuse.

66. Beck, Connie and others. "Rights of Children: A Trust Model." **Fordham Law Review**, 46:669–78, March 1978.

   The rights of children in the legal system, educational system, and within the family are explored. Alternatives to a child staying with an abusing parent are presented.

67. Beckelman, Laurie. "Why the Cry of the Beaten Child Goes Unheard." **New York Times Magazine**, April 16, 1978, pp. 74-88.

Focuses on child abuse intervention. Among the topics discussed are what constitutes child abuse, problems facing someone who attempts to intervene in cases of child abuse, protection of the family's right to privacy, characteristics of abusive parents, and the work of professionals with child abuse. It is suggested that help must come on both societal and individual levels if prevention and management are to be successful.

68. Becker, J.V. and G.G. Abel. "Physical, Psychological, and Economic Victimization of Women." **Quarterly Journal of Corrections**, 1(4):18-24, Fall 1977.

Discusses the relationship between victimization of women and male supremacy in a sexist society. Various forms of victimization, including wife beating and sexual assault, are presented using case studies and statistics to illustrate the problem. It is suggested that a revision of the male dominated criminal justice system would aid in reducing cases of victimization.

69. Bedard, Virginia S. "Wife Beating." **Glamour**, 76:85-86, August 1978.

Examines the problem of wife beating using a case study. Factors which may lead to wife beating, why women stay with abusing husbands, and help for the battered wife are among the topics discussed.

70. Beer, Sally. "A Medical Social Worker's View." **Concerning Child Abuse: Papers Presented by the Tunbridge Wells Study Group on Non-Accidental Injury to Children**. Edited by Alfred White Franklin. Edinburgh: Churchill Livingstone, 1975, pp. 73-77.

Discusses the author's experiences in working with abusing families.

71. Beezley, Patricia and others. "Psychotherapy." **The Abused Child: A Multidisciplinary Approach to Developmental Issues and Treatment**. Edited by Harold P. Martin. Cambridge, Massachusetts: Ballinger Publishing Company, 1976, pp. 201-14.

Details a study which provided psychotherapy for abused children. The characteristics of the children, issues dealt with in therapy, results of therapy, and other methods of psychotherapeutic help for abused children are discussed.

72. Bell, David O. and others. "A Recommendation for Court-Appointed Counsel in Child Abuse Proceedings." **Mississippi Law Journal**, 46:1072-95, Fall 1975.

Following a general discussion of child abuse, a survey of existing child abuse legislation in the state of Mississippi is presented. Recommendations are made for reforming the existing law.

73. Bell, Joseph N. "New Hope for the Battered Wife." **Good Housekeeping**, 183:94+, August 1976.

Discusses the plight of the battered wife and ways in which the victims are helping themselves, including seeking help from others.

74. _____. "Rescuing the Battered Wife." **Human Behavior**, 6:16-23, June 1977.

Presents a general discussion of wife battering, including comments from various people working in the area. Ways to help the victims are highlighted.

75. Bell, S.M. and M.D. Ainsworth. "Infant Crying and Maternal Responsiveness." **Child Development**, 43:1171-90, 1972.

Discusses the breakdown of maternal affection toward an infant as a possible antecedent to later abusing behavior.

76. Bender, Barbara. "Self-Chosen Victims: Scapegoating Behavior Sequential to Battering." **Child Welfare**, 55:417-22, June 1976.

Case studies of two children who felt a compulsive need to be punished following incidences of battering are presented.

77. Bennie, E.H. and A.B. Sclare. "The Battered Baby Syndrome." **American Journal of Psychiatry**, 125(7):975-79, 1969.

Presents findings of a study of ten parents who had abused their children. All ten parents were found to have personality disorders, including feelings of inadequacy. The effects of psychotherapy as a method of treatment are discussed.

78. Bentorim, Arnon. "Therapeutic Systems and Settings in the Treatment of Child Abuse." **The Challenge of Child Abuse**. Edited by Alfred White Franklin. London: Academic Press, 1977, pp. 249-59.

Discusses clinical situations faced by professionals when working with abusing families. A clinical example of a family in therapy is also presented.

79. Benward, Jean and Judianne Densen-Gerber. "Incest as a Causative Factor in Anti-Social Behavior: An Exploratory Study." **Contemporary Drug Problems**, 4:323-40, Fall 1975.

The problem of incest in the histories of female drug users was examined. Results showed a sufficient number of experiences to conclude that incest was a major factor in the development of anti-social behavior in those studied.

80. Berdie, Jane and others. "Violence Toward Youth: Themes From a

Workshop." **Children Today**, 6:7-35, March-April 1977.

In recognition of adolescents as victims of child abuse, a two-day workshop on the subject was held at the University of Minnesota. The workshop is summarized, emphasizing the significance of abuse against children in the twelve to eighteen age group.

81. Berlin, S. and D. Kravetz. "Women as Victims: A Feminist Social Work Perspective." **Social Work**, 26(6):447-60, November 1981.

Calls for a restructuring of values among professionals in social work in order to affect change for the aid of the victimized woman.

82. Bern, Elliot H. "From Violent Incident to Spouse Abuse Syndrome." **Social Work**, 63(1):41-45, January 1982.

Presents a theoretical model that attempts to integrate sociological and psychological views of spouse abuse, and reviews literature and research dealing with these aspects. Violent behavior in male-female relationships is discussed, and distinction is made between a violent incident and a spouse abuse syndrome. Ways in which a person is led from a violent incident into a cycle of abuse are outlined and intervention at specific phases of the cycle is suggested.

83. Besharov, Douglas J. "Building a Community Response to Child Abuse and Maltreatment." **Children Today**, 4:2-4, September–October 1975.

Examines the role of the community in the identification, management and treatment of child abuse.

84. _____. "The Legal Aspects of Reporting Known and Suspected Child Abuse and Neglect." **Villanova Law Review**, 23:458-520, 1977-78.

Explores the legal aspects of reporting all cases of child abuse and neglect. The topics discussed include the protection of individual rights, provisions for services, immunity from liability when reporting, penalties for failure to report, central registries for reporting, protective agencies, confidentiality of records, and issues concerning implementation of laws.

85. _____. "Putting Central Registers to Work: Using Modern Management Information Systems to Improve Child Protective Services." **Chicago-Kent Law Review**, 54:687-752, 1978.

Discusses the development and operation of Central Register systems for storing reports of child abuse and neglect. Criticisms of such systems and methods for their improvement are presented. A discussion of possible abuse and misuse of a central register system is also offered.

86. Beswick, Keith and others. "Child Abuse and General Practice." **British Medical Journal**, 2:800-02, October 1976.

Focuses on a prevention program for child abuse in England. The program is highlighted by a team of medical personnel who work together to identify, and prevent child abuse.

87. "Better Protection for the Defenseless — Tennessee's Revised Mandatory Child Abuse Reporting Statute." **Memphis State University Law Review**, 4:585–93, Spring 1974.

Discusses Tennessee's revised 1973 reporting statute for child abuse and contrasts it with its predecessor. Detailed examinations of the purpose clause, the nature of the report, who must report and the procedures for handling the reports are provided. The role of the community in the effective execution of laws is emphasized.

88. Bevan, Hugh. "Should Reporting be Mandatory?" **Concerning Child Abuse: Papers Presented by the Tunbridge Wells Study Group on Non-Accidental Injury to Children**. Edited by Alfred White Franklin. Edinburgh: Churchill Livingstone, 1975, pp. 133–35.

Discusses the reporting of child abuse and possible procedures for reporting.

89. Billingsley, Andrew and others. "Agency Structure and the Committment to Service." **Public Welfare**, 24:246–51, 1966.

Summarizes material from a study of Child Protective Services currently in progress with the support of the Children's Bureau, Welfare Administration, and the Department of Health, Education and Welfare. Findings indicate that child protective services should be a part of the child welfare function and associated with other child welfare services within the structure of public welfare, rather than put into a public assistance function.

90. Birrell, R.G. and J.H.W. Birrell. "The Maltreatment Syndrome in Children: A Hospital Survey." **Medical Journal of Australia**, 2:1023–29, 1968.

Defines the maltreatment syndrome as physical abuse or deprivation of necessary care or affection in non-accidental circumstances. Discusses cases treated at the Royal Children's Hospital in Melbourne, Australia over a thirty-one month period. Types of injuries, family background, social pathology, and presence of congential abnormalities are among the areas explored.

91. Bishop, Frank. "Perception, Memory, and Pathological Identification as Precipitating Factors in Parental Attacks on Children." **Medical Journal of Australia**, 2:243–45, August 16, 1975.

Case histories of abusing mothers are presented to demonstrate the necessity of ascertaining what the child's behavior means to the mother when abuse occurs. Once this is discovered, the reasons why the mother abused her child may be understood.

92. Bishop, Julia Ann. "Helping Neglectful Parents." **Annals of the American Academy of Political and Social Science**, 355:82–89, September 1964.

States that neglectful parents can be helped and taught to give adequate child care. A community program developed for this purpose is described, emphasizing methods of identification and intervention with parents.

93. Black, Rebecca and Joseph Mayer. "Parents with Special Problems: Alcohol and Opiate Addiction." **The Battered Child**. Edited by C. Henry Kempe and Ray E. Helfer. Chicago: University of Chicago Press, 1980, pp. 104–13.

Discusses a study conducted by the Washington Center for Addictions in Boston which examined post-natal care of children by addicted parents. The study investigated the adequacy of child care, and the incidence and types of child abuse and neglect occurring in these families. Presents treatment statistics for the United States on alcohol and opiate addiction, and explores the possible link between the use of these substances and child abuse.

94. "Black and Blue Marriages." **Human Behavior**, June 1976, pp. 47–48.

Reviews a study conducted in England which examined 100 women who had been battered by their husbands. The study focused on the association between alcoholism and violence, and concluded that for the women interviewed, the use of alcohol by the men in their lives contributed to abusive relationships. The need for care of children involved in these relationships is also explored as a way to prevent them from becoming abusive husbands or battered wives.

95. Blager, Florence and Harold P. Martin. "Speech and Language of Abused Children." **The Abused Child: A Multidisciplinary Approach to Developmental Issues and Treatment**. Edited by Harold P. Martin. Cambridge, Massachusetts: Ballinger Publishing Co., 1976, pp. 83–92.

Discusses a study which reaffirmed the finding that speech and language in abused children may be delayed or distorted, and that speech and language are sensitive neurologic, emotional and social behaviors.

96. Blair, Sandra. "Making the Legal System Work for Battered Women." **Battered Women**. Edited by Donna M. Moore. Beverly Hills: Sage Publications, Inc., 1979, pp. 101–18.

States that the legal system, particularly laws that create and fund programs, is a reflection of society. Civil and criminal laws and the mechanisms that enforce them (police, district attorney, and the court system) are discussed in relation to the batttered woman, and the idea of creating institutions of advocacy for battered women to watch and monitor cases is presented.

97. Blau, M. and others. "Why Parents Kick Their Kids Out." **Parents**, 54:64–69, April 1979.

Focuses on the reasons why parents kick their children out of the home, but also discusses different degrees of child abuse and various therapy groups for child abusers.

98. Bloch, Dorothy. "Fantasy and the Fear of Infanticide." **Psychoanalytic**

Review, 61:5–31, Spring 1974.

Examines children's fears of being murdered by their parents and offers suggestions for the treatment of these children.

99. Blout, Hal R. and Theodore A. Chandler. ''Relationship Between Childhood Abuse and Assaultive Behavior in Adolescent Male Psychiatric Patients.'' **Psychological Reports**, 44(3):1126, June 1979.

Discusses a study which tested Berkowitz's hypothesis that children who are frequently punished may exhibit aggressive, and even assaultive, behavior toward others.

100. Blumberg, Marvin L. ''Psychopathology of the Abusing Parent.'' **American Journal of Psychotherapy**, 28:21–29, January 1974.

Explores the personality traits of abusing parents and advocates various treatment approaches. Factors to be considered in selecting treatment programs for abusing parents are also discussed.

101. _____. ''Treatment of the Abused Child and the Child Abuser.'' **American Journal of Psychotherapy**, 31:205–15, April 1977.

After exploring the emotional and psychological problems of abusing parents, suggestions are made for effective treatment and prevention of child abuse.

102. Blumberg, Myrna. ''When Parents Hit Out.'' **Violence in the Family**. Edited by Suzanne K. Steinmetz and Murray A. Straus. New York: Harper and Row, 1974, pp. 148–50.

Discusses spanking as a form of punishment and examines parents' feelings toward spanking.

103. Boisvert, Maurice J. ''The Battered Child Syndrome.'' **The Battered Child**. Compiled by Jerome E. Leavitt. Morristown, New Jersey: General Learning Press, 1974, pp. 141–46.

Discusses a study conducted in order to establish a typology for the classification and treatment of child abuse, and for planning intervention strategy. Families in which there had been physical abuse of children by parents were examined. The study resulted in the development of detailed typologies, which included uncontrollable battering and controllable abuse.

104. Bolton, F.G., Jr. ''Domestic Violence Continuum — A Pressing Need for Legal Intervention.'' **Women Lawyers Journal**, 66(1):11–17, Winter 1980.

Examines domestic violence in the context of causes and effects, focusing on the necessity and role of legal intervention. Recommends that the legal profession take an active part in domestic violence prevention, that it treat the crime of abuse more seriously, and that victims of violence be represented uniformly.

105. Bolton, F.G., Jr. and others. "Child Maltreatment Risk Among Adolescent Mothers: A Study of Reported Cases." **American Journal of Orthopsychiatry**, 50(3):489–504, July 1980.

Examines a random sample of child maltreatment cases to determine if there is a higher incidence of maltreatment by adolescent mothers than by older mothers. Results indicated that the dynamics were similar for both groups. The findings are discussed, noting limitations of the data used. Implications for further research are presented.

106. Booth, Margaret. "Court Problems in the Management of the Family." **The Challenge of Child Abuse**. Edited by Alfred White Franklin. London: Academic Press, 1977, pp. 192–99.

Discusses laws dealing with the family, the functions of the juvenile court, the role of the Official Solicitor in the legal representation of children, and wardship as a duty of the court.

107. Borland, Marie, editor. **Violence in the Family**. Atlantic Highlands, New Jersey: Humanities Press, 1976. 148 pp.

Focuses on physical violence within the family and its consequences. Examines the social context of violence, medical diagnosis of child abuse, battered wives, police involvement in domestic disputes, legal framework of intrafamilial violence, management of child abuse, and inter-agency cooperation in dealing with cases of domestic violence.

108. Boudouris, J. "Homicide and the Family." **Journal of Marriage and the Family**, 33:667–76, November 1971.

Reviews a study of homicides occurring in Detroit during the period 1926–1968, finding that 30% of them involved "family relations." The data involving these cases are summarized, and rates by demographic characteristics are discussed. Causes of homicide within the family are proposed and methods for reducing the incidence of family violence are suggested.

109. Bourne, Richard. "The Role of Attorneys on Child Abuse Teams." **Chicago-Kent Law Review**, 54:773–83, 1978.

Discusses child abuse teams at the Children's Hospital Medical Center in Boston, Massachusetts. These teams consist of a lawyer, pediatrician, psychiatrist, nurse, social worker, and coordinator. The role of the lawyer is emphasized and examined in detail.

110. Bourne, Richard and Eli H. Newberger. "'Family Autonomy' or 'Coercive Intervention?' Ambiguity and Conflict in the Proposed Standards for Child Abuse and Neglect." **Boston University Law Review**, 57:670–706, July 1977.

Presents a critique of the proposed standards for child abuse and neglect and suggests ways to reform them.

111. Bowley, Agatha H. **Children at Risk: The Basic Needs of Children in the World Today**. Edinburgh: Churchill Livingstone, 1975. 61 pp.

Based on data from work with children at risk and their parents, fundamental needs of these children are defined and discussed. Through actual accounts of family situations, procedures for the care of children at risk are outlined.

112. Brandon, Sydney. "Physical Violence in the Family: An Overview." **Violence in the Family**. Edited by Marie Borland. Atlantic Highlands, New Jersey: Humanities Press, 1976, pp. 1–25.

Discusses the incidence and nature of physical violence in the family and explores factors which may contribute to its occurrence.

113. _____. "The Psychiatric Report in Cases of Non-Accidental Injury." **The Challenge of Child Abuse**. Edited by Alfred White Franklin. London: Academic Press, 1977, pp. 46–55.

Examines the role of the psychiatrist, forensic psychiatrist, and community psychiatrist in cases of child abuse, and discusses the use of the psychiatrist's report in court.

114. Brant, Renee S.T. and Veronica B. Tisza. "The Sexually Misused Child." **American Journal of Orthopsychiatry**, 47(1):80–90, January 1977.

States that sexual misuse of children is often undetected in patients with genital injury or infection. It is suggested that this problem may be a symptom of dysfunction within the family, and guidelines for management of cases are outlined.

115. Breiter, Toni. "Battered Women: When Violence is Linked With Love." **Essence**, 10:74–75 +, June 1979.

As a result of traditional views of women and their role in marriage and society, men and women readily accept a stereotyped view of their relationship with each other. This view is reinforced by other social relations and in the media, and the abuse of women is condoned by the male dominated society. Using this idea as an outline, wifebeating is discussed as a social phenomenon. Topics explored include the incidence of violence within marriage, the universality of the problem, why men batter, why the incidence of marital violence is not reported, the legal system and wife beating, and the role of family privacy and intervention. Ways to break the cycle of marital violence are also suggested.

116. Brenton, Myron. "What Can Be Done About Child Abuse." **Today's Education**, 66:50–53, October 1977.

The role of schools and teachers in the identification and prevention of child abuse is examined. Statistics concerning the incidence of child abuse, reasons why parents abuse their children, and characteristics of abusive parents and abused children are also discussed.

117. Broadhurst, Diane. "Policy-Making: First Step for Schools in the Fight Against Child Abuse and Neglect." **Elementary School Guidance and Counseling**, 10:222–26, March 1976.

A Program designed to detect and prevent child abuse and the policies involved in such a program are outlined.

118. _____. "Project Protection: A School Program to Detect and Prevent Child Abuse and Neglect." **Child Abuse: Perspectives on Diagnosis, Treatment and Prevention**. Edited by Roberta Kalmar. Dubuque, Iowa: Kendall/Hunt Publishing Company, 1977, pp. 108–16.

Examines the efforts of the school to identify and prevent child abuse.

119. _____. "A School Program to Combat Child Abuse." **Education Digest**, 41:20–23, October 1975.

Discusses Montgomery County, Maryland's public school's Project Protection. The primary purpose of this project is to give maximum protection to potential abused children by making sure that the school personnel are alert to the problem of child abuse and are trained to recognize and report it. Indicators of child abuse are presented and curriculums for training future parents are detailed.

120. _____. "What Schools Are Doing About Child Abuse and Neglect." **Children Today**, 7:22–24+, January–February 1978.

Explores the participation of the school in the process of identifying and reporting child abuse and neglect. The multidisciplinary child protection team and the role of the school in it are also discussed. A detailed illustration of the operation of a child abuse committee is provided.

121. Brody, Howard and Betty Gaiss. "Ethical Issues in Screening for Unusual Child Rearing Practices." **Pediatric Annual**, 15:106–12, March 1976.

Focuses on the issue of whether or not a mandatory screening program to identify unusual child rearing practices of parents should be instituted. Positive and negative aspects of such a program are discussed in detail, emphasizing the right of the child to be free from abuse.

122. Brody, Sylvia. "A Mother Is Being Beaten: An Instinctual Derivative and Infant Care." **Parenthood: Its Psychology and Psychopathology**. Edited by E. James Anthony and Therese Benedek. Boston: Little, Brown and Company, 1970, pp. 427–47.

Centers on the relationship between the unconscious fantasy and forms of maternal behavior. Describes the beating fantasy as an unconscious wish represented by three successive statements: my father is beating the child; I am being beaten by my father; a child is being beaten. The beating fantasy is described in relation to types of maternal behavior toward infants. It is concluded that the decision to hit or spank a child is rooted in a defense against the fantasy of being beaten.

123. Bross, Donald C. "Legal Advocacy for the Maltreated Child." **Trial**, 14:29-32, July 1978.

Discusses the role of the attorney in cases of child abuse and neglect, and the preparation of these cases for action by the legal system. A list of resources active in the area of children's law is included.

124. Brown, Harold O.J. "Abortion and Child Abuse." **Christianity Today**, 22:34, October 7, 1977.

Attitudes toward abortion may be correlated with popular conceptions concerning the reasons why parents abuse their children. Child abuse is discussed as a pro-abortionist argument — parents are thought to abuse "unwanted children," and abortion is seen as a kind of solution to this by eliminating them before birth.

125. Brown, John A. and Robert Daniels. "Some Observations on Abusive Parents." **Child Welfare**, 47(2):89-94, February 1968.

Abusive parents were observed from a dynamic perspective, and similarities in backgrounds of these parents were found. It was determined that child abuse was usually accompanied by other family problems, and that the child's behavior activated feelings about problems that still remained unresolved. Treatment techniques for abusive parents are also reviewed.

126. Brown, Linda R. Insalaco. "The Admissibility of Expert Testimony on the Subject of Battered Women." **Criminal Justice Journal**, 4(1):161-79, Fall 1980.

Focuses on the need for jurors, as well as judges, to be educated by an expert in the field with regard to the "battered woman syndrome." It is suggested that with this knowledge, the juror and judge can weigh the evidence and make an intelligent determination as to the reasonableness of the wife's actions in defending herself, and whether or not deadly force was justified in that particular situation. The admissibility and necessity of expert testimony in the case of the battered woman, and the "battered woman syndrome," are among the topics explored.

127. Brown, Rowine Hayes. "The Battered Child." **Medical Trial Technique Quarterly**, 20:272-81, Winter 1974.

Examines the problem of child abuse by discussing the experience of the Cook County Hospital in Chicago. The role of mandatory reporting laws, treatment of abused children, rehabilitation of abusive parents, and the characteristics of abusers are also discussed.

128. _____. "Child Abuse: Attempts to Solve the Problem by Reporting Laws." **Women Lawyers Journal**, 60:73-78, Spring 1974.

Concern over the problem of child abuse led to the development of laws for reporting the offense. The content of reporting laws enacted by various states and U.S. territories are explored and the purposes of such statutes are discussed. The need for additional legislation in the area of child abuse is also examined.

129. Brown, Rowine Hayes and Richard B. Truitt. "Civil Liability in Child Abuse Cases." **Chicago-Kent Law Review**, 54:753–72, 1978.

Discusses law suits initiated on behalf of the child against parents or against physicians who fail to diagnose or treat child abuse. Law suits initiated by parents against a third party are also examined.

130. Brownmiller, Susan. **Against Our Will: Men, Women and Rape**. New York: Simon and Schuster, 1975.

This comprehensive study of rape contains discussions of the sexual abuse and rape of children by family members and others.

131. "*Bruno v. Codd*, New York County Supreme Court." **New York Law Journal**, July 6, 1977, p. 7.

Examines the law in relation to wife abuse.

132. Buchanan, Ann and J.E. Oliver. "Abuse and Neglect as a Cause of Mental Retardation: A Study of 140 Children Admitted to Subnormality Hospitals in Wiltshire." **British Journal of Psychiatry**, 131:458–67, November 1977.

The results of this study showed that three percent of the children studied had definitely been rendered mentally retarded as a result of violent abuse, and that possibly a maximum of eleven percent of the children had been so handicapped. In twenty-four percent of these children, neglect was thought to contribute to a reduction in their intellectual potential.

133. Bullard, Dexter M. and others. "Failure to Thrive in the 'Neglected' Child." **American Journal of Orthopsychiatry**, 37(4):680–90, July 1967.

Through the use of case studies, children who fail to thrive without obvious physical cause are discussed.

134. Burgess, Ann Wolpert and Lynda Lytle Holmstrom. **Rape: Victims of Crisis**. Bowie, Maryland: Robert J. Brady Company, 1974. 308 pp.

In exploring the problem of rape, the case of the child victim is examined.

135. Burgess, Ann Wolpert and others. "Child Sexual Assault by a Family Member: Decisions Following Disclosure." **Victimology: An International Journal**, 2:236–50, Summer 1977.

In order to identify issues faced by the child victim of sexual assault by a family member and the victim's family, forty-four cases were examined. Decisions made by the family concerning ways to handle the problem are emphasized. The major decision made by the family was found to be whether to place their loyalty with the child victim or with the offender.

136. Burgess, Robert L. and Rand D. Conger. "Family Interaction in Abusive, Neglectful, and Normal Families." **Child Development**, 49:1163–73, December 1978.

In an attempt to discover whether patterns in daily interactions within families would distinguish neglectful or abusive families from other families, data was examined from all three groups. It was found that neglectful and abusive parents demonstrated lower rates of interaction, and that they tended to emphasize the negative aspects of their relationships with their children.

137. Burke, Kathleen M. "Evidentiary Problems of Proof in Child Abuse Cases: Why Family and Juvenile Courts Fail." **Journal of Family Law**, 13:819–52, 1973–74.

Discusses Problems of evidence in child abuse cases and suggests modifications to help relax the standards governing burdens of proof, thus helping the court system also.

138. Burt, Marvin. "A New System for Improving the Care of Neglected and Abused Children." **Child Welfare**, 53:167–79, 1974.

Presents results of an analysis, conducted by the Urban Institute in Davidson County, Tennessee, of the services provided for neglected and abused children. When the present system was found to be inadequate, the Tennessee Department of Public Welfare coordinated a demonstration program which was subsequently found to achieve its stated objectives.

139. Burt, Robert A. "Forcing Protection on Children and Their Parents: The Impact of Wyman v. James." **Michigan Law Review**, 69(7):1259–1310, June 1971.

Focuses on the government's power to force assistance for the protection of children when they or their parents are unwilling to accept that assistance. Contrasts the cases of Wyman and Gault, and discusses protecting children from their parents and protecting children from themselves. The Wyman case is re-examined concerning protecting parent and child from excessive "zeal" by the state.

140. Bush, Malcolm. "Institutions for the Dependent and Neglected Children: Therapeutic Option of Choice or Last Resort?" **American Journal of Orthopsychiatry**, 50(2):239–55, April 1980.

Examines claims made about child welfare institutions through the use of survey responses from 370 dependent children. It was found that institutions provided the least supportive form of care.

141. Bush, Sherida. "Child Killers: The Murderer Is Often the Mother."

Psychology Today, 10:28–29, November 1976.

Discusses the results of a study conducted by Kaplun and Reich in which the homicide of children, as recorded in the files of the medical examiner's office in New York City, was examined. The results showed that the mothers were the most frequent offenders in these cases but that they were rarely convicted due to lack of evidence.

142. _____. "Parents Anonymous — A Program that Works." **Psychology Today**, 11:109–10, March 1978.

Reviews the operation and effectiveness of Parents Anonymous, a nationwide self-help organization for abusing parents.

143. _____. "Predicting and Preventing Child Abuse." **Psychology Today**, 11:99, January 2978.

Discusses the results of a study designed to identify the backgrounds, self-concepts, family cohesiveness, attitudes toward child rearing, and other characteristics related to parent-child relationships. Two groups were chosen, one abusing and one not, which matched on demographic characteristics. It was found that both groups shared some characteristics, but differed in the ways in which they dealt with irritating behavior.

144. Butler, Raymond V. "Lend the Client an Ear." **Public Welfare**, 23(2):105–10, April 1965.

Discusses parents as participants in the treatment of neglected children. The concept of Family Unit Treatment is describes, and the caseworker's approach to the family is explored. Concludes by suggesting methods of utilizing the family as a unit of treatment in cases if child neglect.

145. Buzawa, E.S. and C.G. Buzawa. "Legislative Responses to the Problem of Domestic Violence in Michigan." **Wayne Law Review**, 25(3):859–81, March 1979.

Suggests increasing the ability of the police to make warrantless arrests in order to address the lack of judicial flexibility and inadequate law enforcement procedures in cases of family violence. Centralized organization of cases and procedures, and better education concerning domestic violence for law enforcement officers are also recommended.

146. Bysshe, Janette. "A Battered Baby." **Nursing Times**, 72:986–87, June 24, 1976.

Presents the case study of a battered baby brought to a British hospital for treatment. The identification of abuse and its treatment are highlighted.

147. Caffey, John and others. "Child Battery: Seek and Save." **Medical**

Explores the recognition and prevention of child abuse from the perspective of family dynamics. The elements involved in cases of child battering are examined and the possible role of society in fostering child abuse is described.

148. Cameron, J.M. ''Radiological and Pathological Aspects of the Battered Child Syndrome.'' **The Maltreatment of Children**. Edited by Selwyn M. Smith. Baltimore: University Park Press, 1978, pp. 69–81.

Discusses the role that radiology plays in the investigation and diagnosis of battered children. Also describes the role of pathology in the investigation of unnatural death.

149. Cameron, J.M. and others. ''The Battered Child Syndrome.'' **Medicine, Science and the Law**, 6(1):2–21, January 1966.

States that the Battered Child Syndrome has only been recognized as a serious and widespread crime in Britain within the last ten years. Reviews literature and definitions of the battered child syndrome, and discusses medical, social and psychiatric aspects of the problem.

150. Campbell, James S. ''The Family and Violence.'' **Law and Order Reconsidered: A Staff Report to the National Commission on the Causes and Prevention of Violence**, Volume 10. Washington, D.C.: U.S. Government Printing Office, 1969.

Explores the association between family violence and delinquency, stating that the parents of delinquents are less warm and affectionate, and more neglectful and inconsistent in their socialization patterns. Concludes by saying that aggressive parents tend to raise aggressive children, whereas a subtle correction and reward system within the family may create a barrier against violence.

151. Campbell, Ruth. ''Violence in Adolescence.'' **Journal of Analytical Psychology**, 12(2):161–73, 1967.

Centers on a case study of an aggressive and violent sixteen year old boy who exhibits these traits primarily against his parents. The child was referred for analysis, and the progression and results of the program on the child and the parents are reviewed.

152. Canon, Belle. ''National Focus on Domestic Violence.'' **MS.**, February 1979, p. 19.

Discusses the impact of the National Coalition Against Domestic Violence, and reviews progress being made in many areas against the problem.

153. Cantwell, Hendrika B. ''Child Neglect.'' **The Battered Child**. Edited by C. Henry Kempe and Ray E. Helfer. Chicago: University of Chicago Press, 1980, pp. 183–97.

States that child neglect remains a problem because the public either ignores or denies it, and professionals lack information about it. Examines neglect as occuring on a continuum, and not as an isolated incident. The importance of early detection, forms of neglect, physical indicators of neglect, characteristics of neglectful parents, manifestations of neglect, multidisciplinary aspects and approaches to intervention, placement of neglected children, and the roles of the protective service and the courts are among the topics discussed.

154. Carlson, Bonnie E. "Battered Women and Their Assailants." **Social Work**, 22:455–60, November 1977.

Discusses a program which provides assistance to battered women, and examines the causes and effects of marital violence.

155. Carmody, Francis J. and others. "Prevention of Child Abuse and Neglect in Military Families." **Children Today**, 8(2):16+, March–April 1979.

Proposes a program for the prevention of child abuse and neglect in military families, which may be modified for use in civilian communities. In addition to outlining the program, the demographic and social-psychological determinants of child abuse are discussed. Concludes by stating that enough is known about child abuse and neglect to help determine probable causes and to initiate preventive measures. The necessity of a well-planned program to reduce child abuse and neglect is emphasized.

156. Carroll, Claudia A. "The Function of Protective Services in Child Abuse and Neglect." **The Battered Child**. Edited by C. Henry Kempe and Ray E. Helfer. Chicago: University of Chicago Press, 1980, pp. 275–87.

Discusses the role of social service organizations in child abuse intervention, and the criteria of good protective service groups. States that although the public gives social service organizations the job of protecting children in danger of abuse or neglect, little help is received from the public, and children and their rights are given low priority on the public scale of consideration. The functions of the protective services are outlined, and their legal role is examined.

157. Carroll, Joseph C. "The Intergenerational Transmission of Family Violence: The Long-Term Effects of Aggressive Behavior." **Aggressive Behavior**, 3(3):9–99, Fall 1977.

Explores the idea that violence within the family is passed down from generation to generation. Discusses a study which hypothesized that children exposed to a high degree of physical punishment are more likely to resort to violence within the family unit as adults. It was found that people who, as children, had received little affection and a high degree of punishment from their parents were more likely to use violence in their own families, and that family violence is most often transmitted within the same sex.

158. Carter, Jan. "Is Child Abuse a Crime?" **The Challenge of Child Abuse**.

Edited by Alfred White Franklin. London: Academic Press, 1977, pp. 200–05.

Discusses child abuse in the context of the law, science and morality, and presents legal, medical and rehabilitation views of the problem.

159. _____. "Strengthening the Individual." **The Challenge of Child Abuse**. Edited by Alfred White Franklin. London: Academic Press, 1977, pp. 260–68.

Examines the processes involved in strengthening the individual. Also discusses the professional service worker and the child abuser as two separate cultures in the field of child abuse, the concept of "blaming the victim," and the role of the community in shaping the individual.

160. Castle, Raymond L. "Providing a Service." **Concerning Child Abuse: Papers Presented by the Tunbridge Wells Study Group on Non-Accidental Injury to Children**. Edited by Alfred White Franklin. Edinburgh: Churchill Livingstone, 1975, pp. 113–19.

Discusses the battered child syndrome and highlights problems related to the diagnosis, management and treatment of the problem.

161. Cavenaugh, Winifred. "Battered Children Cases in the Courts." **Concerning Child Abuse: Papers Presented by the Tunbridge Wells Study Group on Non-Accidental Injury to Children**. Edited by Alfred White Franklin. Edinburgh: Churchill Livingstone, 1975, pp. 140–46.

Examines the incidence of battered child cases in the courts in England and discusses the procedures involved in such cases.

162. _____. "A Report on the Teaching of Legal Studies in Social Work Courses." **Concerning Child Abuse: Papers Presented by the Tunbridge Study Group on Non-Accidental Injury to Children**. Edited by Alfred White Franklin. Edinburgh: Churchill Livingstone, 1975, pp. 153–54.

Discusses general considerations involved in teaching legal studies in social work courses, and examines the content of the teachings and the implications for cases of abuse.

163. Chadwick, David L. "Child Abuse." **Journal of the American Medical Association**, 235:2017–18, May 3, 1976.

Explores the role of the physician in the identification and treatment of child abuse cases.

164. Chaikin, Douglas A. "Termination of Parental Rights and the Lesser Restrictive Alternative Doctrine." **Tulsa Law Journal**, 12:528–44, 1977.

Reviews abuse and neglect statutes and the termination process contained in these statutes. Constitutional rights affected by these statutes and ways in which constitutional liberties may be safeguarded are also examined.

165. Chamberlain, Michael R. and Gerald M. Eaton. "Protecting the Abused and Neglected Child." **New Hampshire Bar Journal**, 19:25–55, 1977.

Analyzes the laws pertaining to child abuse as enacted by the New Hampshire legislature.

166. Chambers, D.R. "A Coroner's View." **Concerning Child Abuse: Papers Presented by the Tunbridge Wells Study Group on Non-Accidental Injury to Children**. Edited by Alfred White Franklin. Edinburgh: Churchill Livingstone, 1975, pp. 69–70.

Discusses the coroner's involvement in cases of violent, unknown cause, or unnatural deaths of children.

167. Chang, Albert, and others. "Child Abuse and Neglect: Physicians' Knowledge, Attitudes, and Experiences." **American Journal of Public Health**, 66:1199–1201, December 1976.

Various types of physicians were surveyed as to their knowledge and experience with child abuse cases. Results of this survey are presented and conclusions concerning identification, reporting, and treatment are made based on these results. The development of better programs for identification of child abuse cases, educational programs for physicians, and guidelines for the intervention of community agencies are recommended.

168. Chapman, Jack. "Social Work Intervention in Cases of Child Abuse." **The Challenge of Child Abuse**. Edited by Alfred White Franklin. London: Academic Press, 1977, pp. 174–82.

Discusses the roles of social work and probation professionals who deal with the problem and examines the process of separate representation of children in court proceedings involving child abuse.

169. Chase, Naomi F. **A Child Is Being Beaten: Violence Against Children, An American Tragedy**. New York: Holt, Rinehart and Winston, 1975. 225 pp.

Violence against children in America is examined historically. In modern society, child abuse may be attributed to immature parents who find themselves faced with economic, social and interpersonal problems. Failing to cope with the resulting anxiety and stress, parents may turn to violence against a troublesome child. Medical, legal, and social agencies play a significant role in the treatment of abused children and their families, but reform is needed if this treatment is to be successful. Suggestions for the prevention of child abuse include instruction in parenting, greater availability of birth control information, and increased employment opportunities for young parents.

170. Chatterton, Michael R. "The Social Context of Violence." **Violence in the Family**. Edited by Marie Borland. Atlantic Highlands, New Jersey: Humanities Press, 1976, pp. 26–49.

Explores the organization of violence producing processes within society and discusses crimes of violence within this context, including the roles of critical audience groups and the media.

171. Cherry, B.J. and A.M. Kuby. "Obstacles to the Delivery of Medical Care to Children of Neglecting Parents." **American Journal of Public Health**, 61(3):568–73, March 1971.

Focuses on the problem of delivering medical care to neglected children in multi-problem families. States that one of the major obstacles is the fact that some parents are not able to assume the responsibilities of being parents, and that these parents act as agents in determining the distribution of available services to the children. Discusses the experiences of one center in working with parents who neglect their children, and the need for changing attitudes and organization if care is to effectively reach the intended recipient.

172. Chester, Robert and Jane Streather. "Cruelty in English Divorce: Some Empirical Findings." **Journal of Marriage and the Family**, 34(4): 706–10, 1972.

Discusses cruelty as grounds for divorce in England. Examines the judicial definition of cruelty, and the role of court decisions in relaxing the previously stringent interpretations of the definition.

173. "Child Abuse and Neglect in the American Society." **Center Magazine**, 11:70–77, March–April 1978.

Reports on a Center for the Study of Democratic Institutions conference on child abuse and neglect. Topics covered by the conference include legislation, needs of abusive families, contributions of the social system to the problem, the breakdown of the nuclear family, and the role of professionals in the management of child abuse.

174. "Child Abuse Detectives: Early Warnings in the Maternity Ward." **Human Behavior**, 7:67, May 1978.

A Denver research team devised a screening method to use with new parents to help identify future child abusers. The study was found to be successful. In addition to the study itself, danger signals and warning signs of child abuse, and the significance of the parents' own upbringing for the identification of possible future abusers are discussed.

175. "Child Abuse Prompts Plan for State Legislative Action." **Intellect**, 102:283–84, February 1974.

Examines proposed legislation by the Education Commission of the States, which calls on the states to provide for the mandatory reporting of child abuse or neglect by anyone who suspects that child abuse has occurred.

176. "Child Abuse Registry Aids in Prevention." **Pediatric News**, 9:58, April 1975.

The effectiveness of the Dade County, Florida central registry for child abuse reporting is discussed.

177. "Child Abusers: Signaling for Help." **Science News**, 111:214–15, April 2, 1977.

Child abusers may use physical symptoms as signals for help. Three cases where this is suspected are presented.

178. "Children in Peril." **Nation**, 214(10):293–94, March 6, 1972.

States that child abuse reflects the degradation of a society and its values. Discusses the premise that many abusing parents are psychotic, who had been abused themselves as children, and abuse their own children in order to relieve the frustration they feel about their own childhoods.

179. Clements, Theodore. "Child Abuse: The Problem of Definition." **Creighton Law Review**, June 1975, pp. 729–42.

Discusses whether the lack of a precise and limited legal definition of child abuse leads to confusion concerning reporting regulations, and subsequent ineffective intervention by the state.

180. Cohen, Harriette. "Criminal Liability of Parent for Omission Causing Death of Child." **Maryland Law Review**, 21(3):262–68, Summer 1961.

Discusses two cases in which parents were found to be grossly negligent and a child subjected to abuse or neglect died as a result.

181. Cohen, Melvin, and others. "Family Interaction Patterns, Drug Treatment, and Change in Social Aggression." **Violence in the Family**. Edited by Suzanne K. Steinmetz and Murray A. Straus. New York: Harper and Row, 1974, pp. 120–26.

Examines a study conducted by the authors which explored a social system approach to family therapy. It was found that drug therapy must be consistent with family interaction patterns in order to avoid provoking further aggression.

182. Cohen, Morton I., and others. **Neglected Parents: A Study of Psychosocial Characteristics**. Denver: The American Humane Association, Children's Division, 1967. 28 pp.

Reviews a study which was conducted to determine characteristics of clients of The Massachusetts Society for the Prevention of Cruelty to Children. The purpose of this study was to give caseworkers data in order to understand the characteristics and operating factors of its clients. Findings showed that the clients were generally low income families, uneducated, unskilled, highly mobile, unstable, and unable to satisfy goals and aspirations. It is emphasized, however, that the population examined covers a wide spectrum of types, and that few classifications covered all clients. The study concluded that if a treatment program is to be successful, it must consider the characteristics of its clients on an individual basis.

183. Cohen, Stephan J. and Alan Sussman. "The Incidence of Child Abuse in the United States." **Child Welfare**, 54:432–43, June 1975.

Focuses on the absence of accurate, consistent statistics on the incidence of child abuse in the United States. Reasons for the variability of estimates are suggested and caution is given concerning the use of these estimates in support of legal and social projects.

184. Cohn, Anne Harris. "An Evaluation of Three Demonstration Child Abuse and Neglect Treatment Programs." **Journal of the American Academy of Child Psychiatry**, 18:283–91, 1979.

Findings from the first national evaluation of programs concerning the treatment of abused and neglected children are reviewed. Problems with the programs and their resolutions are discussed, and the need for improved programs is suggested.

185. Cohn, Anne Harris, and others. "Evaluating Innovative Treatment Programs in Child Abuse and Neglect." **Children Today**, 4(3):10–12, May–June 1975.

Discusses a demonstration program in the field of child abuse and neglect which had been initiated by three federal agencies. The eleven projects studied, why they they were chosen for evaluation, the design of the program, and policy recommendations using evaluation findings are described.

186. Coigney, Virginia. **Children Are People Too: How We Fail Our Children and How We Can Love Them**. New York: William Morrow and Company, Inc., 1975. 228 pp.

Discusses the way Americans feel about their children, emphasizing the idea that children are property and that because of this, certain demands are made on them, resulting in "abuses" committed under the guises of love and welfare for the child. Attitudes toward children are examined, and the influence of economic and social conditions on these attitudes are explored. In addition, one chapter is devoted to a detailed discussion of child abuse. "The United Nations Declaration of the Rights of the Child," "The Bill of Rights" of the United States Constitution, and a bibliography are included.

187. Collie, James. "The Police Role." **Concerning Child Abuse: Papers Presented by the Tunbridge Wells Study Group on Non-Accidental Injury to Children**. Edited by Alfred White Franklin. Edinburgh: Churchill Livingstone, 1975, pp. 123–26.

Examines the role of the police in child abuse cases and suggests ways to improve their service.

188. Collins, Alice H. and Diane L. Pancoast. **Natural Helping Networks: A Strategy for Prevention**. Washington, D.C.: National Association of Social Workers, 1976. 144 pp.

Discusses experiences of the authors with natural networks, how they are used, and their effectiveness in prevention.

189. Collins, Marilyn C. **Child Abuser: A Study of Child Abusers in Self-Help Group Therapy**. Littleton, Massachusetts: PSG Publishing Company, Inc., 1978. 128 pp.

   Centers on the careers of child abusers who seek and receive treatment as eventually reaching a point of ''self-acceptance and moral reinstatement.'' The way in which this process develops is explored by looking at the lives of people who sought help from Parents Anonymous, an organization which is based on the principles of self-help group therapy. The moral career of the child abuser and the socialization and neutralization of abusing definitions are among the issues examined. A copy of the interview schedule and a bibliography are also included.

190. Colorado Advisory Committee to the U.S. Commission on Civil Rights. **The Silent Victims: Denver's Battered Women**. Washington, D.C.: U.S. Commission on Civil Rights, 1977. 22 pp.

   Discusses a study which examined battered women and the options available to them in seeking protection, refuge, legal assistance and social services. Literature is reviewed, and the responses of law enforcement and legal agencies are examined.

191. Colucci, N.D., Jr. ''The Schools and the Problem of Child Abuse and Neglect.'' **Contemporary Education**, 48:98–100, Winter 1977.

   The role of the school in identifying and reporting cases of child abuse is explored. The necessity for clear reporting procedures, outlines of the school's responsibilities, and public education programs are discussed.

192. ''Concerning Child Abuse..'' **New Zealand Medical Journal**, 85:191–92, March 9, 1977.

   Examines problems associated with the identification and treatment of child abuse.

193. ''Conviction of Forcible Rape of 15 Year Old Daughter Reversed: *People v. McGillen, 22 N.W. 2d 677 (Michigan)*.'' **Sex Problems Court Digest**, 6(1):2, January 1975.

   Describes the Supreme Court of Michigan's reversal of the earlier conviction of a 60 year old man for raping his 15 year old daughter.

194. Cooksey, Charlotte M. ''The Battered Child — Louisiana's Response to the Cry.'' **Loyola Law Review**, 17(2):372+, 1970–71.

   Presents a historical discussion of child abuse and discusses the legal aspects of the problem, focusing on the application of the criminal law to abusive parents. Traces the reporting of a suspected case of child abuse through the legal system of the juvenile court and presents possible ways for resolving the problem. Concludes by stating that although child abuse reporting laws are a major breakthrough in the resolution of the problem, they are not a solution in themselves. The ultimate goal must be the protection of the child and the restoration of the family structure, and it should be determined if existing laws are making sufficient progress in this direction.

195. Cooper, Christine. "Child Abuse and Neglect — Medical Aspects." **The Maltreatment of Children**. Edited by Selwyn M. Smith. Baltimore: University Park Press, 1978, pp. 9–68.

Discusses the need for experienced medical personnel in the area of child abuse, particularly concerning psychological damage to the child, prevention, and the physical injuries sustained by the child.

196. _____. "The Doctor's Dilemma — A Pediatrician's View." **Concerning Child Abuse: Papers Presented by the Tunbridge Wells Study Group on Non-Accidental Injury to Children**. Edited by Alfred White Franklin. Edinburgh: Churchill Livingstone, 1975, pp. 21–29.

Examines the management of child abuse cases by medical personnel and social workers, and the involvement of police and the legal system. Presents a summary of the cases of non-accidental injuries seen at Newcastle from 1965 through 1971, using tables and graphs.

197. _____. "Three Abusing Families." **The Challenge of Child Abuse**. Edited by Alfred White Franklin. London: Academic Press, 1977, pp. 5–15.

Presents three case studies of child abuse which illustrate the causes of the problem and the difficulties involved in its identification and management.

198. Corey, Eleanor J.B., and others. "Factors Contributing to Child Abuse." **Nursing Research**, 24:293–95, July–August 1975.

Compares demographic variables for abused and non-abused children who had been hospitalized over a nine year period. Significant differences were found between the two groups for all of the variables considered, including sex, age, and marital status of the mother.

199. Cormier, Bruno. "Psychodynamics of Homicide Committed in a Marital Relationship." **Corrective Psychiatry and Journal of Social Therapy**, 8(4): 187–94, 1962.

Discusses the psychodynamics of murder committed within a marital relationship, focusing on the psychopathology of the perpetrator. In the cases examined, the murder was committed by the husband following a history of conflict between the husband and wife.

200. Costantino, Cathy. "Intervention With Battered Women: The Lawyer-Social Worker Team." **Social Work**, 26(6):456–60, November 1981.

States that intervention with battered women falls within the juristiction of both the social work and legal professions, but neither effectively meets the needs of the clients. Reasons for this are examined and a model for multidisciplinary intervention is proposed.

201. Cottom, Kris. "Resistance to Incestuous Assault." **Fight Back! Feminist Resistance to Male Violence**. Edited by Frederique Delacoste and Felice Newman. Minneapolis: Cleis Press, 1981, pp. 26-27.

Presents a personal analysis of the problem of incestuous assault, and outlines a proposal for its prevention. States that a child cannot protect herself from incestuous assault — to protect the child, attitudes must be changed and men must be educated not to view a child or child-like attributes as erotic.

202. Council of Europe. **The Causes and Prevention of Child Abuse**. Strasbourg: Council of Europe, 1979. 48 pp.

Examines the problem of child abuse. Topics explored include an historical survey of the problem, definitions of child abuse, causes and management, the role of the police and the legal system, the incidence and morbidity of child abuse, diagnosis, the issue of confidentiality, and the discipline and punishment of children.

203. Court, Joan. "Nurture and Nature: The Nurturing Problem." **Concerning Child Abuse: Papers Presented by the Tunbridge Wells Study Group on Non-Accidental Injury to Children**. Edited by Alfred White Franklin. Edinburgh: Churchill Livingstone, 1975, pp. 106-12.

Discusses the lack of proper nurturing of young children and its relationship to child abuse.

204. Court, Joan and A. Kerr. "The Battered Child Syndrome — 2: A Preventable Disease?" **Nursing Times**, 67(23):695-97, June 10, 1971.

Reviews symptoms of child abuse and presents aspects of parents' treatment of children. Characteristics of abusive parents are examined, and the treatment of abused children and their parents is discussed.

205. Crawford, Christina. "Conspiracy of Silence." **Ladies' Home Journal**, November 1981, pp. 69 & 161-70.

Presents statistics and describes cases of child abuse, stating that no community is immuned to the problem. Discusses reasons why communities do not mobilize to combat child abuse, and examines efforts being made by groups toward treatment and prevention.

206. "Criminal Law — Rape — Husband Cannot be Guilty of Raping His Wife." **Dickinson Law Review**, 82:608-16, Spring 1978.

Discusses the case of State v. Smith (Essex County Court of New Jersey) which held that its rape statute did not permit prosecution for rape when the perpetrator is legally married to the prosecutrix, and reviews other relevant cases. Concludes that the court could have legitimately rejected this long-standing common rule.

207. Curtis, George C. "Violence Breeds Violence — Perhaps?" **The Battered Child**. compiled by Jerome E. Leavitt. Morristown, New Jersey: General Learning Press, 1974, pp. 74–75.

Examines the assertion that children treated violently may grow up to be murderers and perpetrators of other crimes of violence. The theoretical and empirical grounds for this assertion are explored.

208. D'Agostino, Paul A. "Dysfunctioning Families and Child Abuse: The Need for an Interagency Effort." **Public Welfare**, 30(4):14–17, Fall 1972.

Describes steps taken by the Boston community to manage child abuse. The program involves the united efforts of the local welfare department and private organizations to organize a therapeutic infant care center, and an interagency, indisciplinary group directed at the prevention of child abuse. Outlines the purpose of the program and the criteria for selecting the children and the staff. Examines the impact of united efforts in the area, emphasizing the need for community involvement.

209. Danckworth, Edward T. "Techniques of Child Abuse Investigations." **Police Chief**, 43:62–64, March 1976.

States that in investigating cases of suspected child abuse, a police officer must take steps to protect the child immediately. Subsequent steps taken by the officer include the gathering of evidence, interviewing involved or knowledgeable persons, and examining any existing medical records. In addition to discussions of police procedure in child abuse cases, indicators which may alert police to possible abuse are highlighted.

210. David, Charles A. "The Use of the Confrontation Technique in the Battered Child Syndrome." **American Journal of Psychotherapy**, 28:543–52, October 1974.

A case study is presented which illustrates the effective use of confrontation in the treatment of abusive parents.

211. Davidson, Terry. **Conjugal Crime: Understanding and Changing the Wifebeating Pattern**. New York: Hawthorn Books, Inc., 1978.

Presents a comprehensive discussion of the problem of marital violence, including historical precedents for condoning wifebeating, how marital violence affects children, and characteristics of batterers and battered wives. A directory of shelters throughout the country, procedures to be followed by the victim if she chooses to seek legal assistance, a list of available publications, and addresses of programs and organizations interested in the problem are also provided.

212. Davidson, Terry. "Wifebeating: A Recurring Phenomenon Throughout

History." **Battered Women: A Psychosociological Study of Domestic Violence**. Edited by Maria Roy. New York: Van Nostrand Reinhold Company, 1977, pp. 2–23.

Presents a detailed discussion of laws concerning wifebeating from an historical perspective.

213. Davies, Jean M. "The Battered Child Syndrome: Detection and Prevention." **Nursing Mirror**, 140:56–57, June 1975.

In the British system of child abuse detection and prevention, the health visitor plays a significant role, and is in a strategic position of trust, in the community. The health visitor's role is outlined, and other methods of identification and prevention are explored.

214. _____. "A Health Visitor's Viewpoint." **Concerning Child Abuse: Papers Presented by the Tunbridge Wells Study Group on Non-Accidental Injury to Children**. Edited by Alfred White Franklin. Edinburgh: Churchill Livingstone, 1975, pp. 78–81.

Presents a framework for dealing with suspected cases of battering, and discusses the action to be taken. Recommendations are made for future management and prevention in relation to the work of the health visitor.

215. _____. "When the Agency Must Intervene." **Public Welfare**, 23(2):102–05, April 1965.

Discusses public agency intervention in child abuse and neglect cases, focusing on diagnosis by the case worker and his professional responsibility toward the child, the parents, the agency and the community.

216. Davis, Charles Ray. "Torts Action by Wife Against Husband for Personal Injuries." **Mississippi Law Journal**, 34(3):348–49, May 1963.

Examines a case in which a wife brought legal action against her husband for assault and battery as the result of a beating. The lower court found for the husband on the grounds that a wife cannot sue her husband for tort in California. The higher court reversed this decision, stating that the rule of interspousal immunity for intentional torts is abandoned, and that one spouse may sue the other in tort where the tort is intentional.

217. Davis, Gwendolyn and Judith Higgins. "Child Abuse: A Bibliography." **School Library Journal**, 23:29–33, November 1976.

Presents an annotated bibliography on child abuse which emphasizes materials of interest to educators.

218. Davoren, Elizabeth. "Foster Placement of Abused Children." **Children Today**, 4(3):41, May–June 1975.

Outlines the problems associated with foster placement of abused children.

219. _____. "Working With Abusive Parents: A Social Worker's

View.'' **Children Today**, 4:38–43, May–June 1975.

Focuses on the role of the social worker in the treatment of abusive parents. Factors which make the social worker effective and the role of support services are among the topics explored.

220. ''Dealing With Child Abusers.'' **Science Digest**, 76:70–71, October 1974.

Discusses various ways of handling parents who abuse their children.

221. ''The Death of a Child.'' **New Society**, 39:434, March 3, 1977.

Examines the case of Wayne Brewer, in which the child was returned by the court to his parents following a battering incident, and was subsequently beaten to death.

222. DeCourcy, Peter and Judith DeCourcy. **A Silent Tragedy: Child Abuse in the Community**. New York: Alfred Publishing Company, 1973. 230 pp.

Presents 12 case histories of child abuse, including police and psychological reports of the incidents, and of the parents and children involved. The ineffectiveness of current methods for dealing with such cases is discussed, and modifications of social and legal procedures are suggested. A list of agencies in the United States concerned with child abuse, and a brief bibliography are included.

223. DeFrancis, Vincent. ''Laws for Mandatory Reporting of Child Abuse Cases.'' **The Battered Child**. Compiled by Jerome E. Leavitt. Morristown, New Jersey: General Learning Press, 1974, pp. 106–11.

Discusses the need for legislation requiring that evidence of physical abuse in children be reported, particularly by doctors and medical personnel. States that the central objective should be the protection of the child, rather than the punishment of the parents, and suggests a number of approaches to achieve this end. Topics examined include the need for a reporting law and the purpose of such a law, the emotional climate of the child abuse situation, and social planning for children. Presents tables which summarize state laws concerning age juristiction of the child abuse laws, when privileged communications may be waived, and compulsory or permissive laws. Concludes by emphasizing that mandatory reporting laws are only a tool for identifying the abused child, and will not end the problem.

224. DeFrancis, Vincent. ''Protecting the Child Victim of Sex Crimes Committed by Adults.'' **Federal Probation**, 35(3):15–20, September 1971.

States that child victims of adult sex offenders are frequently victims of parental neglect and that the community fails to recognize the problem. Defines the problem and discusses the nature of the acts committed against children, the characteristics of victims and offenders, reporting the offense, and family problems which may lead to abuse.

225. _____. ''The Status of Child Protective Services.'' **The Battered**

Child. Edited by C. Henry Kempe and Ray E. Helfer. Chicago: University of Chicago Press, 1980, pp. 127–45.

Presents findings of a study conducted to assess the status and availability of child protective services. The objectives of the study were to determine which states and communities were currently engaged in providing protective services to neglected and abused children, to identify the auspices and legal bases under which these programs were provided, to assess the size and scope of each program, and to evaluate the degree to which the programs served the needs of the community. Child protective services are defined, and community cooperation is discussed.

226. Delacoste, Frederique and Felice Newman, editors. **Fight Back!: Feminist Resistance to Male Violence**. Minneapolis: Cleis Press, 1981. 398 pp.

Selections deal with many forms and aspects of violence against women including incest, resistance against violence, victim's rights, battered women's refuges, physical and sexual abuse, organizing against male violence, and the politics of male violence against women. A 52 page directory of resource organizations for victims of rape, battering and incest is included.

227. Delaney, James J, "The Battered Child and the Law." **Helping the Battered Child and His Family**. Philadelphia: J.B. Lippincott Company, 1972, pp. 187–207.

Examines child abuse as a crime, including the criminal process, criminal laws, and predictable results. States that an acquitted parent often feels vindicated and sees his conduct as justified; thus, his battering conduct may be reinforced. Discusses the fact that an adequate children's code is a prerequisite to child protection and presents elements which should be included in an adequate child abuse law. The need for community concern and involvement is explored and the legal processes involved in child abuse cases are detailed.

228. DeLesseps, Suzanne. "Child Abuse." **Editorial Research Reports**, 1:67–84, January 30, 1976.

Discusses statistics concerning the incidence and nature of child abuse, the rights of children, and identification projects developed by the community to curtail child abuse.

229. Dellapa, Fred. "Mediation and the Community Dispute Center." **Battered Women: A Psychosociological Study of Domestic Violence**. Edited by Maria Roy. New York: Van Nostrand Reinhold Company, 1977, pp. 239–49.

Presents a hypothetical case of wifebeating in which the victim receives no satisfaction from the legal system. Discusses the punitive nature of the criminal justice system and the establishment of a program which is community oriented and provides for better management of minor criminal cases.

230. Delnero, Harriet. "The Medical Center Child Abuse Consultation Team." **Helping the Battered Child and His Family**. Edited by C. Henry Kempe and Ray E. Helfer. Philadelphia: J.B. Lippincott Company, 1972, pp. 161–76.

Examines a child abuse consultation team within a hospital which work together with the hospital staff to implement a therapeutic program for the family. The function of the social worker and child abuse coordinator are detailed.

231. Delsordo, James D. "Protective Casework for Abused Children." **The Battered Child**. Compiled by Jerome E. Leavitt. Morristown, New Jersey: General Learning Press, 1974, pp. 46–51.

Discusses a study made in 1962 of 80 cases in which children had been seriously abused by their parents. The study was based on a sample of cases handled within a three year period by the Pennsylvania Society to Protect Children From Cruelty. The major factors considered were the degree of injury inflicted, the probability of abuse recurring, and physical and psychological availability of casework help to parents.

232. Del Tosto, D. "Battered Spouse Syndrome as a Defense to Homicide Charge Under the Pennsylvania Crimes Codes." **Villanova Law Review**, 26(1):105–34, November 1980.

States that battered spouses would be charged with third degree murder instead of first, due to a lack of premeditated intent.

233. DeMause, Lloyd. "Our Forebearers Made Childhood a Nightmare." **Psychology Today**, 8:85–88, April 1975.

Child care and attitudes toward children are discussed from an historical perspective. The slow recognition of children as individuals in their own right hindered the acknowledgement of child abuse as a problem in society. The shift from physical to psychological discipline is highlighted, and the twentieth century is mentioned as the first to acknowledge that children do have rights and that the problem of child abuse does exist.

234. Dembitz, Nanette. "Child Abuse and the Law — Fact and Fiction." **The Record of the Association of the Bar of the City of New York**, 24(9):613–27, December 1969.

States that mistakes in passage of the child abuse act encumbered rather than improved the protection of children and the administration in Family Court. Discusses the difficulties of proof in child abuse cases, medical testimony, problems in securing reliable testimony from children, the extent of the problem, and the characteristics of abusing parents. Concludes by examining possible ways to solve the problem of child abuse.

235. Densen-Gerber, Judianne and F. Hutchinson. "Medical-Legal and Societal Problems Involving Children — Child Prostitution, Child Pornography and Drug Related Abuse; Recommended Legislation." **The Maltreatment of Children**. Edited by Selwyn M. Smith. Baltimore: University Park Press, 1978, pp. 317–50.

Discusses child prostitution, pornography and drug related abuse using case studies to illustrate the problem. Possible causative related behavior and the reporting provisions of child abuse and neglect statutes in various states are also examined.

236. Densen-Gerber, Judianne, and others. "Incest and Drug-Related Child Abuse — Systematic Neglect by the Medical and Legal Professions." **Contemporary Drug Problems**, 6:135–72, Summer 1977.

Examines the service systems and statutes of various states concerning child abuse and neglect, and presents case studies of drug-related child abuse. Each case study is evaluated in light of statutes and services. It is concluded that there is adequate evidence to support a causal relationship between substance abuse and child abuse. This should be considered by the service systems when dealing with child abuse cases, and should be integrated into statutes.

237. DePanfilis, Diane. "Clients Who Refer Themselves to Child Protective Services." **Children Today**, 11(2):21–25, March–April 1982.

Focuses on the Voluntary Intervention and Treatment Program in Erie, Pennsylvania which demonstrates ways in which public child protective service agencies can incorporate programs to encourage voluntary self-referrals by parents with actual or potential problems of child abuse or neglect.

238. Derdeyn, Andre P. "A Case for Permanent Foster Placement of Dependent, Neglected, and Abused Children." **American Journal of Orthopsychiatry**, 47(4):604–14, October 1977.

Discusses permanent foster placement as a means of best meeting the needs of children in jeopardy.

239. _____. "Child Abuse and Neglect: The Rights of Parents and the Needs of Their Children." **American Journal of Orthopsychiatry**, 47:377–87, July 1977.

Examines recent legislation concerning the custody of children, the rights of parents, and the needs of the child in cases of abuse and neglect.

240. Dickens, Bernard M. "Legal Responses to Child Abuse." **Family Law Quarterly**, 12:1–36, Spring 1978.

Explores the legal system's intervention into the family, when it is necessary and the basic problems involved in legal intervention. Basic legal principles and the interests and values effected by legal determinations are also examined.

241. Disney, Dorothy Cameron. "I Was a Battered Wife." **Ladies' Home Journal**, 96:18+, April 1979.

Discusses one woman's experience as a battered wife.

242. Dobash, R. Emerson and Russell P. Dobash. "Love, Honour and Obey: Institutional Ideologies and the Struggle for Battered Women." **Contemporary Crisis**, 1:403-15, 1977.

Examines wifebeating in terms of the ideologies which legitimize it. Efforts to prevent wife battering are also examined.

243. _____. **Violence Against Wives**. New York: The Free Press, 1979. 339 pp.

Discusses violence against wives as an expression of patriarchial domination. Wives as victims and the legacy of the "appropriate victim," the structure of the nuclear family as a contributory factor in wife abuse, and social situations in which violence occurs are explored. Responses of relatives, friends, police and the legal system are also examined. Presents a selected bibliography of relevant literature.

244. _____. "Wives: The 'Appropriate' Victims of Marital Violence." **Victimology: An International Journal**, 2:426-42, 1977-78.

The ideologies and legal, religious, and cultural factors which legitimize violence against women by their husbands are reviewed.

245. Doek, Jack E. "Child Abuse in the Netherlands: The Medical Referee." **Chicago-Kent Law Review**, 54:785-826, 1978.

Focuses on the role of "confidential doctors" appointed to deal specifically with child abuse. The problem of child abuse in the Netherlands before the initiation of this program is explored, and the advantages and disadvantages of such a system are highlighted. The application of this method to other countries, such as the United States, is examined.

246. Doerr, Aleta E. "Reporting Child Abuse and Neglect: Oregon's Legislation." **Oregon Law Review**, 57:444-55, 1978.

Presents a definition of child abuse as stated in Oregon's present law. Upon analyzing the Oregon law concerning child abuse, it was found that the law fails to set forth clear guidelines for mandatory reporting, and should be revised to supply a clearer definition. The statute must also encourage the identification of the problem and lead to satisfactory state intervention.

247. Doris, John L. "Child Abuse and Neglect: An Introduction to the Family Life Development Center." **Human Ecology Forum**, 5(2):4-7, Autumn 1974.

Relates the story of Mary Ellen Wilson, a severely battered child, who was the first recorded recipient of institution help for a child abuse victim. As a result of this case, which was handled through The American Society for the Prevention of Cruelty to Animals, the New York Society for the Prevention of Cruelty to Children was formed. Examines the growth of public awareness of the problem, and details, with commentary, the New York State law concerning child abuse. The establishment of a Family Life Center at Cornell University is also discussed.

248. Dow, Mildred. "Policy Involvement." **Violence in the Family**. Edited by Marie Borland. Atlantic Highlands, New Jersey: Humanities Press, 1976, pp. 129–35.

Discusses the role of the police in domestic disputes and problems of enforcing legislation with respect to cases of child abuse and domestic violence.

249. Drake, Frances M. "The Position of the Local Authority." **Concerning Child Abuse: Papers Presented by the Tunbridge Wells Study Group on Non-Accidental Injury to Children**. Edited by Alfred White Franklin. Edinburgh: Churchill Livingstone, 1975, pp. 85–94.

Examines the working methods of social work in cases of child abuse, and the powers and constraints of the local authority in these cases.

250. Drews, Kay. "The Child and His School." **Helping the Battered Child and His Family**. Edited by C. Henry Kempe and Ray E. Helfer. Philadelphia: J.B. Lippincott Company, 1972, pp. 115–23.

Relates a study in which questionaires were sent to one-half of the school districts in the United States in order to ascertain if schools were prepared, and willing, to provide help for battered children and their families. Details the incidence of handling child abuse cases by the school and the methods employed to handle them, school and agency cooperation, and the inadequacy of standard operating procedures. An appropriate standard operating procedure is suggested.

251. Duis, Perry R. and Glen E. Holt. "The Conscience of Chicago." **Chicago**, 29(12):162 & 168–69, December 1980.

Describes Jessie Binford's sixty year crusade against child abuse in Chicago.

252. Duncan, Darlene. **Handbook for Battered, Abused Women**. Hollywood, California: CAN-DU Publications, 1977. 34 pp.

Examines alternatives available to abused women who seek help.

253. Duncan, Elaine. "Recognition and Protection of the Family's Interests in Child Abuse Proceedings." **Journal of Family Law**, 13:8033–38, 1973–74.

Discusses legal proceedings in child abuse cases and complications which may arise during these proceedings. The rights of the parent and child, circumstances warranting the termination of parental rights, and the subsequent removal of the child from home are also explored.

254. Duncan, Jane Watson and Glen M. Duncan. "A Study of Some Homicidal Adolescents." **American Journal of Psychiatry**, 127(1):74–78, 1971.

Presents five cases of adolescents who killed their parents, and the sequence of events that led to the act. Criteria is suggested for assessing the potential for homicidal behavior within the family.

255. Duncan, Lois. "My Husband Batters Our Daughter." **Ladies' Home Journal**, 98(8): 10+ , August 1981.

Discusses a case of child abuse by presenting the mother's, father's, and counselor's comments on the situation.

256. Dunstan, Gordon R. "Means to Good Ends: A Theological View." **The Challenge of Child Abuse**. Edited by Alfred White Franklin. London: Academic Press, 1977, pp. 240–48.

Examines social and theological issues and the family, emphasizing the need for a common morality and the importance of the Christian religion.

257. Duquette, Donald N. "Liberty and Lawyers in Child Protection." **The Battered Child**. Edited by C. Henry Kempe and Ray E. Helfer. Chicago: University of Chicago Press, 1980, pp. 316–29.

Discusses the role of the lawyer in child protection cases and details the roles of the child's attorney, the protective services attorney, and the parents' attorney.

258. Durbin, Karen. "Wife Beating." **Ladies' Home Journal**, 91(6):62–67, June 1974.

Examines the issue of wife beating, with the aid of case studies to illustrate the nature of the problem.

259. Duryea, Perry, and others. "Child Maltreatment: A New Approach in Educational Programs." **Children Today**, 7:13–16+, September–October 1978.

Discusses an educational program conducted by the National Alliance for the Prevention and Treatment of Child Abuse and Maltreatment. This program consists of symposia conducted in various cities in the United States. Issues of concern included punishment as a possible deterrent to child abuse, society intervening in the family if the possibility of harm to a child exists, and the imposition of child rearing practices on others.

260. Earl, Howard G. "Ten Thousand Children Battered and Starved." **The Battered Child**. Compiled by Jerome E. Leavitt. Morristown, New Jersey: General Learning Press, 1974.

Describes types and presents questions and answers concerning various aspects of child abuse. Problems confronting physicians in abuse cases are also examined.

261. Easley, Kevin O. *"State v. Smith*: Presumption of Husband's Coercion Over Wife." **North Carolina Central Law Journal**, 9:208–15, Spring 1978.

A common law doctrine in the state of North Carolina states that if a criminal act is committed by a woman in the presence of her husband, it is presumed that her husband had threatened or coerced her into committing the act. If this presumption is disproved, the wife cannot be convicted. The case of *State v. Smith*, in which a wife appealed a conviction on the grounds that she had been coerced by her husband is explored. The appeal did not overturn the decision of the lower court. It is suggested that this presumption, and the defense of marital coercion, be abolished.

262. Easson, William M. and Richard M. Steinhilber. "Murderous Aggression by Children and Adolescents." **Archives of General Psychiatry**, 4:27–35, January 1961.

States that murderous violence committed by children occurs when it is fostered by the parents. Literature on the psychogenesis of murder is examined, and cases dealing with the problem are presented. Concludes by saying that in all of these cases, psychopathology was present in the family, and that parents condoned the assaults.

263. Ebeling, Nancy B. "Preventing Strains and Stresses in Protective Services." **Child Abuse: Intervention and Treatment**. Edited by Nancy B. Ebeling and Deborah A. Hill. Acton, Massachusetts: Publishing Sciences Group, Inc., 1975, pp. 47–51.

Discusses the feelings and attitudes of protective service workers in working with abused and neglected children, and how these feelings are handled in order to make the work more comfortable for the worker and more effective for the client.

264. _____. "Thoughts on Intervention." **Child Abuse: Intervention and Treatment**. Edited by Nancy B. Ebeling and Deborah A. Hill. Acton, Massachusetts: Publishing Sciences Group, Inc., 1975, pp. 3–9.

Examines intervention from the point of view of the community and states that successful community intervention depends to a large extent on community attitudes.

265. Ebeling, Nancy B. and Deborah A. Hill, editors. **Child Abuse: Intervention and Treatment**. Acton, Massachusetts: Publishing Sciences Group, Inc., 1975. 182 pp.

Provides a therapeutic approach to child abuse by presenting selections which deal with case finding, recognizing and dealing with the emotional reactions to child abuse, management of the program, diagnosis and treatment, community resources and involvement, and the law and child abuse.

266. Eber, L.P. "The Battered Wife's Dilemma." **Hastings Law Journal**,

32(4):895–931, March 1981.

Explores motives, remedies and criminal categories in the area of wife beating. Concludes that existing remedies, shelters and self-defense requirements are inadequate.

267. Edmiston, Susan. "If You Loved Me, You Wouldn't Hurt Me." **Redbook**, 153:99–100+, May 1979.

Women relate their experiences as battered wives, and the author discusses the problem of wifebeating. Places to get help in various areas of the country are listed.

268. Education Commission of the States. Child Abuse and Neglect Project. **Child Abuse and Neglect in the States: A Digest of Critical Elements of Reporting and Central Registries**. Denver, Colorado: Education Commission of the States, 1976. 21 pp.

Summarizes the reporting system for child abuse and neglect in each state. Each summary includes who must report, who is permitted to report, the form of the report and when it should be made, to whom the report should be made, penalties for not reporting, and immunities for those who do report.

269. Edwards, John N. and Mary Ball Brauburger. "Exchange and Parent-Youth Conflict." **Journal of Marriage and the Family**, 35(1):101–08, 1973.

Discusses a study which observed 188 middle class families and found an exchange system existing between parents and children, and that when this system broke down, conflict resulted. Examines ways in which adolescents increase independence by accepting fewer rewards from parents, and ways in which this contributes to the conflict situation.

270. Edwards, Richard L., and others. **Resource Manual on Family Violence**. Knoxville, Tennessee: University of Tennessee School of Social Work, 1979. 214 pp.

Presents resource materials which focus on skill development and strategies for treatment rather than on increased awareness about the problem of family violence. Selections on identification, reporting, and case management are included.

271. Egeland, Byron and Don Brunnquell. "An At-Risk Approach to the Study of Child Abuse." **Journal of the American Academy of Child Psychiatry**, 18:219, 1979.

Relates a study which followed 275 high-risk mothers and children through the child's first year of life. Discusses the differences between mothers within this group who abused their children, and those who did not. Differences between abused and well-treated children are also examined.

272. Egeland, Byron and L. Alan Sroufe. "Attachment and Early Maltreatment." **Child Development**, 52(1):44–52, March 1981.

compares cases of maltreated children with cases of children who received good care. Results showed that the maltreated group had a low proportion of secure attachment following its first year of life. On the other hand, in the group of well treated children, patterns of attachment were present.

273. Egeland, Byron and Brian Vaughn. "Failure of 'Bond Formation' as a Cause of Abuse, Neglect, and Maltreatment." **American Journal of Orthropsychiatry**, 51(1):78–84, January 1981.

Results of a study showed that among a group of high-risk mothers, limited contact with the child at birth was not related to later disorders of mothering.

274. Eisenberg, Alan D. and E.J. Seymour. "The Self-Defense Plea and Battered Women." **Trial**, 14:34–42, July 1978.

Discusses specific cases of women who kill battering husbands and plead self defense. Issues explored include failure of the legal system to enforce human rights within the family, why victims stay with battering husbands, battering as a defense, the flight rule (the victim must take advantage of all escape rules before she may defend herself), current legislation, and legislation in process.

275. Eisenberg, Sue E. and Patricia L. Micklow. "The Assaulted Wife: 'Catch 22' Revisited." **Women's Rights Law Reporter**, 3:138–61, Spring–Summer 1977.

Wifebeating is viewed as an index of the devaluation of women and is not regarded as a crime. This discussion attempts to determine whether wifebeating is actually a crime or a social problem.

276. Elbow, Margaret. "Theoretical Considerations of Violent Marriages." **Social Casework**, 58:515–26, November 1977.

Discusses the theoretical considerations of marital violence, emphasizing intervention by professionals. Guidelines for intervention are presented and four abuse syndromes are described. Professionals are urged to be aware of the potential for homicide in violent marriages and to avoid trying to "rescue" the victim, as this type of intervention may lead to additional frustration and resentment on the part of the abusive husband.

277. Elder, Glen H. and Charles E. Bowerman. "Family Structure and Child-Rearing Patterns: The Effect of Family Size and Sex Composition." **American Sociological Review**, 28(6):891–905, 1963.

States that family size and the sex of the children have a significant effect on the type of punishment they receive, particularly physical discipline.

278. Elkind, James, and others. "Current Realities Haunting Advocates of Abused Children." **Social Casework**, 58:527–31, November 1977.

Discusses problems associated when professionals are working with abusive families, and the reactions of staff to these problems. Suggests ways to make the professional's work in this area "more tolerable."

279. Elliott, Frank A. "The Neurology of Explosive Rage: The Dyscontrol Syndrome." **Battered Women: A Psychosociological Study of Domestic Violence.** Edited by Maria Roy. New York: Van Nostrand Reinhold Company, 1977, pp. 98–109.

Examines the dyscontrol syndrome as an important cause of wife and child abuse. Treatment for the syndrome is also explored.

280. Elmer, Elizabeth. "Abused Children and Community Resources." **International Journal of Offender Therapy**, 11(1):16–23, 1967.

Considers and evaluates various methods for handling child abuse cases. The most effective measures are suggested, and comments are made on the new mandatory laws passed in the United States.

281. _____. "Child Abuse: The Family's Cry for Help." **Journal of Psychiatric Nursing**, 5(4):332–41, 1967.

Suggests that child abuse is usually a result of social problems within the family which result in accumulated stress, rather than an act of willful abuse. The roles of the community, medical personnel, and the extended family in prevention and management of child abuse cases are also discussed.

282. _____. "Child Abuse: A Symptom of Family Crisis." **Crisis of Family Disorganization**. Edited by E. Pavenstedt. New York: Behavioral Publications, 1971.

Discusses a follow-up study conducted at the Children's Hospital in Pittsburgh. Results showed that in almost all cases, the mother was responsible for the abuse, and that stress caused the mothers to resort to violence against the child. The need for prevention is emphasized, and methods for prevention and management are suggested.

283. _____. "A Follow-Up Study of Traumatized Children." **Pediatrics**, 59:273–79, February 1977.

Describes a follow-up study in which victims of abuse were matched with victims of accidents. Many conditions in the families from both groups were found to be similar and it is suggested that conditions of living in lower class communities may act as a strong influence on the child's development, perhaps as strong an influence as is exerted by child abuse.

284. _____. **Fragile Families, Troubled Children**. Pittsburgh: University of Pittsburgh Press, 1977. 160 pp.

Discusses the results of a study which compared seventeen abused children with seventeen who had received injuries as a result of accidents. The cases and controls were matched on demographic and socioeconomic variables. Another group was also added to the study. This group was matched on the same characteristics as the other two groups, but the children in this group

47

suffered no injuries from reported accidents before the age of one year. It was concluded that many of the controls as well as the cases turned out to be intellectually retarded and developed social and emotional problems. The authors emphasize the fact that demographic variables must be considered when analyzing the effects of child abuse on the victim. An index and bibliography are included.

285. _____. "Hazards in Determining Child Abuse." **Child Welfare**, 45:28–33, 1966.

Focuses on the necessity of social evaluation of families suspected of abuse. Problems of definition are discussed and a study of children at Children's Hospital in Pittsburgh whose physical symptoms indicated the possibility of abuse is examined. States that only by evaluating such variables as the history of caretakers, patterns of child care, and behavior patterns of children will it be possible to distinguish abusive from non-abusive families.

286. _____. "Identification of Abused Children." Children, 10:180–84, 1963.

Discusses a study of 50 former patients of the Children's Hospital in Pittsburgh. Defines abuse and neglect, and examines the processes used by the medical profession for the identification of victims of child abuse.

287. _____. "Studies of Child Abuse and Infant Accidents." **The Mental Health of the Child**. National Institute of Mental Health. Washington, D.C.: U.S. Government Printing Office, 1971, pp. 343–70.

Reports findings of a study and follow-up which examined 50 families with children suffering from injuries which indicated abuse or neglect. Characteristics of abusing mothers and the presence of major health problems in abusing and non-abusing mothers are discussed, emphasizing stressful situations which may lead to abuse.

288. Elmer, Elizabeth and others. "Child Abuse Training: A Community-Based Interdisciplinary Program." **Community Mental Health Journal**, 14(3):179–89, Fall 1978.

States that trained personnel in the area of child abuse are scarce, and describes a training program which focuses on the cooperative efforts of personnel from different disciplines. The organization of the program, training for personnel, formulation of curriculum, evaluation measures, and the implementation of the program in the community are among the subjects discussed.

289. Elwell, Mary Ellen. "Sexually Assaulted Children and Their Families." **Social Casework**, 60:227–35, April 1979.

Discusses gaps in recent research on children who have been sexually assaulted, implications of the findings, and topics for future studies. The incidence of sexual assaults on children, emotional effects of the attack, typologies of sexually abused children, the victim-offender relationship, categories of victimization, and crisis therapy for the victim are examined.

290. English, Peter. "Husband Who Rapes His Wife." **New Law Journal**, 126:1223-25, December 9, 1976.

Examines the rule which states that a man cannot legally rape his wife. This rule as applied by the English law is considered to be outdated. Associated issues such as false accusations are also explored.

291. Erlanger, Howard S. "Social Class Differences in Parents' Use of Physical Punishment." **Violence in the Family**. Edited by Suzanne K. Steinmetz and Murray A. Straus. New York: Harper and Row, 1974, pp. 150-58.

Examines the relationship between social status and techniques of parental punishment of children.

292. Evans, Alan L. "Eriksonian Measure of Personality Development in Child Abusing Mothers." **Psychological Reports**, 44(3):963-66, June 1979.

Mothers were administered the Eriksonian development test, which was designed to assess personality developmental stages. Abusive mothers, as expected, scored lower on measures of the first six developmental stages than did non-abusing mothers. Implications of the findings for future study is discussed.

293. Fairburn, A.C. and A.C. Hunt. "Caffey's 'Third Syndrome' – A Critical Evaluation." **Medicine, Science and the Law**, 4(2):123-26, April 1964.

Describes 7 cases in which multiple fractures were found in infants and which investigation proved to be the result of parental violence. Circumstances which may lead to family violence are discussed.

294. Faller, Kathleen Coulborn, editor. **Social Work With Abused and Neglected Children**. New York: The Free Press, 1981. 256 pp.

Articles discuss the scope and nature of child abuse, types and causes of maltreatment, characteristics of abused children, treatment and assessment, and the decision to remove a child from an abusive home. The interdisciplinary approach to successful management of the problem is also examined.

295. **Family Violence Prosecution Manual**. Santa Barbara, California: Office of the District Attorney, 1980. 90 pp.

Outlines the policy of the Santa Barbara County District Attorney's office concerning family violence cases. A brief bibliography, a list of agencies in the Santa Barbara area which aid battered women, concerns of violence victims, and sample documents used in family violence cases are also presented.

296. Fanaroff, A.A. and others. "Follow-up of Low Birth Weight Infants — The

Predictive Value of Maternal Visiting Patterns." **Pediatrics**, 49:287–90, 1972.

Discusses maternal visiting of low-birth weight infants as indicative of the way the mother will treat the child later. It was found that mothers who did not visit the infant often had a higher incidence of abuse and neglect than did frequent visitors.

297. Fanshel, David. "Decision Making Under Uncertainty: Foster Care for Abused or Neglected Children?" **American Journal of Public Health**, 71(7):685–86, July 1981.

Examines an article by Runyan and others in the same issue of the journal, and states that it provides insight into the challenge posed by child abuse and neglect cases as it relates to the decision to place a child in a foster home. Findings and their significance are summarized.

298. Faulk, M. "Men Who Assault Their Wives." **Battered Women: A Psychosociological Study of Domestic Violence**. Edited by Maria Roy. New York: Van Nostrand Rheinold Company, 1977, pp. 119–26.

Presents the results of 23 interviews conducted with men who were in police custody for seriously assaulting their wives. The nature of the charges, outcome of the trial, the relationship of offender and victim, previous offenses, and previous "warnings" are among the areas examined.

299. _____. "Sexual Factors in Marital Violence." **Medical Aspects of Human Sexuality**, 11:30–43, October 1977.

Discusses the possibility of sexual problems acting to provoke violence within a marriage.

300. Fay, Shirl E. "The Social Worker's Use of the Court." **Child Abuse: Intervention and Treatment**. Edited by Nancy B. Ebeling and Deborah A. Hill. Acton, Massachusetts: Publishing Sciences Group, Inc., 1975, pp. 121–27.

Examines the social worker's decision to initiate court action in cases of child abuse.

301. Feinstein, Howard M. and others. "Group Therapy for Mothers With Infanticidal Impulses." **The Battered Child**. Compiled by Jerome E. Leavitt. Morristown, New Jersey: General Learning Press, 1974, pp. 62–65.

Describes a study which addressed itself to the hypothesis that women who present infanticidal thoughts as a significant part of their psychopathology have biographical and other characteristics in common. A second hypothesis examined is that group psychotherapy offers special advantages for treating women with the impulse to harm their children. Case studies are presented to illustrate the issues raised.

302. Felder, Samuel. "A Lawyer's View of Child Abuse." **The Battered Child**. Compiled by Jerome E. Leavitt. Morristown, New Jersey: General Learning Press, 1974, pp. 82–89.

Presents a lawyer's view of child abuse, including causes for parents behavior, the role of the lawyer in child abuse cases, history of child abuse legislation, the New York law in 1969 and 1970, and criminal prosecutions in child abuse cases. The need for additional protective services is suggested.

303. Feldman, Kenneth W. "Child Abuse by Burning." **The Battered Child**. Edited by C. Henry Kempe and Ray E. Helfer. Chicago: University of Chicago Press, 1980, pp. 147–62.

Discusses burn injury as a consequence of abuse. The problems encountered by a physician in treating the victim, effective treatment planning, assistance to the family to prevent additional injury, and patterns of various types of burns are among the topics explored.

304. Ferro, Frank. "Protecting Children: The National Center on Child Abuse and Neglect." **Childhood Education**, 52:63–66, November–December 1975.

Describes the progress made by the National Center on Child Abuse and Neglect toward the prevention of child abuse, emphasizing the role of the educational system in the identification and prevention of abuse. A detailed description of a project designed to investigate the role of educational personnel in the control of child abuse and neglect, and funded by the Center, is also presented.

305. Field, Martha H. and Henry F. Field. "Marital Violence and the Criminal Process: Neither Justice nor Peace." **Social Service Review**, 47(2):221–40, 1973.

States that marital crimes account for a large proportion of crimes of violence. Statistics are detailed which support this statement, and a general discussion of marital violence is presented.

306. Fields, Marjory. "Does This Vow Include Wife Beating?" **Human Rights**, 7:40–45, Summer 1978.

Wife beating is discussed as a civil rights problem. Examines the incidence, seriousness, treatment and prevention of wife battering, and analyzes prevailing stereotypes of the battered wife and the violent home. Suggests that solutions can be realized only when perspectives which condone domestic violence are changed.

307. _____. "Representing Battered Wives, or What to Do Until the Police Arrive." **Family Law Reporter**, 3(22):4025–29, April 1977.

Describes options available to battered women, focusing on legal alternatives. Special problems to be expected by a woman choosing to report abuse to the police are outlined.

308. _____. "Wife Beating: The Hidden Offense." **New York Law Journal**, 175(83):1-7, April 1976.

The dimensions and characteristics of wifebeating are examined, focusing on the role of the legal system in cases of family violnece. The absence of adequate services for battered wives is also discussed, and the establishment of shelters to aid abused women is explored.

309. Fields, Marjory and Elyse Lehman. **A Handbook for Beaten Women: How to Get Help if Your Husband or Boyfriend Beats You**. Brooklyn, New York: Brooklyn Legal Services Corporation, 1981. 32 pp.

A self-help guide for battered women who want to change their situations. Offers step-by-step instructions for obtaining help from the legal system. Medical, legal, emotional, financial, and other pertinent information is also included.

310. Finkelhov, David. **Sexually Victimized Children**. New York: The Free Press, 1979. 228 pp.

Examines the sexual victimization of children, both within the home and outside. The social and family backgrounds of victimized children, the role of marital conflict, and incest are among the topics explored. Distinguishes between sexual abuse, physical abuse, and rape, and discusses possible reasons why they occur.

311. Fiora-Gormally, Nancy. "Battered Wives Who Kill: Double Standard Out of Court, Single Standard In?" **Law and Human Behavior**, 2(2):133-65, 1978.

States that the time has come for a close scrutiny of the laws regarding murder, manslaughter, and self defense, and of the applicability of these to the battered wife as defendant. Examines the elements of each and the legal distinctions between them. Presents a brief description of the "reasonable man" standard as it applies to elements of manslaughter and explores the sociocultural definitions of woman and wife, with a view toward comparing these norms with the behavior of a reasonable man under attack. Details the life pattern of the battered wife syndrome, and discusses the necessity for some adaptation of the standards of self-defense and manslaughter, in order to reconcile them with society's contradictory standards for a reasonable woman.

312. Flammang, C.J. "Interviewing Child Victims of Sex Offenders." **Rape Victimology**. Edited by LeRoy G. Schultz. Springfield, Illinois: Charles C. Thomas, 1975, pp. 245-56.

Discusses police procedure for interviewing the child victim of a sexual offense and the problems associated with cases involving children.

313. Fleming, G.M. "Cruelty to Children." **British Medical Journal**, 5549:421-22, 1967.

States that the incidence of child abuse is difficult to estimate due to the difficulty of obtaining legal proof, and the social service system relying less on action by the courts than on family casework. Discusses the characteristics of abusing parents and the range of injuries sustained by abused children. The importance of cooperation among medical, legal and social agencies in the treatment of child abuse is emphasized.

314. Fleming, Jennifer Baker. **Stopping Wife Abuse: A Guide to the Emotional, Psychological, and Legal Implications for the Abused Woman and Those Helping Her**. Garden City, New York: Anchor Press/ Doubleday, 1979. 532 pp.

Provides a detailed examination of the problem of wife abuse. Working with the victim, the legal system, legislation pertaining to wife abuse, children exposed to domestic violence, counseling as treatment for the abuser and the abused, and shelter and support services are among the topics explored. A list of programs, by state, which provide services to battered women is presented, and a short bibliography of pertinent literature is included.

315. Flynn, John P. "Recent Findings Related to Wife Abuse." **Social Casework**, 58:13–20, January 1977.

Summarizes research on spouse abuse conducted in Kalamazoo, Michigan. Topics examined include attitudes toward family violence, the incidence of family violence, socioeconomic indicators, precipitating factors, the history of violence in assailants, and services available to violent families. Concludes that community resources are not sufficient to deal with the problem.

316. Flynn, William R. "Frontier Justice: A Contribution to the Theory of Child Battery." **American Journal of Psychiatry**, 127(3):375–79, September 1970.

Discusses child abuse as being dependent upon structural and dynamic elements within a person who cares for children. Reports on two cases of mothers who abused one of their children, concluding that defective defense ego structures are frequently responsible for child abuse, and parents who deny and repress anger in themselves project it onto their children.

317. Fojtik, Kathleen M. **Wife Beating: How to Develop a Wife Assault Task Force and Project**. Ann Arbor, Michigan: NOW Domestic Violence and Spouse Assault Fund, Inc., 1976. 42 pp.

Details procedures involved in developing a wife assault task force and project. Appendices include a legal definition of assault, how to document the incidence of wife assault, an example of a wife assault complaint, court watching procedure in wife assault cases, a wife assault mailing list for the state of Michigan, and a questionaire for assaulted wives. A summary of a study on wife beating conducted in the Kalamazoo area and copies of articles on wife beating are also presented, and a bibliography is included.

318. Follingstad, Diane R. "A Reconceptualization of Issues in the Treatment of

Abused Women: A Case Study." **Psychotherapy: Theory, Research and Practice**, 17(3):294–303, Fall 1980.

Discusses the need for reconceptualizing the personality profile of abused women as a result of living in an abusing situation, rather than as the antecedent that provokes abuse from the spouse. Outlines a strategy for therapeutic intervention through a case study that advocates changing beliefs and developing skills prior to instituting change in the abused woman's environment.

319. Follis, Peggy. "Recognizing Non-Accidental Injury in Children." **Nursing Times**, 71:2034–35, December 1975.

The operation of an interdisciplinary team developed for the management of child abuse cases is examined.

320. Fonseka, S. "A Study of Wife-Beating in the Camberwell Area." **The British Journal of Clinical Practice**, 28:400–02, December 1974.

Presents the results of a study of victims of wifebeating in the Camberwell area of England. The incidence, related factors, and patterns of injury were examined.

321. Fontana, Vincent J. "Child Abuse: Tomorrow's Problems Begin Today." **Catholic Lawyer**, 22:297–304, Autumn 1976.

Discusses the problem of child abuse, its prevention, and treatment. Fallacies which retard progress in the area of battered children are also examined.

322. _____. "Child Abuse in Megalopolis." **New York State Journal of Medicine**, 76:1799–1802, October 1976.

Describes child abuse in New York City as representative of child abuse in cities with similar characteristics.

323. _____. "An Insidious and Disturbing Medical Entity." **The Battered Child**. Compiled by Jerome E. Leavitt. Morristown, New Jersey: General Learning Press, 1974, pp. 187–91.

Examines the problem of child abuse, including symptoms of maltreatment, the maltreatment syndrome in children, reporting of cases, agency obligations in cases of suspected abuse, the use of the legal and welfare systems, and the role of the courts in cases of child abuse. Concludes that the maltreatment of children is a pediatric disease as well as a parental disease. It is preventable, and can be diagnosed, recognized and treated. The importance of cooperation and integration among various agencies for child protection is stressed.

324. _____. "The Maltreated Child of Our Times." **Villanova Law Review**, 23:448–57, 1977–78.

Following a discussion of the maltreatment of children, the role of the physician in the management of these cases is described. A multidisciplinary inpatient and outpatient program is explored.

325. _____. "To Prevent the Abuse in the Future." **Trial**, 10:14–18, May–June 1974.

In order to more accurately and effectively deal with the problem of child abuse, the author proposes that the term "Battered Child Syndrome" be changed to "Maltreatment Syndrome." The reasons for this proposal are outlined.

326. _____. **Somewhere a Child Is Crying: Maltreatment – Causes and Prevention**. New York: Macmillan Publishing Company, Inc., 1973. 268 pp.

Defines the maltreatment syndrome and presents a detailed discussion of child abuse. Topics examined include families and the cycle of violence, children's rights, the legal system in child maltreatment cases, parents who abuse their children, and treatment of child abuse cases.

327. _____. "We Must Stop the Vicious Cycle of Child Abuse." **Parents Magazine**, December 1975, p. 8.

Presents statistics concerning the incidence of child abuse and lists available resources and services.

328. _____. "Which Parents Abuse Children?" **The Battered Child**. Compiled by Jerome E. Leavitt. Morristown, New Jersey: General Learning Press, 1974, pp. 195–99.

Reprints a letter from an abusing parent who sought and received help in solving her problem. Discusses characteristics of abusing parents, and evidence which may indicate child abuse to a physician. The physician's resistance to involvement in child abuse cases is also examined.

329. Fontana, Vincent J. and Douglas J. Besharov. **The Maltreated Child: The Maltreatment Syndrome in Children, a Medical, Legal and Social Guide**. Springfield, Illinois: Charles C. Thomas, Publisher, 1977. 156 pp.

Presents an historical perspective of the problem and describes the "maltreatment syndrome" in children. Identification of the problem and its social manifestations are also discussed. In the examination of preventative measures, medical, social and legal responsibilities are explored, and the Model Child Protection Act of 1975 is presented. The work is highlighted by case reports and illustrations.

330. Fontana, Vincent J. and Esther Robinson. "A Multidisciplinary Approach to the Treatment of Child Abuse." **Pediatrics**, 57:760–64, May 1976.

Outlines a treatment program for child abuse in New York City in which teams of professionals from the medical, social, and psychiatric services work together to provide a comprehensive system of management and prevention.

331. Fontana, Vincent J. and others. "The Maltreatment Syndrome in Children." **New England Journal of Medicine**, 269(26):1389–94, December 26, 1963.

Presents cases of the maltreatment of children by parents and discusses the problem. Focuses on the need for immediate attention and protection of children, and outlines the responsibilities of the community, the medical, and the legal systems in cases of child abuse.

332. Ford, D. "The Emergence of the Child as a Legal Entity." **The Maltreatment of Children**. Edited by Selwyn M. Smith. Baltimore: University Park Press, 1978, pp. 393–413.

Discusses the child as a possession from an historical perspective and examines the concept of the child as a separate individual in the eyes of the law.

333. Forrer, Stephen E. "Battered Children and Counselor Responsibility." **Child Abuse: Perspectives on Diagnosis, Treatment, and Prevention**. Edited by Roberta Kalmar. Dubuque, Iowa: Kendall/Hunt Publishing Company, 1977, pp. 117–22.

Discusses the role of the school counselor in preventing child abuse. Topics examined include counseling the abuser and the abused, the counselor and the community, functioning of the child abuse council, and the participation of the counselor in community mental health responses to child abuse.

334. Fosson, Abe R. and Ho Ho Kaak. **Child Abuse and Neglect Case Studies**. Flushing, New York: Medical Examination Publishing Company, Inc., 1977. 196 pp.

Presents an in-depth analysis of fifty case histories of child abuse and neglect. Treatment, prevention, identification, and an assessment of the abusive environment (social, emotional, and domestic factors) are examined.

335. Foster, Henry H. "Violence Towards Children: Medical Legal Aspects." **Violence and Responsibility**. Edited by Robert L. Sadoff. New York: SP Medical and Scientific Books, 1978, pp. 117–23.

Offers a general discussion of violence against children, emphasizing the need for protection to prevent abuse, the limited effectiveness of the law as a means of social control, and the importance of cooperation among professionals when dealing with child abuse. Also examines the problem of child abuse as a reflection of a general deterioration in the values of today's society.

336. Francke, Linda Bird. "Battered Women." **Newsweek**, 87:47–48, February 2, 1976.

Presents a general discussion of wifebeating. Topics discussed include the incidence of the problem, class linkages or lack of them, difficulties in documenting the occurance of wife battering, police intervention, role of the courts, and ways in which women are assisting battered women with the development of shelters, hotlines, and crisis centers.

337. Franklin, Alfred White, editor. **The Challenge of Child Abuse**. London: Academic Press, 1977. 298 pp.

Presents the proceedings of a conference sponsored by the Royal Society of Medicine which was held on June 2–4, 1976. Selections discuss battering in relation to deviant behavior, protective casework in relation to child abuse, psychiatric report of cases of child abuse, alternative family care, the nature of aggression and its application to child abuse, court problems in management of family cases, punishment and rehabilitation, and society's obligation to the family.

338. _____. "Child Abuse as a Challenge." **The Challenge of Child Abuse**. Edited by Alfred White Franklin. London: Academic Press, 1977, pp. 271–83.

Discusses the public's demand for a scapegoat and the role of subcultures and cultures on family behavior. Also examines improved family health and its role in society, and the issues of prediction, prevention, and confidentiality in regard to child abuse.

339. _____. **Concerning Child Abuse: Papers Presented by the Tunbridge Wells Study Group on Non-Accidental Injury in Children**. Edinburgh: Churchill Livingstone, 1975. 189 pp.

Among the topics discussed are the medical aspects of the problem, the social service element, the role of the police and the law, and the education of personnel who deal with child abuse. An overview of the problem and a summary of the book are also presented.

340. _____. "Management of the Problem." **The Maltreatment of Children**. Edited by Selwyn M. Smith. Baltimore: University Park Press, 1978, pp. 83–94.

Describes the objectives and functions of management and discusses the role of institutions and professions in cases of child abuse.

341. _____. **Second International Congress on Child Abuse and Neglect: Abstracts**. Oxford, England: Pergamon Press, 1978. 289 pp.

Presents abstracts of speeches delivered at the Second International Congress on Child Abuse and Neglect, held in London on September 12–15, 1978. Themes of the Congress included the child himself, the family, and the community.

342. Fraser, Brian G. "A Glance at the Past, a Gaze at the Present, a Glimpse at the Future: A Critical Analysis of the Development of Child Abuse Reporting Statutes." **Chicago-Kent Law Review**, 54:641–86, 1978.

Discusses the problem of child abuse, including identification, investigation, intervention and treatment. Presents a detailed common format for reporting statutes which is used by most states, and explores some general problems with legislation. States that legislation is not the solution to the problem of child abuse, but merely a framework to assist in the development of solutions.

343. Fraser, Brian G. "Legislative Approaches to Child Abuse: A Pragnatic Approach." **The American Criminal Law Review**, 12(1):103–24, Summer 1974.

States that in suspected cases of child abuse, there are two potential problems to be addressed: proper response to the child, and what to do with an abusing parent. Discusses methods of approaching the problem, legislative approaches to reporting, the case against against the criminal prosecution of abusing parents, and therapeutic treatment of child abuse.

344. _____. "A Pragmatic Alternative to Current Legislative Approaches to Child Abuse." **American Criminal Law Review**, 12:103–24, Summer 1974.

Explores the issue of mandatory reporting of child abuse cases, noting trends in legislation and basic differences in statutes for the states. Revisions to the child abuse law are suggested.

345. _____. "Towards a More Practical Central Registry." **Denver Law Journal**, 51:509–28, 1974.

Discusses the concept of a central registry for child abuse and presents the state statutory provisions for central registries by state.

346. Fraser, Brian G. and Harold P. Martin. "An Advocate for the Abused Child." **The Abused Child: A Multidisciplinary Approach to Developmental Issues and Treatment**. Edited by Harold P. Martin. Cambridge, Massachusetts: Ballinger Publishing Company, 1976, pp. 165–78.

Examines the need for independent representation for the abused child.

347. Frazier, Claude A. "Child Abuse: Society's Symptom of Stress." **Christianity Today**, 21:6–8, June 3, 1977.

Outlines the responsibility of the Christian in regard to the problem of physical and emotional abuse of children.

348. Freeman, M.D.A. "Violence Against Women: Does the Legal System Provide Solutions or Itself Constitute the Problem?" **British Journal of Law and Society**, 7(2):215–41, Winter 1980.

Provides possible explanations as to why wife beating occurs. Considers the cultural context and legal consequences of the problem and recommends analyzing the issue before suggesting what may be only temporary solutions.

349. Frenzel, Rita. "Claiming My Rights."**Fight Back!: Feminist Resistance to Male Violence**. Minneapolis, Minnesota: Cleis Press, 1981, pp. 39–41.

Presents a personal account of a lesbian mother who was assaulted by her parents and her brother in a fight over custody of her son.

350. Friedman, Kathleen. **Battered Women: Manual for Survival**. Baltimore, Maryland: Women's Law Center, 1976. 14 pp.

Lists resources in the Baltimore area which provide assistance to battered women, and provides advice on ways to proceed when the police or social service personnel are not helpful.

351. _____. "The Image of Battered Women." **American Journal of Public Health**, 67:722+, August 1977.

Presents a general discussion of battered women, focusing on the role of the health profession in the management of the problem.

352. Friedman, Stanford B. "The Need for Intensive Follow-up of Abused Children." **Helping the Battered Child and His Family**. Edited by C. Henry Kempe and Ray E. Helfer. Philadelphia: J.B. Lippincott Company, 1972, pp. 79–92.

States the the implementation of preventive measures with an already abused child to prevent subsequent trauma is often difficult and may limit the practical usefulness of early detection. Describes a study which demonstrated that early identification of abuse is only the first step in preventing further injury, and that methods of professional intervention need to be perfected. Also discusses the characteristics of child abuse, guidelines for early detection, and the role of the hospital emergency department in abuse cases.

353. Friedman, Standford B. and Carol W. Morse. "Child Abuse: A Five Year Follow-up of Early Case Finding in the Emergency Department." **Pediatrics**, 54:404–10, October 1974.

The results of a follow-up to a study conducted by Holter and Friedman are reported. The children chosen for the follow-up study had been judged to be victims of abuse, neglect, or accident in the original study. It was found that the children thought to be victims of accidents subsequently sustained a lower number of serious injuries such as head injuries and burns than did the children in the abused and neglected groups. The authors state, however, that the statistical evidence is not conclusive and that no generalizations can be made on the basis of their findings in this study.

354. Friends, Society of. **The Battered Women Conference Report**. New York: American Friends Service Committee, Community Relations Program, 1977. 45 pp.

Reports on the activities of the conference on battered women, which was sponsored by the American Friends Service Committee, New York

Metropolitan Regional Office, and held on February 12, 1977. Topics explored by the conference include the problem of wife battering, why men batter, aid to battered women, the role of concerned men, and the responses of the society to battered women.

355. Frodi, Ann M. and Michael E. Lamb. "Child Abusers' Responses to Infant Smiles and Cries." **Child Development**, 51(1):238–41, March 1980.

A study in which abusers and non-abusers watched videotypes of crying and smiling infants in order for researchers to observe their reactions is reviewed, and the responses are analyzed.

356. Frodi, Ann M. and others. "Fathers' and Mothers' Responses to the Faces and Cries of Normal Premature Infants." **Developmental Psychology**, 14(5):490–98, September 1978.

Parents were shown videotapes of premature and full term infants crying and not crying. Responses indicated that premature infants may be "at risk" for child abuse.

357. Fromson, Terry L. "The Case for Legal Remedies for Abused Women." **New York University Review of Law and Social Change**, 6:135–74, Spring 1977.

Discusses the problem of wife abuse, emphasizing the legal system's role in its curtailment and prevention. The need for effective legal remedies is explored by examining the magnitude of the problem, the nature of the harm inflicted (physical, emotional and psychological), and the causes of wife battering. The inadequate response of the legal system and the need to reform present laws and procedures are also discussed.

358. Fruchtl, Gertrude and A.E. Brodeur. "Battered Child, Know Enough to Care — Care Enough to Know." **The Catholic World**, 209:156–59, July 1969.

Presents a general discussion of child abuse, including the social, physical, legal, and moral aspects.

359. Gaensbauer, Theodore J. and Karen Sands. "Distorted Affective Communications in Abused Infants and Their Potential Impact on Caretakers." **Journal of the American Academy of Child Psychiatry**, 18:236–50, 1969.

Examines ways in which personality traits of children contribute to disruptions in caretaker-infant interaction and may lead to child abuse or neglect. The implications for treatment of abusers is also discussed.

360. Gager, Nancy and Cathleen Schurr. **Sexual Assault: Confronting Rape in America**. New York: Grosset and Dunlop, 1976. 336 pp.

Rape within marriage and the rape of children are among the topics explored.

361. Gaines, Richard and others. "Etiological Factors in Child Maltreatment: A Multivariate Study of Abusing, Neglecting, and Normal Mothers." **Journal of Abnormal Psychology**, 87(5):531–40, October 1978.

Relates a study which attempted to reinforce the theory of child abuse and neglect which explained maltreatment in terms of many factors, including the personalities of parents, pre-existing deviancy, and environmental stress. Suggestions for subsequent investigations are also made.

362. Galdston, Richard. "Observations on Children Who Have Been Physically Abused and Their Parents." **Child Abuse: Prespectives on Diagnosis, Treatment and Prevention**. Edited by Roberta Kalmar. Dubuque, Iowa: Kendall/Hunt Publishing Company, 1977, pp. 38–44.

Summarizes observations gathered over a five year period on young children admitted to the Children's Hospital Medical Center in Boston due to parental abuse.

363. _____. "Preventing the Abuse of Little Children: The Parents' Center Project for the Study and Prevention of Child Abuse." **American Journal of Orthospychiatry**, 45:32–81, April 1975.

The Parents' Center Project for the Study and Prevention of Child Abuse, established in Brighton, Massachusetts, was designed to look into intervention programs which would not involve the removal of the child from his family. The operation of the day care unit designed for this purpose is outlined and its effectiveness is discussed in light of the progress made by families who had participated in the project.

364. Gaquin, D.A. "Spouse Abuse — Data From the National Crime Survey." **Victimology: An International Journal**, 2(3):32–33, 1977–78.

Data obtained from the National Crime Survey are examined to ascertain the nature of spouse abuse and the characteristics of victims. Tables are provided to illustrate the findings.

365. Garbarino, James. "Changing Hospital Childbirth Practices: A Developmental Perspective on Prevention of Child Maltreatment." **American Journal of Orthopsychiatry**, 50(4):588–97, October 1980.

Suggests that childbirth should be viewed as a social event as well as a psychological and physical one. A program aimed at altering hospital practices so that childbirth be treated as a family-oriented procedure is outlined.

366. _____. "A Preliminary Study of Some Ecological Correlates of Child Abuse: The Impact of Socioeconomic Stress on Mothers." **Child Development**, 47:178–85, March 1976.

Reviews a study in which demographic and socioeconomic variables were examined in an effort to discover their effect on the growth of stress in parents, stress which may lead to child abuse.

367. Garbarino, James and Ann Crouter. "Defining the Community Context for Parent-Child Relations: The Correlates of Child Maltreatment." **Child Development**, 49(3):604–16, September 1978.

Discusses studies which illustrate the use of child abuse report data as social indicators of the quality of family life. The role of family support systems is examined and maltreatment is linked to the balance of stress and reinforcement within the neighborhood context of the family.

368. _____. "A Note on the Problem of Construct Validity in Assessing the Usefulness of Child Maltreatment Report Data." **American Journal of Public Health**, 68(6):598–600, June 1978.

Examines the hypothesis that the relation of child maltreatment rates to socioeconomic levels can be used as criteria for assessing construct validity by using comparisons across time within the same place, across contrasting reporting units during the same time period, and for two forms of social pathology having different reporting characteristics across the same units of analysis. Studies show that socioeconomic criteria may provide a necessary condition for establishing the validity of report data. It is stated that the best approach is to combine an "anthropological" awareness of the realities of reporting with a statistical model such as the one presented here.

369. Garbarino, James and Gwen Gilliam. **Understanding Abusive Families**. Lexington, Massachusetts: D.C. Heath and Company, 1980. 267 pp.

Presents an ecological and developmental perspective on the maltreatment of children and adolescents, and explores the dynamics of abuse as they shift from infancy to childhood to adolescence. Maltreatment is also examined across levels of social systems, and in relation to the problem of social isolation of the family. The community context of child abuse is also analyzed, the the role of the school in identification and management is discussed.

370. Garbarino, James and Deborah Sherman. "High-Risk Neighborhoods and High-Risk Families: The Human Ecology of Child Maltreatment." **Child Development**, 51(1):188–98, March 1980.

Examines a study which matched a pair of neighborhoods on socioeconomic levels, one high-risk and one low-risk, and then drew samples from the families living there. Results supported the theory of the existence of a high-risk neighborhood as a context for problems in family and child development.

371. Gardner, Leslie. "The Gilday Center: A Method of Intervention for Child Abuse." **Child Abuse: Intervention and Treatment**. Edited by Nancy B. Ebeling and Deborah A. Hill. Acton, Massachusetts: Publishing Sciences Group, Inc., 1975, pp. 143–50.

Discusses the development and operation of the Gilday Center, a center set up by the Junior League of Boston to provide child care for "children at risk."

372. Garinger, Gail and James N. Hyde. "Child Abuse and the Central Registry." **Child Abuse: Intervention and Treatment**. Edited by Nancy B. Ebeling and Deborah A. Hill. Acton, Massachusetts: Publishing Sciences Group, Inc., 1975, pp. 171-75.

Explores the potential benefits and costs inherent in the concept of a central registry for identifying abused and neglected children.

373. Garrett, Keren Ann and Peter H. Rossi. "Judging the Seriousness of Child Abuse." **Medical Anthropology**, 2(1):1-48, Winter 1978.

Reviews research which sought to construct a model of seriousness assessments for judging child abuse. Defines child abuse and neglect, and attempts to clarify the types of acts against children which are considered to be serious abuse. Evidence which suggests that seriousness ratings for individual crimes are, in part, related to the social characteristics of offenders and victims is also examined.

374. Gayford, J.J. "Battered Wives." **Violence and the Family**. Edited by J.P. Martin. New York: John Wiley and Sons, 1978, pp. 19-39.

Reviews the literature concerning battered wives and presents findings of a study conducted by the author in which battered wives were surveyed. Factors precipitating violence, effects of violence, family backgrounds of battered wives, psychodynamics of marital violence, characteristics of batterers, and the children of battered women are among the topics explored.

375. _____. "Plight of the Battered Wife." **The International Journal of Environmental Studies**, 10:283-86, 1977.

Presents the results of a survey of 100 battered wives seen at a Women's Aid Crisis Refuge, and also in psychiatric practice. The women's histories and behavior patterns, and the psychosocial implications of them, are discussed. Results suggest that it is possible for a woman to be drawn into a violent marriage by various factors, and that many relationships studied were a "precipitous type" where standard values and courtship patterns were replaced with pre-marital sex and subsequent pregnancy.

376. _____. "Ten Types of Battered Wives." **The Welfare Officer**, 25:5-9, 1976.

Wife battering is discussed through the case studies of ten victims. Recommendations made by a select committee of the House of Commons concerning marital violence are also presented. These recommendations included the establishment of family crisis centers, public education concerning domestic violence, public campaigns against alcoholism, legal reform to protect women from violent husbands, and financial support for voluntary organizations.

377. _____. "Wife Battering: A Preliminary Survey of 100 Cases." **British Medical Journal**, 1:194-97, January 1975.

Presents the results of a survey which interviewed battered wives concerning the incidents. Physical injuries of the victims, medical histories, aetiology of the attack, and various background factors are examined.

378. Gaylin, Jody. "Battered Wives Find It Hard to Get Help." **Psychology Today**, 11:36+, June 1977.

Discusses the work of Richard J. Gelles. His findings demonstrate why violence within a family may be approved by the husbands and wives involved, why women stay in violent marriages, and why police and social service agencies are reluctant to get involved in family violence.

379. _____. "New Help For Battered Children and Their Parents." **Psychology Today**, 11:93–94, June 1977.

The success of the programs instituted by the National Center for Prevention and Treatment of Child Abuse and Neglect is discussed.

380. Geiser, Robert L. **Hidden Victims: The Sexual Abuse of Children**. Boston: Beacon Press, 1979. 191 pp.

Examines the sexual misuse and abuse of children, including incest, child rape, offenders, and treatment. Special attention is given to the battered child as a victim of sexual abuse, and the behavioral problems which develop in these children. A brief selected bibliography is included.

381. Gelles, Richard J. "Abused Wives: Why Do They Stay?" **Journal of Marriage and the Family**, 38:659–68, November 1976.

Explores reasons why abused wives stay with their husbands rather than seek intervention from outside agencies. Focuses on a study which examined various factors involved in family violence, and determined that outside help was ineffective in dealing with the problem.

382. _____. "Child Abuse as Psychopathology: A Sociological Critique and Reformulation." **Violence in the Family**. Edited by Suzanne K. Steinmetz and Murray A. Straus. New York: Harper and Row, 1974, pp. 190–204.

States that the psychopathology model of child abuse is too narrow and not based on strong research. Discusses deficiencies in this model and suggests an alternative one with a flow chart to illustrate the new model.

383. _____. "Demythologizing Child Abuse." **Family Coordinator**, 25:13–41, April 1976.

States that myths concerning the problem of child abuse hinder society's efforts in dealing with it, and the most frequently quoted myths are presented. Concludes that child abuse has always existed, that parents who abuse are not necessarily mentally ill, and that treatment of abusive parents is marred by the stigma that society attaches to the child abuser being treated. Also, most programs developed to treat or prevent child abuse do not sufficiently meet the needs of parents and children.

384. _____. "No Place To Go: The Social Dynamics of Marital Violence." **Battered Women: A Psychosociological Study of Domestic Violence**. Edited by Maria Roy. New York: Van Nostrand Reinhold Company, 1777, pp. 46–63.

Explores the social dynamics of family violence by analyzing the violent situation.

385. _____. "Power, Sex, and Violence: The Case of Marital Rape." **The Family Coordinator**, 26:339–48, October 1977.

Examines rape and the use of physical violence against a spouse by analyzing the case of marital rape. Legal questions involved in an accusation of rape within marriage, and the possibility of an intrinsic relationship between sex and violence in cases of marital violence are among the topics explored.

386. _____. "The Social Construction of Child Abuse." **American Journal of Orthopsychiatry**, 45:363–71, April 1975.

A social construction theory of child abuse is proposed in which child abuse is regarded as a form of social deviance. A method for identifying child abusers is suggested using definitions of abuse, public labeling of behavior as abusive, conditions for the successful application of the label, and the consequences of such a label. The integration of the social systems involved in the social construction of the abuser as deviant is emphasized.

387. _____. "Violence and Pregnancy: A Note on the Extent of the Problem and Needed Services." **The Family Coordinator**, 24:81–86, January 1975.

A study conducted by the author showed that violence during pregnancy occurred in almost 25% of the families reporting cases of marital violence. Five major factors which contribute to violence during pregnancy are proposed and discussed.

388. _____. "Violence in the American Family." **Violence and the Family**. Edited by J.P. Martin. New York: John Wiley and Sons, 1978, pp. 169–82.

Examines family violence in American society. The extent of family violence, the role of norms and attitudes, the roots of family violence, and the structure of American society and its relationship to violence within the family are among the areas explored.

389. _____. "Violence Toward Children in the U.S." **American Journal of Orthopsychiatry**, 48(4):580–92, October 1978.

Presents the results of a survey which examined the incidence, patterns and methods of violence between parents and children. Findings indicate that violence is an extensive and patterned occurance in parent-child interactions. Implications for further research are discussed.

390. _____. **Violent Home — A Study of Physical Aggression Between Husbands and Wives**. Beverly Hills, California: Sage Publications, Inc., 1972. 230 pp.

Discusses a study which sampled 40 families in which known incidents of violence had taken place, and collected data on 40 non-violent families as a control group. Situations and interactions leading to violence are examined and a theory of the family as a breeding ground for violence is proposed.

391. Gelles, Richard J. and Murray A. Straus. "Determinants of Violence in the Family: Toward a Theoretical Integration." **Contemporary Theories About the Family**. Edited by Wesley R. Burr and others. New York: The Free Press, 1976, pp. 549–81.

Discusses violence as an important aspect of family interaction and summarizes various theoretical perspectives concerning interpersonal violence, applying them to family violence. Each theory is presented as a part of a process of family violence.

392. Gentzler, Rie, editor. **Advocacy Programs for Abused Women**. Lancaster, Pennsylvania: Pennsylvania Coalition Against Domestic Violence, 1977.

Provides a guide for establishing a community program for battered women and their children. Services which may be offered are outlined, and sample data forms are included.

393. George, Carol and Mary Main. "Social Interactions of Young Abused Children: Approach, Advoidance, and Aggression." **Child Development**, 50(2):306–18, June 1979.

Describes a study which observed two groups of children, one which experienced stress during interaction with caretakers, and one control group. Findings indicate that the abused children were more likely to be assaulted by their peers, and more frequently avoided friendly overtures.

394. George, J.E. "Spare the Rod: A Survey of the Battered Child Syndrome." **Forensic Science**, 2(2):129–67, May 1977.

Examines the battered child syndrome from an historical perspective. Topics examined include the incidence of child abuse, psychosocial aspects, characteristics of abusive parents and abused children, circumstances surrounding the battering incidents, medical aspects, and legal issues. The need for increased cooperation among agencies to reduce the incidence of child abuse is emphasized.

395. Geracimos, Ann, interviewer. "How I stopped Beating My Wife." **MS.**, 5:53, August 1976.

Presents an interview with a former wife beater. His early life, motivations for beating his wife, and the reasons why he stopped are discussed.

396. Gershenson, Charles P. "Child Maltreatment, Family Stress and Ecological Insult." **American Journal of Public Health**, 67(7):602–04, July 1977.

States that although the family attempts to protect a child from insults into the ecological space in which they live, this protection may manifest itself in maltreatment of the child under severe economic and social conditions. Defines "pediatric social illness" as having a broader and more dynamic definition than does the more limiting label "battered child syndrome," and discusses the interactional or ecological model of child abuse.

397. Gil, David G. "Child Abuse: Levels of Manifestation, Causal Dimensions, and Primary Prevention." **Victimology: An International Journal**, 2:186–94, Summer 1977.

Discusses the levels of manifestation of child abuse and the various dimensions of its causes. Primary prevention is explored, and problems which hinder the progress of effective treatment and prevention programs are examined.

398. _____. "A Conceptual Model of Child Abuse and It's Implications for Social Policy." **Violence in the Family**. Edited by Suzanne K. Steinmetz and Murray A. Straus. New York: Harper and Row, 1974, pp. 205–11.

Examines the social factors which bring about child abuse and outlines the social policy implications, emphasizing the elements which need to be changed in order to reduce child abuse.

399. _____. "A Holistic Perspective on Child Abuse and Its Prevention." **Journal of Sociology and Social Welfare**, 2:110–25, Winter 1974.

Suggests that effective prevention of child abuse must be aided by an integrated approach to the issue. Past failures of an integrated approach are explored and recommendations are made for a broader definition which favors a holistic approach to the problem. This new approach would allow child abuse to be viewed from interpersonal, societal, and institutional levels simultaneously.

400. _____. "A Sociocultural Perspective on Physical Child Abuse." **The Battered Child**. Compiled by Jerome E. Leavitt. Morristown, New Jersey: General Learning Press, 1974, pp. 164–69.

Presents highlights of a nationwide survey conducted by Brandeis University in order to transcend the clinical understanding of child abuse, and to discover the sociocultural dynamics of the problem. The sociological and cultural aspects of child abuse are emphasized, and findings suggest a series of measures as a basis for prevention through education, legislation, the elimination of poverty, and increased use of social services.

401. _____. "Unraveling Child Abuse." **American Journal of Orthopsychiatry**, 45:346–56, April 1975.

Attempts to explain the dynamics of child abuse using different levels of manifestation and causation. The variability and complexity of these dimensions are emphasized.

402. _____. "Violence Against Children." **Journal of Marriage and the Family**, 33(4):637–48, 1971.

Epidemiologic studies, public opinion, and press surveys are analyzed in order to formulate a definition and conceptual model of violence against children. Causal dimensions of child abuse include the culturally sanctioned use of physical punishment in child rearing, psychological and social dysfunction, and poverty and discrimination. Discusses the scope of the problem and suggests social policies directed at prevention.

403. _____. **Violence Against Children: Physical Child Abuse in the United States**. Cambridge, Massachusetts: Harvard University Press, 1970. 204 pp.

Reviews the findings of a study of over 1300 incidents of violence against children in the United States, suggesting that this violence is rooted in culturally determined theories and practices of child rearing. A higher incidence of child abuse was found among the lower educational and socioeconomic classes, in large families, and in broken homes. Concludes that the most serious form of child abuse is inflicted by society, and not by parents, as a result of poverty, hunger, poor educational systems, inadequate medical care, and officially sanctioned abuse in schools and child care facilities.

404. _____. "What Schools Can Do About Child Abuse." **The Battered Child**. Compiled by Jerome E. Leavitt. Morristown, New Jersey: General Learning Press, 1974, pp. 215–20.

Presents a general discussion of the problem and details the role of teachers and school professionals in the identification and reporting of child abuse. Possible ways of reducing the problem are also examined.

405. Gilbert, Marie T. "Behavioral Approach to the Treatment of Child Abuse." **Nursing Times**, 72:140–43, January 29, 1976.

A case study is presented which illustrates the effective use of the behavioral approach to treating abusive parents.

406. Gilmartin, Brian G. "The Case Against Spanking." **Human Behavior**, 8:18, February 1979.

States that children may learn violence through physical punishment. Discusses the result of parents' violent reactions to behavior on their children.

407. Gingold, Judith. "One of These Days — Pow! Right in the Kisser: The Truth About Battered Wives." **MS.**, 5:51–54+.

Presents statistics on the incidence of wife abuse. The cultural factors which condone wife battering, the relationship between alcohol and wife abuse, laws pertaining to the problem, and the role of women's groups in prevention are explored. Reasons why women stay in violent homes and the inequality of the sexes as a root of the violence within marriage are also examined.

408. Giovannoni, Jeanne M. "Parental Mistreatment: Perpetrators and Victims." **Journal of Marriage and the Family**, 33:649–57, 1971.

Focuses on parental mistreatment of children as a manifestation of negative societal forces weighing on the family. Analyzes families in which children had been mistreated and compares them to families in which mistreatment had not occurred. Economic stress among low income families was particularly evident in abusing families.

409. Giovannoni, Jeanne M. and Rosina M. Becerra. **Defining Child Abuse**. New York: The Free Press, 1979. 302 pp.

Identifies the major types of child abuse and prescribes approaches to public policy that might help the state and the family. The need for more specific laws defining child abuse and dictating state intervention is discussed, and more precise definitions to be used in research, statistical reporting, and service evaluation are advocated.

410. Giovannoni, Jeanne M. and Andrew Billingsley. "Child Neglect Among the Poor: A Study of Parental Adequacy in Families of Three Ethnic Groups." **Child Welfare**, 49:196–204, April 1970.

Discusses a study of low income families, examining factors which distinguish adequate parents from neglectful parents. Factors examined include family and social background, age and childbearing patterns, current family structure and stability, income, material resources, social functioning of the mother, informal social systems (neighborhood interactions, relationships with extended relatives), and formal social systems (church, school, political systems). Findings indicate that the low income neglectful parents are under greater environmental and situational stress, and have fewer resources for coping with them. Implications of the results for the practitioner are detailed.

411. Giovannoni, Jeanne M. and others. **Child Abuse and Neglect: An Examination From the Perspective of Child Development Knowledge**. San Francisco, California: R and E Research Associates, Inc., 1978. 105 pp.

Reports on information obtained from reviewing written research on children, and from consulting experts in child-related fields. Focuses on the physical, mental, social and emotional development of the child, and examines problems of definition concerning abuse and neglect, and the contributory factors of the child to an abusing situation.

412. Glenn, Jean. "Kansas and the Children's Trust Fund." **Children Today**, 11(3):21–22, May–June 1982.

Discusses the establishment of a Children's Trust Fund in Kansas which is used primarily for the prevention of child abuse. Projects administered by this organization are detailed.

413. Goldberg, Gale. "Breaking the Communication Barrier: The Initial Interview With an Abusing Parent." **Child Welfare**, 54:274–82, April 1975.

Discusses the behavior of the social worker during the initial interview with an abusing parent. Goals of the social worker during the initial interview include encouraging the parent to communicate openly with the counselor and to feel comfortable with him, to reduce the parents' anxiety about the situation, and to evoke as much information as possible from the parent by using open-ended questions.

414. Golub, Sharon. "The Battered Child: What the Nurse Can Do." **RN**, December 1968, pp. 42–45, 66–68.

Provides a general discussion of child abuse, emphasizing the role of the nurse in management of child abuse cases. Characteristics helpful in identifying abusing parents, statistics on the incidence of the problem, the nurse's relationship with parents, and characteristics of abusing and non-abusing parents are among the topics examined. A list of states where nurses must report cases of child abuse, the age of the children, and penalities for failure to report are also presented.

415. Gonzalez-Pardo, Lillian and Mary Thomas. "Child Abuse and Neglect." **Journal of the Kansas Medical Society**, 78:65–69, February 1977.

Analyzes reports of child abuse and neglect made to the Social Rehabilitation Services or to the Juvenile Court System in Kansas over a three and one-half year period. The incidence of abuse or neglect, types of injuries, patterns and frequency of abuse, attitudes toward abuse, and the particular county of residence of the cases were among the topics considered.

416. Goode, William J. "Force and Violence in the Family." **Journal of Marriage and the Family**, 33(4):624–36, 1971.

Discusses the family as a power system rooted in a certain amount of force, be it actual or threatened. Examines the deterrent value of force and the role of force in socialization. Force culminating in assaultive violence, murder, and child abuse is also explored.

417. _____. "Violence Among Intimates." **Crimes of Violence**. U.S. National Commission on the Causes and Prevention of Violence, Task Force on Individual Acts of Violence. 13:941–77, 1969.

Examines the crime of murder, focusing on the relationship between the victim and the offender. Reasons why intimates manifest violence against one another are discussed and the role of socialization in the prevention or encouragement of violent behavior is explored.

418. Goodman, Emily Jane. "Legal Solutions: Equal Protection Under the Law." **Battered Women: A Psychosociological Study of Domestic Violence**. Edited by Maria Roy. New York: Van Nostrand Reinhold Company, 1977, pp. 139–44.

Discusses wife abuse and the law, emphasizing the law as it is applied in New York State.

419. Goodpaster, Gary S. and Karen Angel. "Child Abuse and the Law: The California System." **Hastings Law Journal**, 26:1081–25, March 1975.

Examines the problem of child abuse and analyzes the operation of California child abuse laws, and the implementation of these laws in Los Angeles county. Problems with the laws are presented and recommendations are made for changing them in order to establish a new system for handling child abuse cases.

420. Gordon, Alan H. and Janet Corcoran Jameson. "Infant-Mother Attachment in Patients With Nonorganic Failure-to-Thrive Syndrome." **Journal of the American Academy of Child Psychiatry**, 18:251–59, 1979.

Explores patterns of attachment in a group of infants diagnosed as nonorganic failure to thrive. Some patients were found to be insecurely attached to their mothers, and the failure to thrive children showed a distinct inhibition of affect during separation from their mothers.

421. Graham-Hall, Jean. "Court Proceedings." **Concerning Child Abuse: Papers Presented by the Tunbridge Wells Study Group on Non-Accidental Injury to Children**. Edited by Alfred White Franklin. Edinburgh: Churchill Livingstone, 1975, pp. 136–39.

Examines the types of court procedures available in cases of non-accidental injury to children and presents criticisms of current juristiction, discussing the possibility of developing more suitable procedures.

422. Gray, Jane and Betty Kaplan. "The Lay Health Visitor Program: An Eighteen-Month Experience." **The Battered Child**. Edited by C. Henry Kempe and Ray E. Helfer. Chicago: University of Chicago Press, 1980, pp. 373–78.

Discusses the lay health visitor program of the department of pediatrics at Colorado General Hospital. This approach prevents the stigma of labeling families at risk for child abuse and neglect, and also satisfies the moral obligation that all families have the opportunity to receive supportive services. Reasons why some families refuse help are also reviewed.

423. Gray, Jane and Ruth Kempe. "The Abused Child at Time of Injury." **The Abused Child: A Multidisciplinary Approach to Developmental Issues and Treatment**. Cambridge, Massachusetts: Ballinger Publishing Co., 1976, 57–65.

Explores factors which influence the child's behavior at the time of abuse and the effect of the medical setting on the child who must subsequently be hospitalized. The issues involved in the management of the abused child in the hospital and the therapeutic value of hospitalization are also examined.

424. Green, Arthur H. "Child Abusing Fathers." **Journal of the American Academy of Child Psychiatry**, 18:270–82, 1979.

Describes the personality traits, psychodynamics, and environmental influences of abusing fathers. Related issues such as use of alcohol and spouse abuse are discussed, and a rationale for intervention and treatment of abusive fathers is suggested.

425. _____. "A Psychodynamic Approach to the Study and Treatment of Child Abusing Parents." **Journal of the American Academy of Child Psychiatry**, 15(3):414–29, Summer 1976.

Examines the psychodynamics of family interaction in abusive families. Child abuse as a dysfunction of parenting is discussed and the use of psychotherapy in the treatment of abusing parents is explored.

426. _____. "Psychopathology of Abused Children." **Journal of the American Academy of Child Psychiatry**, 17(1):92–103, Winter 1978.

Describes the major types of psychopathology and deviant behavior found in abused children and discusses the most prominent areas of dysfunction.

427. _____. "Societal Neglect of Child Abusing Parents." **Victimology: An International Journal**, 2:285–93, Summer 1977.

Discusses services to abused children and their families. Explores the need for a shift in emphasis from placement to crisis intervention. Suggests that parents who abuse their children and are not adequately helped will abuse their children again when they are reunited with them.

428. Green, Arthur H. and others. "Child Abuse: Pathological Syndrome of Family Interaction." **American Journal of Psychiatry**, 131:882–86, August 1974.

Argues that child abuse is a result of dysfunctional parenting rather than a personality disorder.

429. Green, Frederick C. "Child Abuse and Neglect: A Priority Problem for the Private Physician." **Pediatric Clinics of North America**, 22:329–39, May 1975.

Examines the role of the private physician in the identification and treatment of child abuse. Guidelines concerning reporting, identification, and manifestations of child abuse are outlined.

430. Green, Nancy B. "Identifying the Battered or Molested Child." **The Battered Child**. Compiled by Jerome E. Leavitt. Morristown, New Jersey: General Learning Press, 1974, pp. 223–26.

Presents a detailed discussion of identifying the battered or molested child, including physical and emotional factors which may be present.

431. Greene, Nancy B. "A View of Family Pathology Involving Child Molest — From a Juvenile Probation Perspective." **Juvenile Justice**, 28(1):29-34, February 1977.

Focuses on the child who is molested by either his natural father, stepfather, or his mother's common law husband within the home. The child molester's wife, placement of the victim in a living situation outside of the home, and the role of the court in these cases are among the topics discussed. Concludes that innovative programs are needed for neglected child care, and a standardized interview guide would be helpful in facilitating dispositions.

432. Gregory, Margaret. "Battered Wives." **Violence in the Family**. Edited by Marie Borland. Atlantic Highlands, New Jersey: Humanities Press, 1976, pp. 107-28.

Discusses the subject of battered wives by exploring the extent of the problem, types of violence and injuries, characteristics and social background of victims, problems faced by battered women when they seek assistance from service agencies and the law, psychopathology of husband and wife, and the attitudes of society toward the battered wife. Reform in the areas of legal, medical, and social services is suggested.

433. Griffin, Max E. and others. "The Abused Child: A Panel Discussion." **Ohio's Health**, 26:9-19, 1974.

Presents a panel discussion on child abuse. The role and responsibility of medical personnel, procedures followed in cases of child abuse, the interaction of agencies and professionals, problems involved in the management and treatment of abused children, and suggestions for improving care are among the areas explored.

434. Griffiths, A. "The Legacy and Present Administration of English Law: Some Problems for Battered Women in Context." **Cambrian Law Review**, 11:29-39, 1980.

Suggests that the police take a more active role in referring the battered woman to appropriate legal aid.

435. Griggs, Shirley and Patricia Gale. "Abused Child: Focus for Counselors." **Elementary School Guidance and Counseling**, 11:186-94, February 1977.

Discusses the role of the school counselor in the identification of child abuse and neglect.

436. Groth, A. Nicholas and Ann Wolbert Burgess. "Motivational Intent in the Sexual Assault of Children." **Criminal Justice Behavior**, 4(3):253-64, September 1977.

Examines a study which analyzed sexual assault accounts of preadult sexual assault victims and convicted child offenders. Identifies two types of sexual assault and discusses each, and explores the presence of life issues such as power, authority, control, aggression, and dominance. To illustrate the problem, a case study of an 11 year old girl sexually assaulted by her father is presented.

437. Grumet, Barbara R. "The Plaintive Plaintiffs: Victims of the Battered Child Syndrome." **Family Law Quarterly**, 4(3):296–317, September 1970.

Describes the first recorded instance of reported child abuse in the United States, the case of Mary Ellen, found beaten and starved by her stepparents in New York City in 1875. Concerned citizens persuaded the Society for the Prevention of Cruelty to Animals that Mary Ellen, "as a member of the animal kingdom, was entitled to the protection afforded dogs and horses." News of her plight led to the founding of the Society for the Prevention of Cruelty to Children. Also discusses the incidence of child abuse, the task of the physician in child abuse cases, characteristics of battering parents and their families, recidivism for battered child offenses, and possible solutions to the problem. Suggestions are also made for reforming the legal system pertaining to child abuse cases.

438. Gulley, Kenneth G. "The Washington Child Abuse Amendments." **Gonzaga Law Review**, 12:468–91, Spring 1977.

Examines laws pertaining to child abuse which have been enacted and amended by the Washington legislature.

439. Guten, Keri. "Child Abuse: Endless Cycle of Violence." **San Antonio Light**, June 6, 1982, pp. 1M & 5M.

States that child abuse has reached epidemic proportions in this country, and that experts attribute the problem to social stress, the economy, and the violent nature of society. Discusses the cycle of violence which is passed from one generation to another, the causes of child abuse and neglect, and the handling of the problem by the welfare system and the courts.

440. _____. "The Law Acts in the Best Interest of All Children." **San Antonio Light**, June 6, 1982, pp. 1M & 4M.

Examines children's rights as protected by the Texas Family Code, which encourages reporting by guaranteeing that identities remain anonymous. Actions taken by the law and social service agencies in cases of child abuse and neglect are also discussed.

441. Guthrie, Andrew D. "Child Abuse on Main Street — Semantics in the Suburbs." **Child Abuse: Intervention and Treatment**. Edited by Nancy B. Ebeling and Deborah A. Hill. Acton, Massachusetts: Publishing Sciences Group, Inc., 1975, pp. 23–28.

Suggests possible reasons why child abuse is less visible in, and not reported from, the suburbs. Methods of casefinding are discussed and recommendations are made for education programs, community based service agencies, legislation, and family care.

442. Haffner, Sarah. "Wife Abuse in West Germany." **Victimology: An International Journal**, 2:472–76, 1977–78.

Discusses the problem of wife abuse in West Germany, the recognition of the problem by society and government, and the establishment of refuges with and without public funding.

443. Hall, M.H. "A View From the Emergency and Accident Department." **Concerning Child Abuse: Papers Presented by the Tunbridge Wells Study Group on Non-Accidental Injury to Children**. Edited by Alfred White Franklin. Edinburgh: Churchill Livingstone, 1975, 7–20.

Defines the battered child syndrome and discusses the prevalence of abused children, classification of cases, identification and diagnosis of child abuse, and problems in handling child abuse cases.

444. Hammell, Charlotte L. "Preserving Family Life for Children." **The Battered Child**. Compiled by Jerome E. Leavitt. Morristown, New Jersey: General Learning Press, 1974, pp. 38–41.

Discusses the importance of correcting family conditions in order to prevent child abuse. States that if family life is to be preserved, there must be a recognition of parents' needs and an extensive program of intervention and support. Presents case histories of vulnerable families treated by the Delaware County Child Care Service, and examines ways of aiding parents in helping to care for children in order to prevent child abuse and neglect.

445. Hanks, Susan E. and C. Peter Rosenbaum. "Battered Women: A Study of Women Who Live With Violent Alcohol-Abusing Men." **American Journal of Orthopsychiatry**, 47:291–306, April 1977.

Discusses a study which examined families in which women had been repeatedly assaulted by alcoholic husbands. Identifies three distinct types of families of origin and suggests that women carry conditions of their early family situations with them when they marry. Awareness of the woman's background by a treatment professional may help the woman to understand and alter her behavior as a result of treatment.

446. Hanmer, Jalna. "Violence and the Social Control of Women." **Feminist Issues**, 1(2):29–44, Winter 1981.

Focuses on male violence against women, emphasizing the significance and meaning of this violence at the social structural level. The role of violence in male-female relationships, the subordination of women, and the incidence of husband-wife violence are among the issues examined. Sociological explanations of interpersonal violence are criticized, and the relationship between sex and class is explored. Concludes by discussing challenging male dominance, and the use of force by men against women.

447. Hannan, Damian. Patterns of Spousal Accommodation and Conflict in Traditional and Modern Farm Families.'' **Economic and Social Review**, 10:61–84, October 1978.

Presents the results of a survey in which farmers in Ireland were interviewed concerning their marriages. The study focused on the processes of interaction and accommodation within the marriage, and theoretical perspectives concerning these processes are analyzed in light of the results of the study.

448. ''Hard Times for Kids Too.'' **Time**, 105:88, March 17, 1975.

Discusses child abuse as a consequence of economic strain.

449. Harper, Fowler V. ''The Physician, the Battered Child, and the Law.'' **The Battered Child**. Compiled by Jerome E. Leavitt. Morristown, New Jersey: General Learning Press, 1974, pp. 90–93.

Presents a general discussion of child abuse, and examines the physician's responsibility under the law in such cases. Emphasizes the seriousness of the problem and the necessity for the medical profession to protect the child by reporting.

450. Hartman, Mary S. ''Child Abuse and Self-Abuse: Two Victorian Cases.'' **History of Childhood Quarterly**, 2:221–48, Fall 1974.

Discusses two cases of child abuse in which bizarre incidents led to their discovery. One case involved a girl who confessed to the murder of her younger brother, although there was a chance that the girl did not commit the crime. In the other case, a governess was instructed to cure some girls of alleged masturbation and proceeded to beat and starve them. When brought to trial, she could not be tried for her actions, nor were her actions considered abusive, until the children could prove their innocence of the charge of masturbation.

451. Hass, Gerald. ''Child Abuse, the Community, and the Neighborhood Health Center.'' **Child Abuse: Intervention and Treatment**. Edited by Nancy B. Ebeling and Deborah A. Hill. Acton, Massachusetts: Publishing Sciences Group, Inc., 1975, pp. 13–22.

Examines the role of the health center in cases of child abuse and suggests that child abuse is both a family and a community problem.

452. Havens, Leston L. ''Youth, Violence and the Nature of Family Life.'' **Psychiatric Annals**, 2(2):18–21+, 1972.

Family violence is examined in light of current trends in family structure and changing attitudes toward parenting. Suggests that the relationship between the family and society be re-evaluated.

453. Haviland, Mary. ''Starting a Safe Home Network for Battered Women.'' **Fight Back!: Feminist Resistance to Male Violence**. Minneapolis: Cleis Press, 1981, pp. 120–22.

Presents two fundamental questions facing women when starting a safe home network for battered women: What are the origins of the violence?; How does the understanding of these origins affect the kinds of help offered to battered women? Discusses these questions and implications for forming a safe home network. Details the Park Slope Homes Project as an example of a network which relies heavily on volunteers, and discusses the advantages of a safe homes network as a helping unit for battered women.

454. Hays, Richard H. "Child Abuse: An Overview." **Creighton Law Review**, 8:743-56, June 1975.

Explores the problem of child abuse and discusses why parents abuse, identification of the problem, and what children are most likely to be victims. Examines the operation of Child Protective Services in Douglas County, Maryland as an example of a community effort to identify and treat child abuse.

455. Helfer, Mary Edna and Ray E. Helfer. "Communicating in the Therapeutic Relationship: Concepts, Strategies, Skills." **The Battered Child**. Edited by C. Henry Kempe and Ray E. Helfer. Chicago: University of Chicago Press, 1980, pp. 117-27.

Focuses on the importance of communication in a therapeutic relationship. Topics examined include understanding anger and depression during the interview, guidelines for facilitating the interview, the structure and setting of the interview, and special considerations relating to child abuse.

456. Helfer, Ray E. "The Center for the Study of Abused and Neglected Children." **Helping and Battered Child and His Family**. Edited by C. Henry Kempe and Ray E. Helfer. Philadelphia: J.B. Lippincott Company, 1972, pp. 285-97.

Presents the objectives and scope of the center, and discusses the services provided to the community and to families. Concludes that a multidisciplinary approach is required in any attempt to resolve child abuse and neglect. The cycle of violence must be interrupted and new and practical ways must be found to help the children. Centers such as the one discussed are proposed as a feasible and practical approach to the problem.

457. _____. **Child Abuse and Neglect: The Diagnostic Process and Treatment Programs**. Washington, D.C.: U.S. Department of Health, Education and Welfare, 1975. 44 pp.

Provides an overview of the diagnostic and treatment processes for child abuse cases and examines various phases involved in these processes.

458. _____. "Development Deficits Which Limit Interpersonal Skills." **The Battered Child**. Edited by C. Henry Kempe and Ray E. Helfer. Chicago: University of Chicago Press, 1980, pp. 36-48.

Reviews basic developmental deficiences and the mechanisms by which they occurred in order to establish strategies for assisting victims of child abuse.

Emphasizes developmental traits which seem to be most deficient in victims of child abuse and developmental deficiencies which affect interaction between the child and his parents.

459. _____. "Retraining and Relearning." **The Battered Child**. Edited by C. Henry Kempe and Ray E. Helfer. Chicago: University of Chicago Press, 1980, pp. 391–400.

Discusses the ways in which one learns skills, and provides examples of how to teach a young adult who had a very deficient childhood the skills of interacting with other people.

460. _____. "Why Most Physicians Don't Get Involved in Child Abuse Cases and What to Do About It." **Children Today**, 4:28–32, May–June 1975.

Reasons why physicians are reluctant to get involved in child abuse cases and increased involvement by medical personnel is recommended.

461. Helfer, Ray E. and C. Henry Kempe, editors. **The Battered Child**. Chicago: University of Chicago Press, 1968. 268 pp.

Essays discuss the universality of child abuse, the history of the problem, role of the medical profession in identification and treatment, characteristics of abusing parents, and the responsibilities of the legal system in protecting both parents and children.

462. _____. "The Child's Need for Early Recognition, Immediate Care and Protection." **Helping the Battered Child and His Family**. Edited by C. Henry Kempe and Ray E. Helfer. Philadelphia: J.B. Lippincott Company, 1972, pp. 69–78.

Discusses emergency care of abused children and presents guidelines for the emergency room physician which include ways to confront parents, signs and symptoms which warrant consideration as possible indicators of child abuse, and how to determine the safety of a home for the child.

463. _____. "The Consortium: A Community-Hospital Treatment Plan." **Helping the Battered Child and His Family**. Edited by C. Henry Kempe and Ray E. Helfer. Philadelphia: J.B. Lippincott Company, 1972, pp. 177–84.

Outlines a child abuse treatment program which mandates that problems of communication and distrust be resolved before the program can be implemented successfully. The program is based on the concept that the initial phase of a child abuse case must be considered as a diagnostic medical and social problem. The coalition between the community and the hospital is emphasized as necessary for the program to be successful.

464. Helfer, Ray E. and John S. Wheeler. "Child Abuse and the Private Pediatrician." **The Battered Child**. Compiled by Jerome E, Leavitt. Morristown, New Jersey: General Learning Press, 1974, pp. 199–203.

Presents details of a case brought to one of the authors, a pediatrician, in private practice. Summarizes the pattern seen in abusive families and discusses the formation of a rehabilitation program in Allentown, Pennsylvania. The significance of early identification, and acquisition of motivated persons willing to carry through with the difficult first stages of development are emphasized. Concludes by outlining the role and responsibility of the private pediatrician.

465. Helpern, Milton. "Fatalities From Child Abuse and Neglect: Responsibility of the Medical Examiner and Coroner." **Pediatric Annals**, 5:42–57, March 1976.

Discusses the responsibilities of the coroner and medical examiner in regard to discovering the actual cause of death in children, focusing on inconsistencies in reporting violent or suspicious deaths. Cooperation between police, coroner, medical examiner, and reporting physician is emphasized.

466. Hendricks-Matthews, Marybeth. "The Battered Woman: Is She Ready for Help?" **Social Casework**, 63(3):131–37, March 1982.

Briefly reviews literature on battered women, emphasizing literature dealing with helping systems. Examines issues which must be considered if intervention is to be efficient and effective, including the woman's degree of learned helplessness, her system of causal attribution, and her locus of control. The impact of intervention on the client and implications for further research are also discussed.

467. Hendrix, Melva and others. "The Battered Wife." **American Journal of Nursing**, 78(4):650–53, April 1978.

Considers the nature of the problem and discusses theories concerning wife battering. Recognizing the battered wife and ways nurses can offer assistance to her and her children are also examined. Efforts to introduce legislation making wife battering a crime are also reviewed.

468. Henry, D.R. "The Psychological Aspects of Child Abuse." **The Maltreatment of Children**. Edited by Selwyn M. Smith. Baltimore: University Park Press, 1978, pp. 205–19.

Reviews literature on the psychological aspects of child abuse and discusses the problems associated with some child abuse studies.

469. Hepburn, John R. "Violent Behavior in Interpersonal Relationships." **Sociological Quarterly**, 14(3):419–29, Summer 1973.

Analyzes interpersonal violence resulting in physical injury that occurs in a dyadic relationship, is not promoted by an underlying motive extraneous to the interaction, and does not involve premeditation. Concludes by saying that violent behavior does not happen at random, but is constructed within a situation through a process of interaction which involves perceived threat and threat reducing tactics, and retaliation which may lead to violence.

470. Hepburn, Ronald W. "The Moral Strengthening of the Individual." **The Challenge of Child Abuse**. Edited by Alfred White Franklin. London: Academic Press, 1977, pp. 219–28.

Discusses the relevance of moral and religious issues in cases of child abuse.

471. Herbruck, Christine C. **Breaking the Cycle of Child Abuse**. Minneapolis: Winston Press, Inc., 1979. 206 pp.

Relates stories of people who had abused their children and finally turned to Parents Anonymous for help. In the course of the stories, the following topics are discussed: defining the problem; the cycle of abuse; stress and abuse; high-risk indicators of troubled parenting; choosing alternatives to abuse; implications of change and the desire for a solution. Parents Anonymous as a therapeutic tool is examined in detail.

472. Herman, Bernice Jane. "A Cucumber From Roberta." **Mental Health**, 60:19–21, Summer 1976.

Discusses the work of Child and Family Advocates of Evanston, a non-profit group which works with abusive families in Evanston, Illinois.

473. Herre, Ernest A. "A Community Mobilizes to Protect Its Children." **Public Welfare**, 23(2):93–97, April 1965.

Describes a pilot project conducted by the Family Service Agency of Milwaukee in 1959 — the Protective Service Unit of Milwaukee County. Its functions included providing emergency services, carrying responsibility for long-term treatment, and coordinating community activities pertaining to abused children.

474. Herrenkohl, E.C. and R.C. Herrenkohl. "A Comparison of Abused Children and Their Non-Abused Siblings." **Journal of the American Academy of Child Psychiatry**, 18:260–69, 1979.

Examines the role of the child-related characteristics in precipitating abuse. Characteristics considered included physical handicaps, mental retardation, congenital factors, and parental perceptions of the child's differences.

475. Hilberman, Elaine and Kit Munson. "Sixty Battered Women." **Victimology: An International Journal**, 2:460–70, 1977–78.

Examines the psychological effects of marital violence on sixty women who had been referred to a rural health clinic for psychiatric evaluation and were found to be victims of marital violence. Identification and treatment issues involved in marital violence are also explored.

476. Hill, Deborah A. "Child Abuse: Early Casefinding in a Hospital Setting." **Child Abuse: Intervention and Treatment**. Edited by Nancy B. Ebeling and Deborah A. Hill. Acton, Massachusetts: Publishing Sciences Group, Inc., 1975, pp. 17–22.

Discusses the social worker as casefinder and describes the characteristics a social worker looks for in identifying a potentially abusing family.

477. Hill, Deborah A. "The Development of Children's Advocates, A Community Approach." **Child Abuse: Intervention and Treatment**. Edited by Nancy B. Ebeling and Deborah A. Hill. Acton, Massachusetts: Publishing Sciences Group, Inc., 1975, pp. 179–82.

Examines the development of children's advocates within the community as an example of agencies and the community working together to improve services for children in need and their families.

478. _____. "Emotional Reactions to Child Abuse Within a Hospital Setting." **Child Abuse: Intervention and Treatment**. Edited by Nancy B. Ebeling and Deborah A. Hill. Acton, Massachusetts: Publishing Sciences Group, Inc., 1975, pp. 37–40.

Describes the emotional reactions evoked when an abused child is admitted to a hospital, and the difficulties created by these reactions when medical personnel are forced to deal compassionately with the parent.

479. Hindman, Margaret. "Child Abuse and Neglect: The Alcohol Connection." **Alcohol Health and Research World**, 1(3):pp. 2–7, Spring 1977.

States that parents with alcohol problems have a high potential for child abuse and neglect. Situations in which child abuse and neglect are most likely to occur, characteristics of abusers and victims, and treatment needs and alternatives are among the topics discussed.

480. Hirsch, Mariam F. **Women and Violence**. New York: Van Nostrand Reinhold Company, 1981. 385 pp.

Discusses various types of violence against women and devotes a chapter exclusively to battered women.

481. Hoffman, Ellen. "Policy and Politics: The Child Abuse Prevention and Treatment Act." **Public Policy**, 26(1):71–78, Winter 1978.

Examines the legislative history of the Child Abuse Prevention and Treatment Act, focusing on the interaction of policy and politics in shaping that legislation.

482. Hoggett, Brenda. "Care Proceedings: A Question of Priorities." **The Solicitor's Journal**, 120:727–29, November 5, 1976.

Discusses care proceedings and safety orders as methods used by the legal system to prevent children from being harmed in their homes. A recent court case is used to illustrate the operation of the law in such circumstances.

483. Holmes, S.A. and others. "Working With the Parent in Child Abuse Cases." **Child Abuse: Perspectives on Diagnosis, Treatment, and Prevention**. Edited by Roberta Kalmar. Dubuque, Iowa: Kendall/Hunt Publishing Company, 1977, pp. 123–36.

Examines child abuse from a social work perspective, emphasizing the treatment of abusing parents.

484. Holter,Joan C. and Stanford B. Friedman. "Principles of Management in Child Abuse Cases." **American Journal of Orthopsychiatry**, 38(1):127–36, January 1968.

Describes possible approaches to identifying child abuse cases and suggests a team diagnosis approach to the problem.

485. Hoover, Eleanor L. "Mommie Post Mortem — The Awful Truth About Joan Crawford." **Human Behavior**, 8:16–17, February 1979.

Discusses Joan Crawford as a child abuser, and a biography of her life written by her daughter. Some general points are made about child abuse.

486. Horn, Jack C. "A Touch of Class? Views of Leroy Pelton." **Psychology Today**, 12:50, December 1978.

Emphasizes the role of politics in labeling one social class as more abusive than another, for the purpose of allowing professionals to better classify, and treat, problems such as child abuse as a disease rather than as a sociological or poverty-related problem which has no political appeal.

487. _____. "Hidden Factors in Violent Families." **Psychology Today**, 12:46, December 1978.

Discusses Gelles' work with violent families, and his conclusion that factors such as geographic location of residence, educational level, or socioeconomic status can't be used as predictors of violence within a family.

488. Horn, Pat. "The Child-Battering Parent: Sick But Slick." **Psychology Today**, 8:32–33, December 1974.

Summarizes the psychological characteristics often found in abusing parents. The results of various psychological tests administered to abusing and non-abusing parents are also presented. These tests showed that abusive parents had higher scores on tests which measured aggression and control, and also higher scores on a test designed to identify respondents who falsify answers.

489. Howard, Janet. "Battered and Raped: The Physical/Sexual Abuse of Women." **Fight Back!: Feminist Resistance to Male Violence**. Edited by Frederique Delacoste and Felice Newman. Minneapolis: Cleis Press, 1981, pp. 71–84.

Discusses rape and battering as the two primarily examples of physical and sexual violence against women. Myths concerning both are presented, and the police and legal system's responses to domestic violence are examined. Concludes by describing what is being done to help combat rape and battering.

490. Howell, Jackie N. "The Role of Law Enforcement in the Prevention,

Investigation, and Treatment of Child Abuse.'' **The Battered Child**. Edited by C. Henry Kempe and Ray E. Helfer. Chicago: University of Chicago Press, 1980, pp. 306-315.

Discusses the expansion of the police role in child abuse cases, including improved training programs, better interagency cooperation, specialized units, early intervention, and treatment and referral services.

491. Hubenak, Priscilla M. ''Due Process for Parents in Emergency Protection Proceedings Under the Texas Family Code — Suggestions for Improving the System.'' **Houston Law Review**, 15:709-14, March 1978.

Examines the issues of due process and parental rights, including problem areas such as standards for removal of a child from the home, the initial presentation of the child to the court, and hearing procedures. Suggestions are made for improving emergency protection procedures in Texas.

492. Hudson, Walter W. and Sally Rau McIntosh. ''The Assessment of Spouse Abuse: Two Quantifiable Dimensions.'' **Journal of Marriage and the Family**, 43(4):873-85, November 1981.

Discusses the need for appropriate tools with which to measure spouse abuse, and presents a new scale of measurement called the Index of Spouse Abuse (ISA). This scale evaluates change in the degree or severity of physical and non-physical abuse as perceived by female respondents. Examines findings concerning the reliability and validity of this scale and concludes that it is a psychometrically sound tool that can be used to measure abuse inflicted upon women by spouses.

493. Hurt, Maure. **Child Abuse and Neglect: A Report on the Status of the Research**. Washington, D.C.: U.S. Department of Health, Education, and Welfare. Office of Human Development/Office of Child Development, 1975. 63 pp.

Reviews the status of research on the problem of child abuse and neglect. Describes the background of the problem, problems of definition, people involved, the environment of abuse and neglect, and intervention into the family for purposes of prevention or reduction of the problem. Appendices include the text of the Child Abuse Prevention and Treatment Act, abstracts of current federal research, and an annotated bibliography.

494. Hussey, Hugh. ''The Battered Child Syndrome: Unusual Manifestations.'' **Journal of the American Medical Association**, 234:856, November 24, 1975.

Reviews literature concerning unusual manifestations of the battered child syndrome.

495. Hyman, Clare A. and Ruth Mitchell. ''A Psychological Study of Child Battering.'' **Health Visitor**, 48:294-96, August 1975.

Summarizes a study conducted by the Battered Child Research Department of the NSPCC which explored the "psychological functioning" of battered children and their families. The psychological characteristics of family members are emphasized.

496. "I Was a Battered Wife." **Good Housekeeping**, 188:34–42, May 1979.

One woman relates her experiences as a battered wife and describes the ways she sought help for her problem.

497. "Incidence of Child Abuse." **Children Today**, 11(1):27–28, January–February 1982.

Presents statistics of child abuse released by the National Center on Child Abuse and Neglect.

498. "Indiana's Statutory Protection for the Abused Child." **Valparaiso University Law Review**, 9:89–133, Fall 1974.

Examines the general statutory provisions provided by the Indiana Legislature for the protection of the abused child.

499. Inglis, Ruth L. **Sins of the Fathers: A Study of the Physical and Emotional Abuse of Children**. New York: St. Martin's Press, 1978. 220 pp.

Presents an extensive examination of child abuse. Attitudes toward children, background of child abuse, characteristics of abusing parents, societal attitudes toward the problem, prevention and treatment, and the effect of battering on the mind of the child are among the issues examined. Detailed discussions of family therapy, and the relationship between child abuse and single parenting are also presented.

500. International Association of Chiefs of Police. "Training Keys," Numbers 245 and 246. **Battered Women: A Psychosociological Study of Domestic Violence**. Edited by Maria Roy. New York: Van Nostrand Reinhold Company, 1977, pp. 144–63.

Presents two training keys designed to familiarize and train police to deal with family violence.

501. Issacs, Jacob L. "The Role of the Lawyer in Child Abuse Cases." **Helping The Battered Child and His Family**. Edited by C. Henry Kempe and Ray E. Helfer. Philadelphia: J.B. Lippincott Company, 1972, pp. 225–41.

Discusses the role of the lawyer in child abuse cases, emphasizing experience as a determinant of the lawyer's proper role. The need for, and the role of, counsel for the abused child are reviewed and the role of counsel for the parent is summarized.

502. Issacson, Lon B. "Child Abuse Reporting Statutes: The Case for Holding Physicians Civilly Liable for Failing to Report." **San Diego Law Review**, 12:743–77, June 1975.

Explores the proposition that non-reporting physicians of suspected cases of child abuse may incur civil liability for injuries subsequently received by these children.

503. Jacobs,J. "Child Abuse, Neglect and Deprivation and the Family." **The Maltreatment of Children**. Edited by Selwyn M. Smith. Baltimore: University Park Press, 1978, pp. 245–316.

Discusses children and violence, and explores the problem of child abuse and the role of various social institutions in its treatment and prevention.

504. Jacobson, Beverly. "Battered Women: The Fight to End Wife Beating." **Civil Rights Digest**, 9:2–11, Summer 1977.

States that wife beating is not a class-linked phenomenon and discusses the cultural and social conditions which may lead to it. The role of fear in the battered wife syndrome, attempts at prevention and protection, the significance of the criminal justice system in relation to wife beating, and the incidence of the problem is explored. The work of Marjorie Fields, an attorney who works with battered women, is also discussed.

505. James, Howard. **The Little Victims: How America Treats Its Children**. New York: David McKay Company, Inc., 1975. 374 pp.

Discusses children who are abused, handicapped, retarded, or delinquents, and how society treats them. Presents an extensive discussion of child abuse and child sexual abuse. Concludes with an examination of possible solutions, including systems that have proved to work and what can be done to save the children.

506. James, Jennifer and others. "Physician Reporting of Sexual Abuse of Children." **Journal of the American Medical Association**, 240:1145–46, September 1978.

Describes a study in which physicians were surveyed as to the frequency of their contact with sexually abused children, the type of abuse involved, the usual procedure for reporting, and the treatment provided to the patient. Findings support the hypothesis that physicians are not reporting cases of sexual abuse of children as directed by law. Also supported is the view that the actual frequency of cases exceeds the number reported.

507. Jayaratne, Srinika. "Child Abusers as Parents and Children: A Review." **Social Work**, 22:5–9, January 1977.

Discusses the theory that abused children frequently grow up to be abusive parents. Suggests that little empirical evidence exists to support this theory and comparison studies should be made to add validity to statements concerning this issue.

508. Jenkins, Richard L. and Andrew Boyer. "Effects of Inadequate Mothering and Inadequate Fathering on Children." **International Journal of Social Psychiatry**, 16(1):72–78, Winter 1969–70.

Relates the findings of a study which explored the elements related to deficient mothering and fathering in children in a clinical population. Results showed that children who lacked mothering tended to be hostile, resentful, engage in rebellious delinquent acts, and are also depressed and anxious.

509. Jenkins, Richard L. and others. "Interrupting the Family Cycle of Violence." **Journal of the Iowa Medical Society**, 60(2):85–89, 1970.

Explains the cycle of violence theory of abuse, stating that in addition to a battered child possibly becoming a battering parent, a battered child may also batter younger children. A case history is examined to illustrate this problem.

510. Jensen, Rita Henley. "Battered Women and the Law." **Victimology: An International Journal**, 2:585–90, 1977–78.

Explores the response of the criminal justice system when battered women seek help from the law. Changes in the New York laws which pertain to wife beating and some relevant court cases are also examined.

511. Jobling, Megan. "Battered Wives: A Survey." **Social Service Quarterly**, 47:142–46, April–June 1974.

Examines the problem of battered wives. Topics discussed include characteristics of men who batter and why they batter, the main types of assault inflicted, the use of alcohol as a factor in battering, characteristics of the children of battering mothers, available services for violent families and the willingness of these services to take action, and the characteristics of women which make them likely victims of abusive husbands. Suggestions are made for management of the problem and for prevention.

512. Johnson, Betty and Harold Morse. **The Battered Child: A Study of Children With Inflicted Injuries**. Denver: Denver, Colorado Welfare Department, 1968. 22 pp.

Relates a study conducted by the Division of Services for Children and Youth of the Denver Welfare Department. Findings indicate that abusing parents often have needs which have not been met, and that they are unaware of age-appropriate behavior for children. Characteristics of abusing parents are discussed, focusing on parental "acting out" of their own needs by inflicting injury on children.

513. _____. "Injured Children and Their Parents." **The Battered Child**. Compiled by Jerome E. Leavitt. Morristown, New Jersey: General Learning Press, 1974, pp. 18–23.

States that the major concern of professional persons responsible for protecting children should be how to insure the safety of children returned to abusing parents. Discusses a study conducted by the Division of Services for Children and Youth of the Denver Department of Welfare, which reviewed its work with families where a child had been injured by parents. Findings indicated that about 80% of the children were no longer in danger of subsequent injury. Concludes by discussing ways in which the community and protective services can work together to help families and protect children.

514. Johnson, John M. "Program Enterprise and Official Cooptation in the Battered Women's Shelter Movement." **American Behavioral Scientist**, 24(6):827–42, July–August 1981.

Reports on the organizational and resource development of the shelter movement, its success and relationship to official funding sources, and the welfare state corruption and official cooptation involved in many shelter programs. In addition to academic and research involvements in this field, personal experiences of a shelter cofounder represent sources for these analyses.

515. Johnson, Sally. "Abused Wives Strike Back." **Majority Report**, 4:9, May 3, 1975.

Discusses the formation of Abused Women's Aid in Crisis (AWAIC) in New York City to offer self-help and counseling services to abused women.

516. Johnston, Pamela. "Attack From the Right." **Fight Back!: Feminist Resistance to Male Violence**. Minneapolis: Cleis Press, 1981, pp. 85–92.

Outlines an organization's attempt to discredit and close a shelter for battered women. Discusses the policies and economics of operating the shelter, and the politics and philosophy behind establishing the shelter.

517. Jones, Carolyn Okell. "The Fate of Abused Children." **The Challenge of Child Abuse**. Edited by Alfred White Franklin. London: Academic Press, 1977, pp. 108–21.

Analyzes the common path of child abuse and discusses the implictions for future therapeutic intervention on behalf of the abused child.

518. Jordan, BIll and Jean Packman. "Training for Social Work With Violent Families." **Violence and the Family**. Edited by J.P. Martin. New York: John Wiley and Sons, 1978, pp. 325–43.

Examines the training of social workers to deal with violent families, the problems encountered in working with family violence, and the role of the social worker in the treatment process.

519. Justice, Blair and David F. Duncan. "Life Crisis as a Precursor to Child Abuse." **Public Health Reports**, 91:110–15, March–April 1976.

Discusses the relationship between life changes and the incidence of child abuse as illustrated by a study of abusing parents and matched controls. It was found that the abusing parents had experienced more intense life changes than had the control group. It is suggested that intense life changes, both positive and negative, can create a high degree of stress which may hamper the parent's ability to cope with a child.

520. Justice, Blair and Rita Justice. **The Abusing Family**. New York: Human Sciences Press, 1976. 288 pp.

Matched groups of abusive and non-abusive parents were interviewed. As a result of these interviews, a model of the abusive family was constructed. Change, both excessive and stressful, characterized the lives of the abusive families. In addition, the attachment between mother and child was not a mutually strong, bonding one. Methods of therapy for abusive families are presented and the effectiveness of therapy on the parent is discussed. A bibliography is included.

521. Justice, Blair and others. "Judges Views of Child Abuse: A Survey of Attitudes and Experience." **Psychological Reports**, 41(3):887–90, December 1977.

Reports on the results of a questionaire distributed to judges in Texas concerning child abuse and neglect.

522. Justice, Rita and Blair Justice. "Evaluating Outcome of Group Therapy for Abusing Parents." **Corrective and Social Psychiatry and Journal of Behavior Technology Methods and Therapy**, 24:45–48, January 1978.

Evaluates the effectiveness of group therapy for abusive parents by discussing a study conducted for this purpose.

523. _____. "TA Work With Child Abuse." **Transactional Analysis Journal**, 5:38–41, January 1975.

Describes the use of transactional analysis techniques in the treatment of child abusing parents.

524. Kadushin, Alfred and Judith A. Martin. **Child Abuse — An Interactional Event**. New York: Columbia University Press, 1981. 304 pp.

Reports on research which attempted a detailed examination of the immediate parent-child interaction which culminated in physical abuse, with particular reference to child behavior as the stimulus for initiation of the episode. Implications for therapy with abusing families are also discussed.

525. Kaiser, Gunther. "Child Abuse in West Germany." **Victimology: An International Journal**, 2:294–306, Summer 1977.

Discusses recent research on child abuse conducted in West Germany.

526. Kaizen, Mark S. "Child Abuse: The Role of Adoption as a Preventative Measure." **The John Marshall Journal of Practice and Procedure**, 10:546–66, Spring 1977.

Examines the role of adoption in preventing child abuse. Proposals for legislative reform which would increase the role of adoption in the prevention of child abuse are also discussed.

527. Kalmar, Roberta, editor. **Child Abuse: Perspectives on Diagnosis, Treatment and Prevention**. Dubuque, Iowa: Kendall/Hunt Publishing Company, 1977. 150 pp.

Reviews various aspects of child abuse. Topics discussed include the child as victim, the parent as victim and victimizer, and prevention and treatment. A brief summary of each article to be presented precedes each section and resources for clinicians are provided.

528. Kameman, Sheila B. "Eight Countries: Cross-National Perspectives on Child Abuse and Neglect." **Children Today**, 4(3):34–37, May/June 1975.

Discusses a study conducted by the Columbia University School of Social Work. The major objective of the study was to determine whether a personal or general social service system in dealing with child abuse was emerging in various countries. The study stressed operational definitions and descriptive reporting.

529. Katz, Sanford N. and others. "Child Neglect Laws in America." **Family Law Quarterly**, 9(1):1–372, Spring 1975.

Surveys child neglect statutes in all fifty states, the District of Columbia, Guam, Puerto Rico, and the Virgin Islands. Presents an overall view of the research, tables summarizing definitions, elements of purpose clauses, grounds for determining neglect, ages of children, reporting neglect, neglect hearings, statutes, termination of parental rights, and immunities and privileges in reporting. A state by state digest of how each basic component is handled is also offered.

530. Kaufman, Irving. "The Physically Abused Child." **Child Abuse: Intervention and Treatment.** Edited by Nancy B. Ebeling and Deborah A. Hill. Acton, Massachusetts: Publishing Sciences Group, Inc., 1975, pp. 79–86.

Focuses on the personality factors found in parents who physically abuse their children.

531. Kaul, Mohan L. "Physical Child Abuse and Its Prevention." **Intellect**, February 1977, pp. 270–72.

Presents a general discussion of child abuse and an epidemiological approach (viewing child abuse as a disease) in the interests of prevention is suggested. The causes, definition, scope, and characteristics of abusers and victims are among the topics explored.

532. Kaye, Loraine. "Establishing a Task Force for Battered Women." **American Journal of Nursing**, 78(4):653, April 1978.

Discusses the establishment of a task force for battered women in Waukesha, Wisconsin.

533. Keller, O.J. "Hypothesis for Violent Crime." **American Journal of**

Correction, 37(2):7, March–April 1975.

Explores a correlation between violent crime and the large number of unwanted, abused and battered children. Statistics of child abuse in some cities of the country are also presented.

534. Kellum, Barbara A. "Infanticide in England in the Later Middle Ages." **History of Childhood Quarterly,** 1(3):367–89, 1974.

Discusses the difficulty of measuring the incidence of infanticide during the Middle Ages and suggests reasons why it was practiced extensively during that time.

535. Kempe, C. Henry. "Approaches to Preventing Child Abuse: The Health Visitors Concept." **American Journal of Diseases of Children,** 130:941–47, September 1976.

Approaches to the prevention of child abuse are explored. Indicators for early detection of abuse or the potential for abuse, and the role of the health visitor in prevention are highlighted.

536. _____. "Incest and Other Forms of Sexual Abuse." **The Battered Child.** Edited by C. Henry Kempe and Ray E. Helfer. Chicago: University of Chicago Press, 1980, pp. 198–214.

Defines sexual abuse and discusses the problem, incidence, underreporting, management of victims, and the nature of sexual abuse.

537. _____. "Pediatric Implications of the Battered Baby Syndrome." **Archives of Diseases in Childhood,** 46(245):28–37, 1971.

Views the battered child syndrome as an extreme form of an entire spectrum of the abuse and neglect of children. Statistics concerning the incidence of the problem, characteristics of abusing parents, and contributory factors are presented. Concludes by suggesting that early management should include separation of the child from its parents, and a treatment program which focuses on the needs of the parents as well as the child.

538. Kempe, C. Henry and Ray E. Helfer, editors. **The Battered Child.** Chicago: University of Chicago Press, 1980. 440 pp.

The first part of this book reviews background material in order to put the problem into perspective. Basic concepts are discussed, and historical and cross-cultural aspects of the problem are reviewed. The effect of crisis and stress on parent-child interaction is also analyzed and the influences of abuse on child development are summarized. The second part of the book focuses on assessment of the problem, and the third part discusses methods of intervention and treatment.

539. _____. **Helping the Battered Child and His Family.** Philadelphia: J.B. Lippincott Company, 1972. 313 pp.

States the purpose of this book is to suggest a child abuse treatment program, to demonstrate that people from a variety of backgrounds can be helpful to the abused child and his family, and to provide practical approaches for people providing help. Presents a general introduction to the problem and offers a bibliography.

540. _____. "Innovative Therapeutic Approaches." **Helping the Battered Child and His Family**. Edited by C. Henry Kempe and Ray E. Helfer. Philadelphia: J.B. Lippincott Company, 1972, pp. 41–54.

Focuses on the limited availability of skilled psychiatrists and social workers in the field, and suggests treatment personnel alternatives. Discusses the roles of "Parent Aides," visiting nurses, homemaker services, crisis nurseries, and Mothers Anonymous groups.

541. Kempe, C. Henry and others. "The Battered Child Syndrome." **Journal of the American Medical Association**, 181(1):17–24, 1962.

States that child battering is not merely a problem among the poor, but occurs within all social classes. Discusses child abuse as a result of parents' own battering experiences during childhood, and as an identification with a battering parent. Other social and psychological factors affecting the incidence of child abuse are also examined.

542. Kempe, Ruth S. And C. Henry Kempe. **Child Abuse**. Cambridge, Massachusetts: Harvard University Press, 1978.

The nature and management of child abuse are explored. Issues examined include the characteristics of abused children and their parents, the extent of the problem, sexual abuse, prevention and treatment, the role of the community in child abuse management, and the rights of children. An index and a suggested reading list are included.

543. Kempe, Ruth S. and others. "The Infant With Failure-to-Thrive." **The Battered Child**. Edited by C. Henry Kempe and Ray E. Helfer. Chicago: University of Chicago Press, 1980, pp. 163–82.

States that failure-to-thrive is one of the most important conditions to be considered in abused and neglected children. Reviews the incidence of this problem in the United States, and defines both organic and non-organic conditions. Diagnosis and management, including reporting to protective services and possible treatment plans, are discussed.

544. Kieviet, Thomas G. "The Battered Wife Syndrome: A Potential Defense to a Homicide Charge." **Pepperdine Law Review**, 6:213–29, Fall 1978.

Examines the method used by the legal system to deal with marital violence and discusses its effectiveness. The use of self-help by battered wives as a possible remedy against the violence of their husbands is discussed and the present legal perspectives on intrafamilial homicide are explored. The defense of battering as a motive for homicide is also examined.

545. "Killing Excuse: Wives Murdering Husbands Because of Abuse." **Time**, 110:108, November 28, 1977.

Briefly discusses three cases of women who had killed their husbands during domestic violence and were not found guilty of murder. The role of public opinion in law enforcement is also explored.

546. Kinard, E. Milling. "Emotional Development in Physically Abused Children." **American Journal of Orthopsychiatry**, 50(4):686–96, October 1980.

Presents the results of a study which compared 30 physically abused children with a matched control group. Psychological tests were administered to both groups which measured aggression, self-concept, socialization with other children, and establishment of trust. Differences between each group are found in each area studied.

547. Kohlman, Richard J. "Malpractice Liability for Failing to Report Child Abuse." **California State Bar Journal**, 49:118–23 + , March–April 1974.

Discusses the problem of child abuse and the law's response to it. The responsibility of the physician to report suspected cases of child abuse and the possible civil liabilities for failure to report are emphasized.

548. Korbin, Jill E. "The Cross-Cultural Context of Child Abuse and Neglect." **The Battered Child**. Edited by C. Henry Kempe and Ray E. Helfer. Chicago: University of Chicago Press, 1980, pp. 21–35.

States that current understanding of child abuse is based on behavior in western cultures. Presents a cross-cultural perspective in order to understand a more universal context of child abuse, including culturally appropriate definitions of the problem. Also explores misunderstandings concerning child abuse due to different cultural practices.

549. Krause, Harry D. "Child Welfare, Parental Responsibility and the State." **Family Law Quarterly**, 6(4):377–403, Winter 1972.

Focuses on child welfare and deals with parental non-support and neglect. Recommends the re-examination of the states' neglect and dependency laws to make sure that welfare agencies can take over when parents fail.

550. Kretschman, Karen L. **Selected Bibliography on Child Abuse and Neglect**. Austin: University of Texas School of Law, 1976. 26 pp.

Provides a brief introduction to the subject of child abuse and discusses government documents as sources of information on the problem. The bibliography itself lists government documents which pertain to child abuse, and briefly annotates them.

551. Krieger, Ingeborg. "Food Restriction as a Form of Child Abuse in Ten Cases of Psychosocial Deprivation Dwarfism." **Clinical Pediatrics**, 13(2):127–33, February 1974.

Discusses the cases of ten children who were found to have a psychosocial deprivation syndrome due to food being withheld by the mothers. Food restriction as a form of child abuse is examined and intensive psychotherapy for the mothers is suggested.

552. Kristal, Helen F. and Ford Tucker. "Managing Child Abuse Cases." **Social Work**, 20:392–95, September 1975.

Discusses a multidisciplinary treatment program for the management of child abuse which was developed at the University of Rochester.

553. Kumagai, Fumie and Gearoid O'Donoghue. "Conjugal Power and Conjugal Violence in Japan and the U.S.A." **Journal of Comparative Family Studies**, 9:213–21, Summer 1978.

Compares marriage patterns in Japan and the U.S., emphasizing the patterns of conjugal conflict resolution, decision making, and the relationship between the decision making process and how a couple resolves its differences within marriage.

554. Kutun, Barry. "Legislative Needs and Solutions." **Battered Women: A Psychosociological Study of Domestic Violence**. Edited by Maria Roy. New York: Van Nostrand Reinhold Company, 1977, pp. 277–87.

Reviews a survey which had been distributed to agencies associated with law enforcement. The survey demonstrated that no public office kept separate records for spouse abuse cases and it was, therefore, impossible to tell how many incidents had occurred per year. Areas in need of reform are examined in light of this survey.

555. Lamb, Robert L. "New Child Abuse Law Explained." **Pennsylvania Medicine**, 79:30, February 1976.

Explains the Child Protective Services Law enacted in 1975 by the Pennsylvania Legislature. The law is highlighted by the mandatory reporting of suspected cases of child abuse with immunity, and the mandating of every county in the state to establish a child protective service.

556. Langer, William L. "Infanticide: A historical Survey." **History of Childhood Quarterly**, 1(3):353–67, 1974.

Defines infanticide and discusses it from a historical perspective.

557. Langley, R. and R.C. Levy. "Wife Abuse and the Police Response." **FBI Law Enforcement Bulletin**, 47(5):4–9, May 1978.

Examines the incidence of wife abuse and discusses typical responses of the police. Suggests that police intervention be based on a criminal law approach, and that wife beating be added to the uniform crime reporting system.

558. Langley, Roger and Richard C. Levy. **Wife Beating: The Silent Crisis.**

New York: E.P. Dutton, 1977. 237 pp.

Examines wifebeating by using women's accounts of battering by their husbands. Also explored are the methods available to a woman who seeks outside help, and ways in which a wife may liberate herself from a violent home.

559. Larsen, Jo Ann. "Remedying Dysfunctional Marital Communication." **Social Casework**, 63(1):15–23, January 1982.

Discusses the management and modification of a couple's communication patterns, and the removal of negative and problematic communication as an effective manner of therapy for distressed marriages.

560. Lascari, Andre D. "The Abused Child." **Journal of the Iowa Medical Society**, 62:229–32, 1972.

Explores the problem of child abuse, focusing on abusive parents.

561. Lauer, Brian and others. "Battered Child Syndrome: Review of 130 Patients With Controls." **Pediatrics**, 54:67–70, July 1974.

Discusses a study conducted at San Francisco General Hospital in which admissions for child abuse are compared demographically with other pediatric admissions. It is noted that the number of admissions for child abuse rose steadily over time, while the admissions for other conditions remained stable.

562. Laughlin, John and Myra Weiss. "An Outpatient Milieu Therapy Approach to Treatment of Child Abuse and Neglect Problems." **Social Casework**, 62(2):106–9, February 1981.

Describes a project which addressed the delivery problem that a county child protective service faces in attempting to control and mitigate occurrences of abuse and neglect. The project found that the child abuse community centers were responsive to the needs of the service, and that this effected significant improvement in service delivery.

563. Laury, Gabriel V. "The Battered Child Syndrome: Parental Motivation, Clinical Aspects." **Bulletin of the New York Academy of Medicine**, 46(9):676–85, 1070.

Examines possible reasons why parents batter their children. States that underlying motivations generally reflect parental hostility, which may not be directly related to the child.

564. "Law to Protect Children." **New England Journal of Medicine**, 271(4):210, July 23, 1964.

Describes the Massachusetts child abuse reporting law, enacted on June 15, 1964, which makes reporting mandatory if the victim is under sixteen years of age.

565. Leavitt, Jerome E., compiler. **The Battered Child, Selected Readings**. Morristown, New Jersey: General Learning Press, 1974. 268 pp.

Presents articles dealing with various aspects of the child abuse problem, including characteristics of the battered child and abusing parents, role of the legal system in the disposition of cases, role of social service workers, medical aspects of the problem, and treatment and prevention. A bibliography, references, section summaries and study questions are also included.

566. _____. "The Battered Child." **The Battered Child**. Compiled by Jerome E. Leavitt. Morristown, New Jersey: General Learning Press, 1974, pp. 208-10.

Examines the incidence of child abuse, the role of educators in identification, work with parents and children, and the importance of sensitivity to the needs of the child when dealing with abuse cases.

567. Lefkowitz, Monroe and others. "Punishment, Identification, and Aggression." **Merrill-Palmer Quarterly of Behavior and Development**, 9(3):159-74, 1963.

Discusses the relationships among punishment, identification, and aggression in reference to children. Findings indicate that non-physical punishment was unrelated to either aggression or identification, and that the use of physical punishment was also unrelated to social status.

568. Leghorn, Lisa. "Social Responses to Battered Women." **FAAR Newsletter**, May–June 1977, pp. 15-19.

Discusses the need to identify the social system with the problem of wife abuse in order to understand why the problem occurs and how to deal with it. Also emphasizes the importance of sharing information with others in order to educate and enlighten people to the realities of the problem and to affect social change.

569. Leistyna, J.A. "Advocacy for the Abused Rural Child." **Children Today**, 7:26-26+, May–June 1978.

Examines the operation of a child protection team in rural Virginia. The responsibility of advocacy for the rural child and where it should fall, and the requirements for effective advocacy are featured.

570. Lena, Hugh F. and Seymour Warkov. "Occupational Perceptions of the Causes and Consequences of Child Abuse/Neglect." **Medical Anthropology**, 2(1):1-28, Winter 1978.

Examines perceptions of child abuse held by child welfare service systems, including judges, teachers, police, medical personnel and social service agencies. Patterns of interpretation for these groups were identified and the effects of the interpretations on work experiences are explored.

571. LeValley, Joseph D. "Safe-House Network for Rural Victims." **MS.**, 11(4):19, October 1982.

A battered woman living in a rural area may encounter difficulties when seeking help. To remedy this situation, an Iowa community established a safe-house network to aid and shelter battered women. The need for such a program is discussed and the operation of the Iowa network is described.

572. Levin, Marj Jackson. "The Wife Beaters." **McCalls**, 102:37, June 1975.

Discusses the problem of wife beating and attempts to curtail it.

573. Levine, Abraham. "Child Neglect: Reaching the Parent." **The Social and Rehabilitation Record**, 1(7):26–27 +, July–August 1974.

Defines child neglect and presents statistics concerning the incidence of the problem. Describes research which focuses on treatment of the neglectful parent and discusses the needs of children and parents.

574. Levine, Montague B. "Interpersonal Violence and Its Effect on the Children: A Study of Fifty Families in General Practice." **Medicine, Science, and the Law**, 15:172–76, July 1975.

Discusses a study of fifty families in which violence had occurred between parents in order to ascertain the effects of it on the children. It was concluded that interpersonal violence renders children "at risk."

575. Levinger, George. "Source of Marital Dissatisfaction Among Applicants for Divorce." **American Journal of Orthopsychiatry**, 36(5):803–7, October 1966.

Compares marital complaints of husbands and wives, and also lower and middle class marriages. Data show that wives complained of physical abuse eleven times more frequently than did husbands.

576. Lewis, Dorothy O. and others. "Violent Juvenile Delinquents: Psychiatric, Neurological, Psychological and Abuse Factors." **Journal of the American Academy of Child Psychiatry**, 18:307–19, 1979.

Compares various factors of extremely violent incarcerated boys with those of less violent ones. It was found that the more violent children were more likely to have experienced and witnessed extreme physical abuse. Factors contributing to delinquency and implications for therapy are also discussed.

577. Lieberknecht, Kay. "Helping the Battered Wife." **American Journal of Nursing**, 78(4):654–56, April 1978.

States that in order to give women the most support, it is necessary to understand the battered woman's situation, her needs, and how to help her meet these needs. It is also important to recognize and deal with common misconceptions. Ways to help the woman take charge of her life following an abusing experience are suggested.

578. Light, Richard J. "Abused and Neglected Children in America: A Study of Alternative Policies." **Harvard Educational Review**, 43(4):556-98, November 1973.

In order to estimate the incidence of child abuse, several sources of data are examined, and social and demographc features are discussed. Potential social policies are analyzed, including national health screening, education in child rearing, and the development of profiles of abusing families. The effectiveness of policies and suggested improvements in policies are also discussed. Concludes by recommending more systematic and carefully designed investigations of reporting systems in order to ascertain the most effective programs to reduce child abuse and neglect.

579. Lindenthal, Jacob and others. "Public Knowledge of Child Abuse." **Child Welfare**, 54:521-23, July 1975.

To determine the extent of the public's knowledge of child abuse, adults were interviewed concerning their exposure to information on the subject. Although about seventy percent of the people surveyed had heard something about child abuse, less than twenty-five percent of them were aware of protective and preventative services available in their own community. In addition, attitudes toward abusers were found to be liberal.

580. Lion, John R. "Clinical Aspects of Wifebattering." **Battered Women: A Psychosociological Study of Domestic Violence**. Edited by Maria Roy. New York: Van Nostrand Reinhold Company, 1977, pp. 126-36.

Explores the role of the victim in domestic violence, the dynamics of the violent situation, and treatment for wifebattering which involves treatment of both parties. Examples are presented to illustrate the complexity of the problem.

581. Lipner, Joanne D. "Attitudes of Professionals in the Management and Treatment of Child Abuse." **Child Abuse: Intervention and Treatment**. Edited by Nancy B. Ebeling and Deborah A. Hill. Acton, Massachusetts: Publishing Sciences Group, Inc., 1975, pp. 31-35.

Discusses the experiences of the author as a social worker with one particular case of child abuse.

582. _____. "The Use of Community Resources in Work With Abusive Families." **Child Abuse: Intervention and Treatment**. Edited by Nancy B. Ebeling and Deborah A. Hill. Acton, Massachusetts: Publishing Sciences Group, Inc., 1975, pp. 131-35.

Examines the use of community resources in working with child abuse cases, including the work of paraprofessionals and volunteers.

583. Lippi, Laura. "Jersey Asks: Are You a Woman or a Spouse?" **Majority Report**, 7(16):5, January 7-20, 1978.

Briefly describes two bills passed by the New Jersey State Assembly dealing with battered spouses. Five professionals discuss wife abuse from different perspectives: a woman who runs a shelter for battered women; a police sergeant; a social worker; a psychologist; and an attorney.

584. "Little Mary Ellen." **Parade**, November 29, 1981, p. 17.

Relates the story of Mary Ellen, the first recorded case of a battered child receiving assistance from a public agency. This case led to the establishment of the New York Society for the Prevention of Cruelty to Children.

585. Lloyd-Still, John D. and Barbara Martin. "Child Abuse in a Rural Setting." **Pennsylvania Medicine**, 79:56–60, March 1976.

Child abuse in rural areas is explored using data gathered from a rural medical center in Pennsylvania. It was found that child abuse in the study area was similar to child abuse occurring in most other areas. The authors also discuss the importance of cooperation among agencies when dealing with child abuse cases.

586. Lobenz, Norman. "One Woman's War Against Child Abuse." **Good Housekeeping**, 181:82 + , July 1975.

Discusses the operation of SCAN (Suspected Child Abuse and Neglect) and examines the nature of the child abuse problem.

587. Loizos, Peter. "Violence and the Family: Some Mediterranean Examples." **Violence and the Family**, Edited by J.P. Martin. New York: John Wiley and Sons, 1978, pp. 183–96.

Describes situations of violence in the family in rural communities of the Mediterranean and argues that belief in family honor as a moral code may lead to violence, especially by men against women.

588. Long, Robert T. and Oliver Cope. "Emotional Problems in Burned Children." **New England Journal of Medicine**, 264(22): 1121–27, June 1, 1961.

Presents psychologic observations on nineteen children with burn injuries. Observation showed that a high incidence of family disturbance accompanied the burn incidents, and the emotional reactions of the children hindered recovery.

589. Lord, Edith and David Weisfield. "The Abused Child." **Childhood Deprivation**. Edited by Albert R. Roberts. Springfield, Illinois: Charles C. Thomas, Publisher, 1974, pp. 64–83.

States that abusive parents are not usually criminals or mentally ill, but rather, are parents who are uninformed or misinformed about effective parenting. An overview of the problem is presented and the probable reasons why parents batter are discussed.

590. Lorens, Herbert D. and Jules Rako. "A Community Approach to the

Prevention of Child Abuse." **Child Abuse: Perspectives on Diagnosis, Treatment and Prevention**. Edited by Roberta Kalmar. Dubuque, Iowa: Kendall/Hunt Publishing Co., 1977, pp. 104–07.

Describes a program developed in one community in order to identify and intervene in cases where children are designated as "vulnerable." Some typical cases are presented.

591. Lourie, Ira S. "The Phenomenon of the Abused Adolescent: A Clinical Study." **Victimology: An International Journal**, 2:268–76, Summer 1977.

Explores the unique factors of adolescent abuse. The study related here indicates that there is much variability in patterns of abuse of adolescents, the abused adolescents frequently have developmental problems in the areas of separation and control, and that parents who abuse adolescents are most likely having problems in their own development as adults.

592. Lowenberg, D.A. "Conjugal Assaults: The Incarcerated or Liberated Woman." **Federal Probation**, 41:10–13, June 1977.

Discusses the victim witness advocate program which was developed in order to increase the willingness of the public to report crimes and to participate in the prosecution process. Also explored are the reasons why battered women stay in their violent homes, the legal process and available services for battered women, ways of educating the community to the problem, and the supportive services of the program's staff and of other agencies.

593. Lynch, Annette. "Child Abuse in the School-Age Population." **Journal of School Health**, 45:141–48, March 1975.

Discusses a program which was organized to aid a school district in the management of child abuse and neglect. The program consisted of a reporting process whereby the school personnel could report directly to the director of the program who would, in turn, refer the family to the child welfare agency. Suggestions are made for the improved handling of child abuse cases by school personnel.

594. Lynch, Catherine G. and Thomas L. Norris. "Services for Battered Women: Looking for a Perspective." **Victimology: An International Journal**, 2:553–62, 1977–78.

Examines the problems involved in providing services to battered women. The needs of the victim, resources necessary for a functioning agency, the diversity of various agencies, and the responses of programs to victims' needs are among the issues explored. Suggestions for further work in this area are made.

595. Lynch, Margaret A. "Child Abuse: The Critical path." **Journal of Maternal and Child Health**, July 1976, pp. 25–29.

Discusses child abuse as the result of a process and series of specific events which begin before the child is born and continue until the abuse begins. An analysis of family history is examined as a method of recognizing warning signs of abuse and perhaps stop the abuse before it begins.

596. _____. "Ill-Health and Child Abuse." **The Lancet**, 2:317–19, August 16, 1975.

Presents a study which examined the relationship between bonding failure and child abuse. Suggests treatment of parents during pregnancy and early infancy in order to prevent child abuse.

597. _____. "Risk Factors in the Child: A Study of Abused Children and Their Siblings." **The Abused Child: A Multidisciplinary Approach to Developmental Issues and Treatment**. Edited by Harold P. Martin. Cambridge, Massachusetts: Ballinger Publishing Co., 1976, pp. 43–56.

Discusses abuse as an extreme effect of bonding failure between parent and child, focusing on the high risk factors identifiable in the child.

598. Lynch, Margaret A. and Jacqueline Roberts. "Predicting Child Abuse: Signs of Bonding Failure in the Maternity Hospital." **British Medical Journal**, 1:624–26, March 5, 1977.

Presents results of a case-control study conducted in a maternity hospital. Factors frequently found in the case group (abused children or children in a high risk category) included unemployed parents, babies born prematurely, evidence of emotional disturbance, referral to a social welfare agency, mother 20 years old or younger, admission of the child to a special care unit. Recommends that procedures be developed to predict the probability of abuse.

599. Lystad, Mary H. "Violence at Home: A Review of the Literature." **American Journal of Orthopsychiatry**, 45(3):328–45, April 1975.

Recent literature on intrafamilial violence is reviewed and suggestions are made for additional research.

600. MacCarthy, Dermod. "Deprivation Dwarfism Viewed as a Form of Child Abuse." **The Challenge of Child Abuse**. Edited by Alfred White Franklin. London: Academic Press, 1977, pp. 96–107.

Discusses deprivation, rejection and the incidence of deprivation dwarfism as a result of being unfed. An assessment of the mother whose child fails to thrive is also presented.

601. MacFarlane, Kee. "Sexual Abuse of Children." **The Victimization of Women**. Edited by Jane Roberts Chapman and Margaret Gates. Beverly Hills, California: Sage Publications, Inc., 1978, pp. 81–109.

Discusses the sexual abuse of children by examining antecedents and scope of the problem, types of sexual abuse, effects on the victim, the role of socialization in creating victims and abusers, and prescriptions for change.

602. MacKeith, Ronald. "Speculations on Some Possible Long-Term Effects." **Child Abuse: Papers Presented by the Tunbridge Wells Study Group on Non-Accidental Injury to Children**. Edited By Alfred White Franklin. Edinburgh: Churchill Livingstone, 1975, pp. 63–68.

Discusses various injuries inflicted on abused children and the possible long term effects of them.

603. MacKeith, Ronald and others. "Notes on Education." **Concerning Child Abuse: Papers Presented by the Tunbridge Wells Study Group on Non-Accidental Injury to Children**. Edited by Alfred White Franklin. Edinburgh: Churchill Livingstone, 1975, pp. 149–52.

Discusses the education of doctors, social workers, and the police concerning the problem and treatment of child abuse.

604. MacLeod, Celeste. "Legacy of Battering." **Nation**, 218:719–22, June 8, 1974.

States that the cycle of abuse is passed from generation to generation, and that the traditional solution to battering (putting parents in jail and taking away their children) has perpetrated this cycle. Examines a new approach which involves working with parents to teach them how to be good parents. Other programs aimed at combating child abuse are also discussed.

605. Madden, Susan. "Fighting Back With Deadly Force: Women who Kill in Self-Defense." **Fight Back!: Feminist Resistance to Male Violence**. Edited by Frederique Delacoste and Felice Newman. Minneapolis: Cleis Press, 1981, pp. 143–51.

Through the use of newspaper accounts, cases of women who have killed their assailants, including husbands, in self defense are presented.

606. Maden, Marc F. and David E. Wrench. "Significant Findings in Child Abuse Research." **Victimology: An International Journal**, 2:196–224, Summer 1977.

Reviews recent research and literature on child abuse. Deficiencies in research and literature are highlighted and a comprehensive bibliography is presented.

607. Maidment, Susan. "Law's Response to Marital Violence in England and the U.S.A." **International and Comparative Law Quarterly**, 26:403–44, April 1977.

Discusses the present legal framework in England, including criminal and civil proceedings, and the purpose of a law for the protection of battered women. The legal system in the U.S.A. is examined as one in which the special nature of intrafamilial violence is taken into account.

608. Malone, Charles A. "Safety First: Comments on the Influence of External

Danger in the Lives of Children of Disorganized Families." **American Journal of Orthopsychiatry**, 36(1):3–12, January 1966.

Presents findings of a study which focused on the psychological and developmental characteristics of children from multiproblem families.

609. Mann, Andrew. "Society's Obligation to the Family." **The Challenge of Child Abuse**. Edited by Alfred White Franklin. London: Academic Press, 1977, pp. 206–16.

Discusses child abuse, the stresses of family life, the responsibility of the individual within society, the functions of the neighborhood on social life, and the role of professionals in dealing with the family.

610. Marcovitch, Anne. "Refuges for Battered Women." **Social Work Today**, 7(2):34–35, April 15, 1976.

Explains how Acton Women's Aid in Britain offers assistance to women and ways in which it works constructively through the use of shared experiences. Concludes by emphasizing the need for greater understanding of the dynamics of violence in marital relationships for educating vulnerable women.

611. "Maria Colwell and After." **British Medical Journal**, 1:300, February 23, 1974.

Focuses on the lack of cooperation between agencies which deal with child abuse. The problem of identification of abuse and the potential of a family for violent behavior is discussed in light of the Maria Colwell case.

612. "Marital Rape Exemption." **New York University Law Review**, 52:306–23, May 1977.

Explores the rationales underlying the Rape Exemption for husbands. States which have withdrawn from the use of an absolute exemption are also discussed. Suggests that the exemption has no place in modern criminal law.

613. Marks, Alan N. "Role of a Child Psychiatrist as a Consultant to a Hospital Trauma Team." **Child Abuse: Intervention and Treatment**. Edited by Nancy B. Ebeling and Deborah A. Hill. Acton, Massachusetts: Publishing Sciences Group, Inc., 1975, pp. 73–75.

Examines the main functions of the child psychiatrist consultant to a hospital-based child abuse trauma team.

614. Marsden, Dennis. "Sociological Perspectives on Family Violence." **Violence and the Family**. Edited by J.P. Martin. New York: John Wiley and Sons, 1978, pp. 103–33.

Explores family violence as a public issue and presents various sociological perspectives and analyses of the problem.

615. Marsden, D. and D. Owens. "The Jekyll and Hyde Marriages." **New Society**, 32:333–35, May 8, 1975.

Discusses the relationship between abused children and the possibility of them eventually becoming abusing parents. Factors which may trigger family violence are also explored and the possible link between material deprivation and family instability is examined.

616. Martin, David L. "The Growing Horror of Child Abuse and the Undeniable Role of the Schools in Putting an End to It." **American School Board Journal**, 160(11):51–55, November 1973.

States that school officials can help with the problem of child abuse. Statistics on the incidence of child abuse are presented, and the role of the school in reporting, identification, prevention and treatment is detailed.

617. Martin, Del. **Battered Wives**. San Francisco: Glide Publications, 1976. 269 pp. Revised edition: San Francisco: Volcano Press, Inc., 1981, 281 pp.

Inequality and male aggression are emphasized as the roots of marital violence. The legal and social service systems are criticized for their treatment of battered women, and a list of shelters and proposals for new legislation pertaining to intrafamilial violence are presented. Discusses why a woman stays in a violent home, survival tactics, what makes men batter, wife beating and the marriage contract, and remedial legislation. The revised edition also summarizes the work done in the area of family violence from 1976–81, and examines domestic violence as a crime, treatment of the offender, new insight into sex roles, and the battered women's aid movement.

618. _____. "Battered Women: Society's Problem." **The Victimization of Women**. Edited by Jane Roberts Chapman and Margaret Gates. Beverly Hills, California: Sage Publications, Inc., 1978, pp. 111–41.

Discusses battered women by emphasizing the complex nature of the problem, and examining the reluctance of society to recognize the prevalence of domestic violence. Historical attitudes toward women, the marriage contract, the failure of the legal system to deal with marital violence, the inadequacies of the social service system, refuges for battered women, and remedial legislation are among the areas explored.

619. _____. "Lives on the Rocks: The Phoenix Solution." **MS.**, 5:97, August 1976.

Discusses the work of Rainbow Retreat, the first of the now-existing refuges for battered women to be established in the United States.

620. _____. "What Keeps a Woman Captive in a Violent Relationship? — The Social Context of Battering." **Battered Women**. Edited by Donna M. Moore. Beverly Hills: Sage Publications, Inc., 1979, pp. 33–57.

Views wife beating as "an abuse of power," and examines the significance of social imperatives which influence the behavior of husbands and wives (sex role socialization, marriage, the criminal justice system, responses of helping agencies). Also discusses adult violence from a cultural perspective, and presents possible solutions to the problem.

621. Martin, Harold P., editor. **The Abused Child: A Multidisciplinary Approach to Developmental Issues and Treatment**. Cambridge, Massachusetts: Ballinger Publishing Company, 1976. 304 pp.

Selections deal with the developmental issues concerning abused children and the treatment of the abused child.

622. _____. "The Child and His Development." **Helping the Battered Child and His Family**. Edited by C. Henry Kempe and Ray E. Helfer. Philadelphia: J.B. Lippincott Company, 1972, pp. 93–114.

Examines a study conducted by the John F. Kennedy Child Developmental Center at the University of Colorado, which followed 42 abused children over a 3 year period. The study is summarized, defining the sample, methodology and results. Discusses in detail the type of children that were abused, physical development, failure to thrive, subsequent personality development, the potential for rehabilitation for abused children, and changes in the child after varying lengths of time during intervention. Concludes by stating that therapeutic goals must be broadened and methods of intervention should be developed in order to maximize the chances for abused children to develop into healthy adults.

623. _____. "The Consequences of Being Abused and Neglected: How the Child Fares." **The Battered Child**. Edited by C. Henry Kempe and Ray E. Helfer. Chicago: University of Chicago Press, 1980, pp. 347–65.

Discusses the treatment of children with serious and long lasting problems resulting from abuse or neglect. Describes the consequences of abuse for the child, including medical and psychological consequences, developmental problems, and long-term effects of the abusive environment.

624. _____. "Factors Influencing the Development of the Abused Child." **The Abused Child: A Multidisciplinary Approach to Developmental Issues and Treatment**. Edited by Harold P. Martin. Cambridge, Massachusetts: Ballinger Publishing Company, 1976, pp. 139–62.

Explores factors which may be considered when examining the effects of an abusive environment on a child.

625. _____. "Neurologic Status of Abused Children." **The Abused Child: A Multidisciplinary Approach to Developmental Issues and Treatment**. Edited by Harold P. Martin. Cambridge, Massachusetts: Ballinger Publishing Company, 1976, pp. 67–82.

Discusses the neurologic examination of the abused child and special problems and characteristics which are found only with children.

626. _____. "Summing Up and Moving On." **The Abused Child: A Multidisciplinary Approach to Developmental Issues and Treatment**. Edited by Harold P. Martin. Cambridge, Massachusetts: Ballinger Publishing Company, 1976, pp. 275–80.

Presents a summary of important points presented in the book and, in doing so, discusses reforms made by state and federal governments for the protection of children, services to families, and the child as belonging to himself rather than to his parents or to society.

627. _____. "Which Children Get Abused: High Risk Factors." **The Abused Child: A Multidisciplinary Approach to Developmental Issues and Treatment**. Edited by Harold P. Martin. Cambridge, Massachusetts: Ballinger Publishing Company, 1976, pp. 27–41.

Based on the premise that all adults have some potential to abuse their children, abuse is discussed as a spectrum with adults having low to very high potential for abuse. The role of the child in the abuse syndrome, conditions which may put a child at a higher risk of abuse, and the components of the potential for abuse are described.

628. Martin, Harold P. and Patricia Beezley. "Behavioral Observations of Abused Children." **Developmental Medicine and Child Neurology**, 19:373–87, June 1977.

Discusses a study which followed the subsequent physical, intellectual, and neurological development of abused children about four years after their identification as victims of abuse.

629. _____. "Foster Placement: Therapy or Trauma." **The Abused Child: A Multidisciplinary Approach to Developmental Issues and Treatment**. Edited by Harold P. Martin. Cambridge, Massachusetts: Ballinger Publishing Company, 1976, pp. 189–99.

Examines reasons for foster care and suggests ways to make it more therapeutic.

630. _____. "Personality of Abused Children." **The Abused Child: A Multidisciplinary Approach to Developmental Issues and Treatment**. Edited by Harold P. Martin. Cambridge, Massachusetts: Ballinger Publishing Company, 1976, pp. 105–11.

Presents the results of a follow-up study of fifty abused children, emphasizing the role of the environment on the personality of the child.

631. _____. "Therapy for Abusive Parents: Its Effect on the Child." **The Abused Child: A Multidisciplinary Approach to Developmental Issues and Treatment**. Cambridge, Massachusetts: Ballinger Publishing Company, 1976, pp. 251–63.

Discusses ways in which psychotherapy might be considered for abusive parents, and the effects that this form of treatment might have on the child.

632. Martin, Harold P. and Martha Rodeheffer. "Learning and Intelligence." **The Abused Child: A Multidisciplinary Approach to Developmental Issues and Treatment**. Edited by Harold P. Martin. Cambridge, Massachusetts: Ballinger Publishing Company, 1976, pp. 93–104.

Explores the abused child in relation to learning and intelligence with the use of data obtained from formal intelligence tests and school performance.

633. Martin, J.P. "Family Violence and Social Policy." **Violence and the Family**. Edited by J.P. Martin. New York: John Wiley and Sons, 1978, pp. 199–254.

Examines family violence in relation to the measures taken by publicly funded organizations to manage the problem. Detailed descriptions of the work of police, the legal system, medical organizations, social service organizations, and volunteer groups are presented.

634. _____. "Some Reflections on Violence and the Family." **Violence and the Family**. Edited by J.P. Martin. New York: John Wiley and Sons, 1978, pp. 345–52.

Discusses topics likely to recur in explorations of family violence. Topics examined include the legitimacy of force in family relationships, personal factors involved in family violence, and ways to limit family violence.

635. _____, editor. **Violence and the Family**. New York: John Wiley and Sons, 1978. 369 pp.

Examines the experience of family violence, the context of family violence from a number of perspectives, family violence as a social problem, and agencies that deal with this problem. An introduction by the editor and an index are included.

636. Masumura, Wilfred T. "Wife Abuse and Other Forms of Aggression." **Victimology: An International Journal**, 4:46–59, 1979.

Discusses a cross-cultural study which found the abuse of wives to be correlated with other forms of violence within the society.

637. May, Margaret. "Violence in the Family: An Historical Perspective." **Violence and the Family**. Edited by J.P. Martin. New York: John Wiley and Sons, 1978, pp. 135–67.

Explores violence within the family in England and Wales before 1914 by examining conjugal violence in the nineteenth century, the abuse of children, and late Victorian and Edwardian explanations of family violence.

638. Mazura, Adrianne C. "Negligence — Malpractice — Physician's Liability for Failure to Diagnose and Report Child Abuse." **Wayne Law Review**,

23:1187–1201, March 1977.

Discusses child abuse and the medical response to the problem. The possibility of a common law malpractice action against a non-reporting physician, and relevant cases, are also examined.

639. McAllister, Pam. "Feminist Law — Challenging Actions." **Fight Back!: Feminist Resistance to Male Violence**. Edited by Frederique Delacoste and Felice Newman. Minneapolis: Cleis Press, 1981, pp. 212–21.

Examines the "vigilantism" undertaken by women in an attempt to "challenge the patriarchal law to do the job it pretends to do." Examples from actual cases are presented to illustrate the points discussed.

640. McAnulty, Elizabeth H. "Nursing Responsibility on a Child Abuse Team." **Child Abuse: Intervention and Treatment**. Edited by Nancy B. Ebeling and Deborah A. Hill. Acton, Massachusetts: Publishing Sciences Group, Inc., 1975, pp. 69–71.

Discusses the role of the nurse on a child abuse team and the special problems and considerations involved in dealing with the parents and children.

641. McCabe, S. "Unfinished Business — A Note on the Reports of the Select Committees on Violence in Marriage and Violence in the Family." **British Journal of Criminology**, 17(3):280–85, July 1977.

Comments on Britain's Select Committee on Violence in Marriage and the Family and focuses on legal aspects of the problem, including police response and changes in the law. Aid for battered women is also examined.

642. McCathren, Randall R. "Accountability in the Child Protection System: A Defense of the Proposed Standards Relating to Abuse and Neglect." **Boston University Law Review**, 57:707–31, July 1977.

Defends the Standards, emphasizing their ability to provide "true reform."

643. McClintock, F.H. "Criminological Aspects of Family Violence." **Violence and the Family**. Edited by J.P. Martin. New York: John Wiley and Sons, 1978, pp. 81–101.

Criminally violent behavior within the family is discussed by exploring the morphology of family violence in England and Wales, aspects of family violence in Scotland, control of family violence by the criminal justice system, and crime trends and criminal violence within the family.

644. McCloskey, Kenneth D. "Torts: Parental Liability to a Minor Child for Injuries Caused by Excessive Punishment." **Hastings Law Journal**, 11:335–40, February 1960.

Reviews a suit filed by a child's father against her stepmother for injuries received as a result of a beating. Focuses on the controversial immunity doctrine, which grants a parent immunity from suit by a child in a tort action. The court rules that a parent is not immune from suit for injuries arising from punishment which "willfully exceeds" the limit of reasonable punishment. Arguments for and against this ruling are also presented.

645. McCoid, Allan H. "The Battered Child and Other Assaults Upon the Family: Part I." **Minnesota Law Review**, 50:1–58, 1965–66.

Discusses the identification and reporting of child abuse. The rationale and effectiveness of current mandatory reporting statutes are also analyzed.

646. McDermott, John F., Jr. "The Treatment of Child Abuse." **Journal of the American Academy of Child Psychiatry**, 15(3):430–40, Summer 1976.

Focuses on the need for follow-up reports on abused children in order to fulfill special treatment needs children may have beyond removal from an abusive home.

647. McDonald, Anne E. "The Collaborative Aspect of the Hospital Social Worker's Role." **Child Abuse: Intervention and Treatment**. Edited by Nancy B. Ebeling and Deborah A. Hill. Acton, Massachusetts: Publishing Sciences Group, Inc., 1975, pp. 55–59.

Emphasizes the importance of interagency collaboration while discussing the child abuse population, the evaluative process used by many hospitals with cases of child abuse, the role of the hospital social worker, and the interaction between community agencies and professional agencies in dealing with cases of child abuse.

648. McGeorge, John. "Sexual Assaults on Children." **Medicine, Science and Law**, 4(1): 245–53, October 1974.

Presents a general discussion of sexual assaults on children, including assaults occurring within the family. Preventive and protective measures are described, and a survey conducted by the Cambridge Department of Criminal Science on the subject is reviewed.

649. McHenry, Thomas and others. "Unsuspected Trauma With Multiple Skeletal Injuries During Infancy and Childhood." **The Battered Child**. Compiled by Jerome E. Leavitt. Morristown, New Jersey: General Learning Press, 1974, pp. 12–17.

Discusses experiences at the Children's Hospital of Pittsburgh with fifty children who had unsuspected trauma with multiple injuries to the skeleton. Emphasizes the age distribution in this group of parents, and the variety of presenting complaints. Observations are offered by the social service department as to family backgrounds, and interviews with parents are summarized.

650. McKeel, Nancy Lynn. "Child Abuse Can Be Prevented." **American Journal of Nursing**, 78(9):1478–82, September 1878.

States that emotional abuse or neglect almost always goes with any form of abuse, and that child abuse is not an isolated incident. Describes the National Center for Child Abuse and Neglect's formula for abuse, including a formula for abuse which incorporates various elements of the problem. Case histories of child abuse are also presented, and abuse of adolescents is discussed. In addition, the nurse's role in prevention is examined.

651. McKenna, J. James. "A Case Study of Child Abuse: A Former Prosecutor's View." **The American Criminal Law Review**, 12(1):165–78, Summer 1974.

Using one case of child abuse resulting in death of the child, the author outlines the practical problems of prosecuting a case of child abuse, underscoring the need for the continued presence of law enforcement and prosecutorial disciplines in the overall treatment of abusers and their children. Circumstances of the case, problems in trial preparation, the trial itself, the role of the prosecution, and the Maryland child abuse law are also discussed.

652. McQuiston, Mary. "Crisis Nurseries." **The Abused Child: A Multidisciplinary Approach to Developmental Issues and Treatment**. Edited by Harold P. Martin. Cambridge, Massachusetts: Ballinger Publishing Company, 1976, pp. 225–34.

Discusses necessary services for abused children and the goals of treatment, emphasizing the role of the crisis nursery in assisting abusing parents.

653. McQuiston, Mary and Ruth S. Kempe. "Treatment of the Child." **The Battered Child**. Edited by C. Henry Kempe and Ray E. Helfer. Chicago: University of Chicago Press, 1980, pp. 379–90.

Details treatment of abused and neglected children and discusses special considerations, such as keeping the family intact and when to place a child in foster care. Treatment goals and modalities for various age groups are also outlined.

654. Melnick, Barry and John R. Hurley. "Distinctive Personality Attributes of Child Abusing Mothers." **Journal of Consulting and Clinical Psychology**, 33(6):746–49, 1969.

Explores the personality attributes of abusing mothers. An abusive and a control group were matched for demographic factors and compared on certain personality variables. Significant differences which were found, and characteristics of abusive mothers, are described.

655. Melville, Joy. "A Note on Men's Aid." **Violence and the Family**.

Edited by J.P. Martin. New York: John Wiley and Sons, 1978, pp. 311–13.

Discusses the purpose and operation of Men's Aid, a helping center for abusive men.

656. _____. "Some Violent Families." **Violence and the Family**. Edited by J.P. Martin. New York: John Wiley and Sons, 1978, pp. 9–18.

Presents accounts of family violence as compiled from interviews with women who had left their violent homes and gone to refuges.

657. _____. "Women in Refuges." **Violence and the Family**. Edited by J.P. Martin. New York: John Wiley and Sons, 1978, pp. 293–309.

Discusses the experience of living in a refuge for battered women.

658. Michigan Women's Commission. **Domestic Assault: A Report on Family Violence in Michigan**. Lansing, Michigan: Michigan Women's Commission, 1977. 141 pp.

Reports on hearings held by the Michigan Women's Commission in order to obtain information about family violence. Theories on marital violence are also presented, and recommendations are made concerning prevention and treatment of the problem.

659. Midlin, Rowland L. "Background to the Current Interest in Child Abuse and Neglect." **Pediatric Annuals**, 5:10–12, March 1976.

Outlines the history of child abuse and society's treatment of it. The coining of the term "Battered Child Syndrome," the development of mandatory reporting laws, and the initiation of child abuse and neglect programs for prevention and treatment are among the topics discussed.

660. Miller, Laura M. "Family Law — Parental Rights — Principles of *Res Ipsa Loquitur* Apply to Proof of Child Abuse and Neglect." **Texas Tech Law Review**, 9:335–42, Winter 1977–78.

Discusses child abuse and the law, using the Texas case of *Higgins v. Dallas County Welfare Unit* to illustrate the application of the principles of *Res Ipsa Loquitur*. The case allowed the condition of the child to be used as proof of abuse on the part of the parent.

661. Miller, Merle K. and Henry J. Fay. "Emergency Child Care Service: The Evaluation of a Project." **The Battered Child**. Compiled by Jerome E. Leavitt. Morristown, New Jersey: General Learning Press, 1974, pp. 35–37.

Summarizes the results of a year-long project which studied the Emergency Child Care Committee in Springfield, Massachusetts. Results showed the value of the program, and identified some of its strengths and weaknesses.

662. Miller, Nick. **Battered Spouses**. London: G. Bell and Sons, 1975. 69 pp.

Discusses the problem of marital violence and the needs of the battered wife.

663. Mills, B.G. "California's Response to Domestic Violence." **Santa Clara Law Review**, 21(1):1–21, Winter 1981.

Examines California's Domestic Violence Prevention Act, which extends consideration to non-marital relationships. Procedures for police in such cases are also outlined.

664. Minier, Alice. "Dealing With Child Abuse in a Unified Family Court." **Creighton Law Review**, 8:782–90, June 1975.

Discusses the institution of a unified family court in order to improve the judicial handling of child abuse cases. Examines the Hawaii Family Courts Act as an example of such a court.

665. Mirandy, Joan. "Preschool for Abused Children." **The Abused Child: A Multidisciplinary Approach to Developmental Issues and Treatment**. Edited by Harold P. Martin. Cambridge, Massachusetts: Ballinger Publishing Company, 1976, pp. 215–24.

Explores the therapeutic value of a group education setting for abused children, focusing on the preschool setting as the primary unit of therapy for children of that age group.

666. Mitchell, Eleanor. "Domestic Assault." **Women: A Journal of Liberation**, 6(2):26–27, 1981.

Presents a general examination of marital violence, including the incidence and nature of the problem. The development of shelters and other means of helping victims of domestic violence are also discussed.

667. Mitchell, Marilyn Hall. "Does Wife Abuse Justify Homicide?" **Wayne Law Review**, 24(5):1705–31, September 1978.

Discusses homicide as a culmination of marital violence. Wife abuse in the U.S., women and homicide, defenses to homicide, and laws pertaining to wife assault are among the issues examined. Proposals made for law reform in this area include changing the criminal assault laws to make special provisions for cases of wife battering, and reforming the civil laws to eliminate inter-spousal immunity in the area of wife abuse.

668. Mitchell, Ross G. "The Incidence and Nature of Child Abuse." **Developmental Medicine and Child Neurology**, 17:641–44, October 1975.

Explores the incidence, causes, and identification of child abuse. The early identification of child abuse is viewed as essential for effective prevention of future injury.

669. Mitchiner, Myra J. "Providing Preventive and Protective Services to Children in a Public Welfare Agency." **The Battered Child**. Compiled by

Jerome E. Leavitt. Morristown, New Jersey: General Learning Press, 1974, pp. 161–64.

Describes protective service systems in North Carolina, including the responsibility of the caseworker, development of a plan for each child, and the coordination of services so as to use resources of both public assistance and child welfare.

670. Mogielnicki, R. Peter and others. "Impending Child Abuse: Psychosomatic Symptoms in Adults as a Clue." **Journal of the American Medical Association**, 237:1109–11, March 14, 1977.

Three cases are discussed in which parents who abuse their children, or may abuse their children in the future, develop psychosomatic symptoms and subsequently seek medical help. A psychiatric interpretation of this phenomenon is presented and implications of it for recognizing potential child abusers and thus preventing injury to the child are explored.

671. Mohr, J.W. and C.K. McKnight. "Violence as a Function of Age and Relationship With Special Reference to Matricide." **Canadian Psychiatric Association Journal**, 16(1):29–53, 1971.

Discusses the risk to children of homicide by mothers who are severely depressed. A case history is detailed, and personality features of patients are examined.

672. Mondale, Walter F. "Introductory Comments." **Chicago-Kent Law Review**, 54:635–39, 1978.

Presents the conclusions reached at the hearings on child abuse held by the Senate Subcommittee on Children and Youth. The establishment of the National Center of Child Abuse and Neglect, the "Child Abuse Prevention and Treatment Act," and improvements in services offered by the states are also examined.

673. Moore, Donna M., editor. **Battered Women**. Beverly Hills, California: Sage Publications, Inc., 1979. 232 pp.

Selections discuss various aspects of the problem and appendices outline the legal rights of the battered woman, and suggestions for public policies in this area. A Bibliography is also included, and an introduction by the editor which offers a comprehensive overview of the problem is presented.

674. Moore, Donna M. and Fran Pepitone-Rockwell. "Experiences With and Views About Battering." **Battered Women**. Edited by Donna M. Moore. Beverly Hills, California: Sage Publications, 1979, pp. 119–43.

Discusses a conference on battered women, which was held at the University of California at Davis in 1978, and examines research conducted on the participants. Factors considered include demographic characteristics, battering-related experiences, ideas of participants concerning the causes of attitudes toward helping the victim, and the responses of helping agencies.

675. Moore, Jean G. "The Yo-Yo Syndrome: A Matter of Interdisciplinary Concern." **Medicine, Science and the Law**, 15:234–36, October 1975.

Discusses violence as a recurring phenomenon in some families. The plight of children involved in these families is discussed, highlighting the incidence of children who are adversely affected by the violence. An interdisciplinary approach to treatment is recommended in order to help these children.

676. ———. "Yo-Yo Children." **Nursing Times**, 70:1888–89, December 5, 1974.

The instability of violent marriages may necessitate the "parceling out" of children to relatives or friends. This may produce children who are emotionally abused.

677. ———. "Yo-Yo Children — Victims of Matrimonial Violence." **Child Welfare**, 54:557–66, September–October 1975.

The "yo-yo" syndrome is illustrated in detail in case studies of violent marriages. The families are characterized by marital violence and instability, and the children are frequently emotionally abused. A discussion of treatment for these families is also presented.

678. "More on the Battered Child." **New England Journal of Medicine**, 269(26):1437, December 26, 1963.

Focuses on the management of child abuse, using non-legal methods instead of reporting laws in order to give the family every opportunity for therapy.

679. Morgan, Dorothy. "The Place of Family Planning." **Concerning Child Abuse: Papers Presented by the Tunbridge Wells Study Group on Non-Accidental Injury to Children**. Edited by Alfred White Franklin. Edinburgh: Churchill Livingstone, 1975, pp. 71–72.

Explores the place of family planning advice in work with abusive parents.

680. Morris, Marian G. and Robert W. Gould. "Role Reversal: A Necessary Concept in Dealing With the Battered Child Syndrome." **American Journal of Orthopsychiatry**, 33(2):298–99, March 1963.

States that the concept of role reversal is necessary in order to understand the reasons behind parents' abusive behavior. Abusive parents showed no signs of guilt, although they feared punishment from the outside world, and they had no goals for better parent-child relationships. Role reversal is also viewed as necessary in order to adequately protect children through intervention.

681. Morris, Marian G. and others. "Toward Prevention of Child Abuse." **The Battered Child**. Compiled by Jerome E. Leavitt. Morristown, New Jersey: General Learning Press, 1974, pp. 232–37.

This selection is based on the premise that constructive, preventive intervention into the cycle of violence and punishment is necessary for preventing child abuse and neglect. Presents social indicators which have implications for early identification of neglectful and abusive parents, and for the prevention of further abuse or neglect. Concludes that chronic neglect and abuse have been passed down through generations, and that prevention implies not only protecting the child from future abuse, but in breaking the chain which may lead an abused child to abuse his own child. The child's reactions to abuse are discussed, and implications for prevention and protection are also presented.

682. Morse, Abraham E. and others. "Environmental Correlates of Pediatric Social Illness: Preventive Implications of an Advocacy Approach." **American Journal of Public Health**, 67(7):612–15, July 1977.

Examines the results of a study which analyzed the maternal interview and clinical data for child abuse victims and a control group of children who had been treated for other reasons. Significant differences were found in areas of environmental stress, which included employment, housing, and access to essential services.

683. Mounsey, Joseph. "Offenses of Criminal Violence, Cruelty, and Neglect Against Children in Lancashire." **Concerning Child Abuse: Papers Presented by the Tunbridge Wells Study Group on Non-Accidental Injury to Children**. Edited by Alfred White Franklin. Edinburgh: Churchill Livingstone, 1975, pp. 127–30.

Discusses the role of the police concerning cases of non-accidental injury to children and examines specific offenses in Lancashire.

684. Mulvihill, Donald J. and others. "The Interpersonal Relationship Between Victim and Offender." **Crimes of Violence: A Staff Report to the Commission on the Causes and Prevention of Violence**. Volume 11. Washington, D.C.: United States Government Printing Office, 1969.

Compares the percentage of non-primary group relationships with family and other primary group relationships in cases of violent interactions.

685. Munson, P.J. "Protecting Battered Wives — The Availability of Legal Remedies." **Journal of Sociology and Social Welfare**, 7(4):586–600, July 1980.

Reviews traditional ideas concerning wife battering, considers the functioning of the criminal and civil justice systems regarding this offense, and suggests remedies.

686. Mushanga, Tibamanya Mwene. "Wife Victimization in East and Central Africa." **Victimology: An International Journal**, 2:479–85, 1977–78.

Discusses wife victimization as illustrated by data collected from various African societies. Victim precipitation and the role played by change in provoking family conflicts are among the topics discussed. Cultural and societal values which legitimize violence within the family are also examined.

687. Myers, Steven A. "The Child Slayer: A 25-Year Survey of Homicides Involving Preadolescent Victims." **Archives of General Psychiatry** (Chicago), 17:211–13, August 1967.

Examines eighty-three cases of felonious homicide occurring over a 25-year period in the city of Detroit. Sixty children were killed by a parent or close relative, with almost half of the assailants being the victims' mothers. The most common precipitating factor was found to be frank psychosis in the assailant, and was most prevalent among the accused mothers. In addititon, about half of the assailants were judged to be insane and were subsequently committed to state hospitals.

688. NSPCC School of Social Work, London, England. "Yoyo Children: A Study of 23 Violent Matrimonial Cases." **Battered Women: A Psychosociological Study of Domestic Violence**. Edited by Maria Roy. New York: Van Nostrand Reinhold Company, 1977, pp. 249–63.

Discusses a study of 23 cases in which domestic violence was a distinct feature. Patterns found in common are discussed and the effect of the violence on the children, and treatment programs, are examined.

689. Nagi, Saad Z. "Child Abuse and Neglect Programs: A National Overview." **Children Today**, 13–17, May–June 1975.

A national survey on child abuse and neglect was conducted by interviewing agencies and groups which deal with child abuse cases. Topics covered by the survey included the rate of reporting, the placement of abused and neglected children, the effectiveness of intervention programs, and additional services needed to improve methods of identification and treatment. A presentation of the results of this survey highlight the discussion.

690. National Center on Child Abuse and Neglect. **Child Abuse and Case Identification and Reporting**. Washington, D.C.: U.S. Department of Health, Education and Welfare, U.S. Children's Bureau, 1977. 19 pp.

Following a general introduction to child abuse identification and reporting, the role of professionals is discussed and a comparison of professional perspectives is presented.

691. National Center on Women and Family Law, Inc. **Legal Advocacy for Battered Women**. New York: National Center on Women and Family Law, Inc., 1982. 250 pp.

Presents a comprehensive guide for professionals and advocates concerning the legal issues facing battered women, and legislative remedies available. What advocates should know about obtaining proper materials and orders is outlined, and common problems associated with elements of domestic violence are discussed. A list of resources available to the legal advocate is also provided.

692. National Women's Aid Federation, Northwest Region. "Battered Women and Social Work." **Violence and the Family**. Edited by J.P. Martin. New York: John Wiley and Sons, 1978, pp. 315-24.

Discusses reasons why battered women are appropriate subjects for social work involvement, what help can be offered, and the quality of the assistance available.

693. Nelson, Stephen H. "Child Abuse: The Legal Framework in Nebraska." **Creighton Law Review**, 8:771-81, June 1975

Examines Nebraska's laws pertaining to child abuse, emphasizing the lack of a unified and comprehensive system. Recommendations for reform of these laws are also presented.

694. Nelson, Susan. "How Battered Women Can Get Help." **Reader's Digest**, 110:21-23 + , May 1977.

Presents a general discussion of wife battering. Police response, the establishment of shelters for battered women, battered women and the law, and why women stay with abusive husbands are among the topics discussed.

695. New Jersey, State of. **Physically Abused Women and Their Families: The Need for Community Services**. Trenton, New Jersey: Department of Human Services, Division of Youth and Family Services, 1978. 96 pp.

Summarizes the problems of battered women and their children, and identifies the programs and services which may be implemented by the community to meet the needs of abused women and their families. A bibliography is included.

696. New York State, Assembly Select Committee on Child Abuse. **A Guide to New York's Child Protection System**. Albany, New York: New York State Assembly, 1974. 38 pp.

Discusses the concept of New York State's Child Protective Services and the purpose of New York's child protective laws.

697. New York State, Office of Educational Finance and Management Services. **Child Abuse and Maltreatment: Suggestions for School Personnel**. Albany, New York: The University of the State of New York, State Education Department, 1977. 5 pp.

Describes the role that the school personnel play in identifying and reporting suspected cases of child abuse and maltreatment. Legal implications for school personnel and procedures for the development of policies and methods of reporting of child abuse by school districts are included.

698. Newberger, Eli H. editor. **Child Abuse**. Boston: Little, Brown and Company, 1982. 282 pp.

Selections present a comprehensive view of child abuse by reviewing the roles of professionals in various fields and discussing the nature of the problem, prevention, treatment, and the history of child protection. The first section of the book emphasizes the significance of viewing child abuse in the context of family violence and need for intervention programs which recognize child abuse as the result of a complex interaction of psychological and social factors. The second section deals with the treatment and protection of abused children, and emphasizes the importance of cooperation among all professionals who deal with child abuse.

699. _____. "Child Abuse and Neglect: Toward a Firmer Foundation for Practice and Policy." **American Journal of Orthopsychiatry**, 47:374–75, July 1977.

Recommends improved methods of child abuse management and research.

700. _____. "A Physician's Perspective on the Interdisciplinary Management of Child Abuse." **Child Abuse: Intervention and Treatment**. Edited by Nancy B. Ebeling and Deborah A. Hill. Acton, Massachusetts: Publishing Sciences Group, 1975, pp. 61–67.

Discusses the problems associated with the management of child abuse cases and presents suggestions for effective interdisciplinary programs.

701. Newberger, Eli H. and Richard Bourne. "The Medicalization and Legislation of Child Abuse." **American Journal of Orthopsychiatry**, 48(4):593–607, October 1978.

Examines symptoms of family disorganization that are being "medicalized" and "legalized" in order to classify them under child abuse, so that they may be dealt with by professionals whose work is legitimized by these processes. The effects of this system on treatment are discussed, and child abuse is explored as a sociological problem.

702. Newberger, Eli H. and James N. Hyde, Jr. "Child Abuse: Principles and Implications of Current Pediatric Practice." **Pediatric Clinics of North America**, 22:695–715, August 1975.

Case studies are employed to illustrate the unique problems involved in child abuse cases and their treatment. A model system for the management of child abuse is outlined, and the significance of determining the family's ability to protect the child is emphasized.

703. Newberger, Eli and others. "Child Abuse in Massachusetts." **Massachusetts Physician**, 32(1):31–38, January 1973.

Discusses the incidence of child abuse in Massachusetts and present recommendations of the Governor's Advisory Committee on Child Abuse concerning the management, treatment and prevention of child abuse.

704. Newman, Charles L. "Police and Families: Factors Affecting Police Intervention." **Police Chief**, 39(3):25–26 + , 1972.

Examines factors affecting police intervention in family problems. The range of police responsibility is discussed and an experimental training program for police dealing with family violence in New York City is explored.

705. NiCarthy, Ginny. **Getting Free: A Handbook for Women in Abusive Relationships**. Seattle: The Seal Press, 1982. 272 pp.

A self-help manual for battered women. Discusses issues facing battered women who decide to leave their homes and provides information concerning legal, medical and social service help available to her. Also presents self-counseling techniques to aid the abused women in clarifying her feelings about herself and her relationships.

706. Nichols, Beverly B. "The Abused Wife Problem." **Social Casework**, 57:27–32, January 1976.

Discusses the problem of wife beating and the influence of various factors. Suggests that innovative treatment efforts must be developed in order to treat both the victim and the abuser, and that caseworkers should be more assertive in designing treatment programs.

707. Nichols, William C. "Wife Abuse." **Parents Magazine**, 53:26, January 1978.

States that the problem of wife abuse is not defined by income, social status, or educational attainment, and that humiliation is a definite feature of wife beating. Possible solutions to the problem are explored.

708. "No Not Non-Accidental Injury!" **Lancet**, 2:775–76, October 9, 1976.

Presents a brief discussion of the physician's role in the identification and treatment of child abuse.

709. Noble, Sheila M. "The Contributions of the Social Agencies and the Social Worker." **The Maltreatment of Children**. Edited by Selwyn M. Smith. Baltimore: University Park Press, 1978, pp. 351–91.

Examines the contributions of social workers to the treatment of child abuse, and discusses problems associated with social agencies who deal with child abuse.

710. Nordstrom, Jerry L. "Child Abuse: A School District's Response to Its Responsibility." **Child Welfare**, 53:257–60, April 1974.

Discusses a program organized by one school district in order to act as a kind of advocate of the rights of children. The role of a central registry in identifying cases of child abuse is also examined.

711. "Normal Child Abuser: What Stress Can Do to a Mother." **Human**

Behavior, 7:35, July 1978.

Discusses a study conducted by Passman and Mulhern which showed that "normal" mothers (mothers who admitted to no abusive tendencies or emotional problems) could be moved to greater violence toward their children if their level of stress was increased, whether or not the child was the source of the stress.

712. Norman, Mari. "A Lifeline for Battering Parents." **Nursing Times**, 70:1506–07, September 26, 1974.

Views the health visitor's role as vital to the prevention of child abuse. Describes the work of the visitor and urges recognition of this work by other professionals.

713. Nurse, Shirley. "Familial Patterns of Parents Who Abuse Their Children." **Child Abuse: Perspectives on Diagnosis, Treatment and Prevention**. Edited by Roberta Kalmar. Dubuque, Iowa: Kendall/Hunt Publishing Company, 1977, pp. 63–76.

Discusses a study which was conducted to explore the characteristics of abusing parents. Aspects of abuse, parental family history, aspects of family life, relationships between spouses, and demographic characteristics of parents are among the topics examined.

714. Nwako, Festus. "Child Abuse Syndrome in Nigeria." **International Surgery**, 59:613–15, November–December 1974.

Explores the problem of child abuse in Nigeria, highlighting the role of one hospital's staff in detecting child abuse cases among cases of reported accidental injury.

715. Nyden, Paul V. "The Use of Authority." **The Battered Child**. Compiled by Jerome E. Leavitt. Morristown, New Jersey: General Learning Press, 1974, pp. 128–34.

Discusses the child protection movement from a historical perspective. Also examines the prevalence of the problem, asserts that the child protective agency must find its basis in law, and that authority properly applied is a valuable casework tool in safeguarding the child.

716. O'Brien, John E. "Violence in Divorce Prone Families." **Journal of Marriage and the Family**, 33(4):692–98, November 1971.

Presents results of a study which interviewed 150 people recently involved in divorces. 15% of the respondents reported the presence of violence in the marriage, and the perpetrator was most often the husband. Also significant is that most of the violent husbands were under-achievers in their respective occupations. Findings indicate that husband-wife violence has characteristics similar to those of violence in the larger society, most often involving the use of force by people of higher status when they find their position threatened.

717. O'Brien, Shirley. **Child Abuse, A Crying Shame**. Provo, Utah: Brigham Young University Press, 1981. 198 pp.

Defines child abuse, presents statistics on the problem, and outlines its history. Other topics explored include types of abuse and neglect, myths about child abuse, and characteristics of abusive parents and abused children. Concludes by suggesting possible solutions to the problem. The Child Abuse Prevention and Treatment Act (Text of Public Law 93-247) is reprinted, and a bibliography of relevant literature is presented.

718. O'Connor, Shannon P. "Due Process and the Fundamental Right to Family Integrity: A Re-Evaluation of South Dakota's Parental Termination Statute." **South Dakota Law Review**, 24:447–65, Spring 1979.

Reviews the South Dakota parental termination statute in relation to the due process clause of the fourteenth amendment of the Constitution.

719. O'Doherty, N.J. "Subdural Haematoma in Battered Babies." **Developmental Medicine and Child Neurology**, 6(2):192–93, April 1964.

Discusses the diagnosis of subdural haematoma in cases of battered children.

720. Oettinger, Katherine B. "The Abused Child." **The Battered Child**. Edited by Jerome E. Leavitt. Morristown, New Jersey: General Learning Press, 1974, pp. 211–212.

Presents a general discussion of child abuse, discussing reporting of cases, characteristics of abusive parents, backgrounds of abused children.

721. O'Grady-Gregoire, Christine. "Something Old, Something New: The Juvenile Act Relating to Dependency and Termination." **Gonzaga Law Review**, 14:359–68, 1979.

Explores the new Juvenile Court Act of the state of Washington. The Act deals with various issues concerning the parent-child relationship, custody of children, termination of parental rights over a child, the maltreatment of a child by his parents, and the family as a unit.

722. Oglov, Linda and Claire Lalonde. "International Conference Provides Analysis of Child Abuse Problems." **Canadian Medical Association Journal**, 117:170–76, July 23, 1977.

Discusses the program presented by the International Society of Family Law, in June 1977 at McGill University. The issues investigated by this conference included incest, characteristics of abusing parents, treatment and prevention of abused children, causes of physical and sexual abuse of children, and aggression within the family.

723. Oliver, J.E. "The Epidemiology of Child Abuse." **The Maltreatment of Children**. Edited by Selwyn M. Smith. Baltimore: University Park Press, 1978, pp. 95–119.

Discusses the cultural patterns, biological principles, and historical episodes in relation to the abuse of children. Literature on child abuse in the home is reviewed.

724. Oliver, J.E. and Audrey Taylor. "Five Generations of Ill-Treated Children in One Family Pedigree." **The British Journal of Psychiatry,** 119(552):473–80, November 1971.

Describes five generations of abused or neglected children, which are thought to be representative of many others living in the same area where the study was conducted. Implications for prevention in psychiatry are also discussed.

725. Oliver, J.E. and others. "The Extent of Child Abuse." **The Maltreatment of Children.** Edited by Selwyn M. Smith. Baltimore: University Park Press, 1978, pp. 121–74.

Presents a detailed discussion of a study of abused children conducted in Wiltshire, England. The maltreatment of children as a cause of impaired intelligence is also examined.

726. Oliver, Jack. "Some Studies of Families in Which Children Suffer Maltreatment." **The Challenge of Child Abuse.** Edited by Alfred White Franklin. London: Academic Press, 1977, pp. 16–37.

Discusses various aspects of child abuse. The characteristics of abusing families, manifestations of abuse to children, and rehabilitation and treatment are among the topics explored.

727. Olson, David H. and Robert G. Ryder. "Inventory of Marital Conflicts (ICM): An Experimental Interaction Procedure." **Journal of Marriage and the Family,** 32(3):443–48, 1970.

Describes the use of the IMC, which was developed to provide reliable interaction data on conflict resolution between couples. Advantages of this system are outlined, and its potential as a diagnostic as well as a research tool is explored.

728. Olson, Robert. "Index of Suspicion: Screening for Child Abusers." **American Journal of Nursing,** 76:108–10, January 1976.

Offers a procedure which would detect potential abusive parents by analyzing the family structure in terms of behavior patterns thought to lead to the abuse of children. The patterns cited are illustrated with the use of case studies. Implications of this procedure for the prevention of abuse are also presented.

729. Oppe, Thomas E. "Problems of Communication and Co-ordination." **Concerning Child Abuse: Papers Presented by the Tunbridge Study Group on Non-Accidental Injury to Children.** Edited by Alfred White Franklin. Edinburgh: Churchill Livingstone, 1975, pp. 155–61.

States the objectives of management in cases of child abuse according to the consensus view, and the role of each agency in its management.

730. Orriss, Harry D. "Lessons From a Tragedy." **Nursing Times**, 70:140–41, January 31, 1974.

Discusses the case of Maria Colwell, a child who had been returned to her home by social workers and was subsequently beaten to death by her stepfather.

731. Ory, Marcia G. and Jo Anne L. Earp. "Child Maltreatment and the Use of Social Services." **Public Health Reports**, 96(3):238–45, May–June 1981.

Presents the findings of a study in which 100 case histories were selected from social service records in a county department of social services and were examined to ascertain the amount and types of social services that persons identified as having maltreated a child had received. Two groups were created, each with fifty families. One group had been reported to social services for child maltreatment, and the other had not. Differences were found in the amount and type of services used by each group. Results indicated that the level of services needed by protective service clients, and the level that they actually received, should be re-examined.

732. O'Shea, Ann. "Family Violence Bills." **McCalls**, 105:42, January 1978.

Discusses two bills before Congress which were conceived for the purpose of eliminating family violence.

733. Ounsted, Christopher and others. "Aspects of Bonding Failure: The Psychopathology and Psychotherapeutic Treatment of Families of Battered Children." **Developmental Medicine and Child Neurology**, 16(4):447–56, August 1974.

Describes systems of treatment and prevention that are evolving in the Park Hospital for Children in Oxford, England. These systems deal in both inpatient and outpatient treatment.

734. _____. "The Psychopathology and Psychotherapy of the Families: Aspects of Bonding Failure." **Concerning Child Abuse: Papers Presented by the Tunbridge Wells Study Group on Non-Accidental Injury to Children**. Edited by Alfred White Franklin. Edinburgh: Churchill Livingstone, 1975, pp. 30–40.

Discusses the work of the authors with families and mothers who were treated because of fears that they may injure their babies, but who had not done so when they began treatment.

735. "Out of the Closet: Authorities Face Up to the Child Abuse Problem." **U.S. News and World Report**, 80:83–84, May 3, 1976.

Explores attempts by groups to organize for child abuse prevention.

736. Oviatt, Boyd. "After Child Abuse Reporting Legislation — What?" **Helping the Battered Child and His Family**. Edited by C. Henry Kempe and Ray E. Helfer. Philadelphia: J.B. Lippincott Company, 1972, pp. 146-60.

Hypothesizes that public policy must provide for a system of state funding and supervision of protective services, and that the helping professions, particularly social work, must critically examine present methods of providing services for neglected children and their families. Discusses a study conducted by the Children's Division of the American Humane Association which assessed the availability of child protective services. Propositions are offered as guidelines which would assist in the development of adequate services for neglected and abused children and their families.

737. Owens, David. "Battered Wives: Some Social and Legal Problems." **British Journal of Law and Society**, 2:201-11, Winter 1975.

Presents a general discussion of marital violence, emphasizing the social and legal aspects of the problem. British law is viewed as a patriarchal institution as far as marriage and family law is concerned and, therefore, does not meet the needs of the battered wife. The same attitudes toward marriage that form the root of family law also prevail in society, thus legitimizing marital violence. In addition, recommendations are made for curtailing or preventing family violence.

738. Ozzanna, S. Harmony. "A Refuge Is Where Women Can Grow Together." **Majority Report**, 5(22):March 6-20, 1976.

Discusses the Women's Advocates Crisis Shelter in St. Paul, Minnesota, and the affects of the shelter's help on the women served.

739. Page, Mariam O. "Cohesion, Dignity, and Hope for Multiproblem Families." **The Battered Child**. Compiled by Jerome E. Leavitt. Morristown, New Jersey: General Learning Press, 1974, pp. 135-40.

Examines a demonstration project operating in the Vermont Department of Social Welfare to help multi-problem families achieve a better quality of home life for their children.

740. Pagelow, Mildred Daley. "Research on Woman Battering." **Stopping Wife Abuse: A Guide to the Emotional, Psychological, and Legal Implications for the Abused Woman and Those Helping Her**. By Jennifer Baker Fleming. Garden City, New York: Anchor Press/Doubleday, 1979, pp. 334-49.

Provides an overview of research that deals with battered women. Reviews theoretical perspectives underlying the studies. Discusses the lack of consensus in the field, differences and inconsistencies of definitions, and the focus of various studies. Presents recommendations for needed research and suggests ways research can be designed and conducted so that it will be of the greatest value.

741. Palmer, C.H. and J.T. Weston. "Several Unusual Cases of Child Abuse." **Journal of Forensic Sciences**, 21:851–55, October 1976.

Explores the deaths of children in New Mexico which resulted from abuse.

742. "The Paralysis of the Battered Wife." **Human Behavior**, pp. 47–48, May 1977.

Describes research conducted by Richard Gelles with 41 families in which the wife had been the victim of abuse, emphasizing the woman's reluctance to leave her situation.

743. "Parents Anonymous and Child Abuse: Self-Help Group for Abusers." **Intellect**, 103:76–77, November 1974.

Summarizes a panel discussion of child abuse and neglect, which was held at Purdue University. Ways to curtail child abuse are emphasized and the work of the Parents Anonymous Group is detailed.

744. "The Park Slope Safe Home Project Services." **Fight Back!: Feminist Resistance to Male Violence**. Edited by Frederique Delacoste and Felice Newman. Minneapolis: Cleis Press, 1981, pp. 123–25.

Details the organization, services and operation of the Park Slope Safe Home Project. Emphasizes issues of confidentiality and safety, and presents key points for other communities developing similar projects.

745. Parker, Barbara and Dale N. Schumacher. "Battered Wife Syndrome and Violence in the Nuclear Family of Origin: A Controlled Study." **American Journal of Public Health**, 67:760–61, August 1977.

Discusses a study in which women who had applied to the Domestic Relations Division of the Baltimore, Maryland Legal Aid Bureau for legal assistance were interviewed. It was found that women whose mothers had been victims of the battered wife syndrome had greater probability of being battered wives themselves. In addition, abusive husbands were shown to have a lower educational level than non-abusing husbands.

746. Parker, Graham E. "The Battered Child Syndrome." **Medicine, Science and the Law**, 5(3):160–63, July 1965.

Explores the problem of the battered child in the United States, focusing on legislation making reporting by the Medical Profession mandatory, and the medical profession's response to this.

747. Parnas, Raymond. "Police Discretion and Diversion of Incidents of Intra-Family Violence." **Law and Contemporary Problems**, 36(4):539–65, Autumn 1971.

Outlines current police practices for dealing with family violence. Discusses traditional police practice as emphasizing short-term adjustment, and recommends increasing mediation and referral to prevent recurrence of the violence.

748. Parnas, Raymond L. "Prosecutorial and Judicial Handling of Family Violence." **Criminal Law Bulletin**, 9(9):733–69, 1973.

States that many cases of family violence are diverted out of the criminal process by the police, and that when these cases reach the district attorney's office, they are screened and temporarily resolved without prosecution. Several information hearing processes are examined to determine the rationale behind the prosecutor's handling of family dispute cases.

749. Pascoe, Elizabeth Jean. "Shelters for Battered Wives." **McCalls**, 104:51, October 1976.

Discusses the establishment of shelters for battered wives.

750. _____. "Wife Beating: A Community to the Rescue." **McCalls**, 105:81, November 1977.

Examines the role of television station KYW-TV in Philadelphia in aiding battered women. Broadcasts by this station provided the impetus for community action against wife abuse.

751. Pascoe, John M. "Vaccination Status of Maltreated Children." **American Journal of Public Health**, 70(9):1014, September 1980.

Reviews the vaccination status of maltreated children and compares it with that of other children. Findings indicate that despite a high degree of visibility following treatment or confinement for abuse, maltreated children were less likely to receive needed vaccinations than were other pre-school children.

752. Paulsen, Monrad G. "Child Abuse Reporting Laws: The Shape of the Legislation." **Columbia Law Review**, 67(1):1–49, January 1967.

Describes and analyzes the existing child abuse reporting statutes and presents some of the practical experience gained with these enactments. It is felt that the statutory texts themselves do not offer a reliable guide to the way in which cases are actually handled in particular states, and they cannot in themselves ensure an effective program of protection and welfare for the child. The enactment of a reporting statute is significant only if reported children are protected from further injury. Discusses who should report, what injuries are to be reported, the statutory plan for handling reports, and the role of central registries for reporting.

753. _____. "Legal Protections Against Child Abuse." **The Battered Child**. Compiled by Jerome E. Leavitt. Morristown, New Jersey: General Learning Press, 1974, pp. 94–100.

Details four sets of legal provisions that are directly related to child abuse. States that criminal sanctions are a poor means of prevention, and discusses the criminal law in relation to child abuse. The juvenile court's powers over neglected children and court ordered protective supervision are examined, and a detailed discussion of reporting laws is presented.

754. Paulsen, Monrad and others. "Child Abuse Reporting Laws — Some Legislative History." **The George Washington Law Review**, 34(3):482–506, March 1966.

Discusses child abuse reporting laws from an historical perspective, and the impact of the media on the enactment of such laws. The course of reporting bills in the legislature is explained and the future of enactment of satisfactory child abuse reporting legislation is explored.

755. Paulson, Morris J. "Child Trauma Intervention: A Community Response to Family Violence." **Journal of Clinical Child Psychology**, 4:26–29, Fall 1975.

Examines the problem of child abuse, emphasizing the role of the community in its management.

756. Paulson, Morris J. and Phillip R. Blake. "The Physically Abused Child: A Focus on Prevention." **Child Welfare**, 48(2):86–95, 1969.

Presents statistics on child abuse and discusses a study which examined cases of possible mistreatment in Los Angeles. The data suggest that many parents do not accept the responsibilities of their roles, and that preventive intervention requires the identification of high-risk families in order to help the parents.

757. Paulson, Morris J. and others. "The MMPI: A Descriptive Measure of Psychopathology in Abusive Parents." **Journal of Clinical Psychology**, 30:387–90, July 1974.

A study comparing the psychopathology of abusive and non-abusive parents using the MMPI as a measure is presented.

758. _____. "An MMPI Scale for Identifying 'At Risk' Abusive Parents." **Journal of Clinical Child Psychology**, 4:22–24, Spring 1975.

The use of the Minnesota Multiphasic Personality Inventory to diagnose abusive parents is explored. The authors feel that this test has the potential to identify possible child abusers.

759. _____. "Parents Attitude Research (PARI): Clinical vs. Statistical Inferences in Understanding Abusive Mothers." **Journal of Clinical Psychology**, 33:848–54, July 1977.

Discusses the Parent Attitude Research Instrument, a test designed to measure the attitudes of mothers toward parenthood. This test was administered to a group of abusive mothers, and also to a control group. Since the test was shown to accurately classify abusive mothers about two-thirds of the time, the authors caution against using the test alone to predict potential abusive behavior.

760. _____. "Parents of the Battered Child: A Multidisciplinary Group

Therapy Approach to Life-Threatening Behavior." **Life-Threatening Behavior**, 4:18–31, Spring 1974.

Discusses the findings of a study with thirty-one abusing families who underwent therapy in a multidisciplinary group therapy setting.

761. Pavenstedt, Eleanor. "An Intervention Program for Infants From High Risk Homes." **American Journal of Public Health**, 63(5):393–95, May 1973.

Examines criteria for classifying children at risk and states that the battered child is a small fraction of this group which has drawn attention because the injuries are visible and undeniable. States that for intervention to be effective it must begin during the first three years of the child's life, and describes the establishment of a day care unit for "at risk" children from birth through 3 years of age. Emphasizes that the high risk group needs compensatory and corrective care to withstand the pressure of their pathological environment during the succeeding formative years.

762. Pedicord, Diane. "Courts: Seen and Not Heard: The Child's Need for His Own Lawyer in Child Abuse and Neglect Cases." **Oklahoma Law Review**, 29:439–45, Spring 1976.

Examines Oklahoma statutes in regard to right to counsel and reviews the statutes in effect in other states, emphasizing the child's need for independent counsel in child abuse and neglect proceedings.

763. Pelton, Leroy H. "Child Abuse and Neglect: The Myth of Classlessness." **American Journal of Orthopsychiatry**, 48(4):608–17, October 1978.

Argues that evidence does not support belief in child abuse as being a widely distributed problem within society, and states that the wide exceptance of this belief diverts attention from the actual nature of the problem.

764. _____. **The Social Context of Child Abuse and Nelgect**. New York: Human Sciences Press, 1981. 331 pp.

The editor states that this book is a vehicle to help facilitate understanding and appreciation of the alternative perspective on child abuse and neglect, which takes into account social and economic factors. The main themes of the book include the relationship between child abuse and social and economic circumstances, and the necessity for social services and programs to recognize this fact, and the harmful effects of poverty on children and whether or not these effects are mediated by child abuse and neglect.

765. Perdue, Nancy. "Physicians Face Depressing Task of Examining Child Abuse Cases." **San Antonio Light**, June 7, 1982, p. 3A.

Discusses one physician's view of child abuse. States that many children are mistreated because there are stresses that the parents cannot handle, and the only outlet some parents know is violence.

766. Peters, Joseph J. "Children Who Are Victims of Sexual Assault and the

Psychology of Offenders." **American Journal of Psychotherapy**, 30:398–421, July 1976.

Describes cases in which sexual assaults in childhood form the roots of psychiatric problems in adulthood. The author's experience indicates that reports of sexual assaults on children are often ignored at the expense of the psychological health of the child. It is suggested that immediate supportive responses from parents and professionals may help to preserve the emotional health of the victim. Research conducted at the Sex Offender and Rape Victim Center in Philadelphia is also examined.

767. Peterson, Karen. "There's a Link Between Animal Abuse and Child Abuse." **PTA Magazine**, 68:14–16, June 1974.

Children's cruelty to animals may be an indicator of child abuse in the family and also a predictor of possible violence in the child's adult life.

768. Pfeifer, Donald R. and Catherine Ayoub. "An Approach to the Prophylaxis of Child Abuse and Neglect." **Journal of the Oklahoma State Medical Association**, 69:162–67, May 1967.

Describes a comprehensive program for child abuse and neglect intervention which was developed for the purposes of identification, treatment and education.

769. Pfouts, Jane H. and Connie Renz. "The Future of Wife Abuse Programs." **Social Work**, 26(6):451–55, November 1981.

Examines current efforts in the treatment of battered women and discusses four possible intervention programs for the future.

770. Pickett, John. "The Management of Non-Accidental Injury to Children in the City of Manchester." **Violence in the Family**. Edited by Marie Borland. Atlantic Highlands, New Jersey: Humanities Press, 1976, pp. 61–87.

Describes in detail the system developed in Manchester for the notification, intervention, coordination, and review of cases of non-accidental injury.

771. Pickett, John and Andy Maton. "Protective Casework and Child Abuse: Practice and Problems." **The Challenge of Child Abuse**. Edited by Alfred White Franklin. London: Academic Press, 1977, pp. 56–80.

Discusses the role of the social workere in cases of child abuse and describes the social work processes involved with these cases.

772. Pierron, G. Joseph. "Child Abuse and Neglect: The Legal Challenge." **Journal of the Kansas Bar Association**, 46:167–81, Fall 1977.

Explores the law concerning child abuse, emphasizing the Kansas Child Protection Act.

773. Piers, Maria W. **Infanticide**. New York: W.W. Norton and Company, Inc., 1978. 139 pp.

Discusses the reality of infanticide by using cases as illustrations of the problem. The chain reaction of violence and attitudes toward infanticial mothers are among the topics explored. A bibliography and index are included.

774. Pitcher, Rudolph A., Jr. "The Police." **Helping the Battered Child and His Family**. Edited by C. Henry Kempe and Ray E. Helfer. Philadelphia: J.B. Lippincott Company, 1972, pp. 242–55.

States that the role of law enforcement agencies in child abuse cases is vague, and that these agencies must be recognized as having a legitimate interest in the social problem created by families in which children are victims of physical violence. Studies suggest a relationship between people who were abused as children and subsequent delinquency and criminal behavior. Since the role of the police is the prevention of these behaviors, they should be given clear roles in child abuse management and prevention.

775. Pizzey, Erin. **Scream Quietly or the Neighbors Will Hear**. Short Hills, New Jersey: Ridley Enslow Publishers, 1977. 154 pp.

Discusses the relationship between battered women and the effect on their children, the backgrounds of abusive men, attitudes of the police and medical personnel, and treatment of battered women by social service agencies. The majority of the work is devoted to the author's own experiences as a battered wife and the establishment of Chiswick Women's Aid, a refuge for battered women in England.

776. Plaine, Lloyd. "Evidentiary Problems in Criminal Child Abuse Prosecutions." **Georgetown Law Journal**, 63:257–73, October 1974.

Explores the differences between child abuse and other criminal assaults. Problems of admissable evidence and difficulties inherent in prosecuting child abuse cases are among the issues discussed.

777. Pleck, Elizabeth. "Wife Beating in Nineteenth-Century America." **Victimology: An International Journal**, 4:60–74, 1979.

The plight of the abused wife in the nineteenth century and the protection afforded them are examined. It is concluded that the system for dealing with the problem during that time was as effective as the system in effect today.

778. Pogrebin, Letty Cottin. "Do Women Make Men Violent?" **MS.**, 3:49–55+, November 1974.

Explores the question of whether a woman's presence incites male violence. Evidence to the contrary is presented and the social conditions which make women victims and men aggressors are discussed. It is concluded that women are relatively powerless and have little control over their own "destinies," and that women would not invite a crime of which they would be the victims.

779. Polansky, Norman A. "Help for the Helpless." **Smith College Studies in Social Work**, 49(3):169–91, June 1979.

Examines the thesis that a high proportion of families identified as neglectful live outside of the usual helping networks. The significance of child neglect as a major cause of social ills because of its relationship to emotional illness, child and adult criminality, and mental retardation is also discussed.

780. Polansky, Norman A. and others. **Damaged Parents: An Anatomy of Child Neglect**. Chicago: University of Chicago Press, 1981. 271 pp.

States that damaged children become damaged parents because they know no other way of life, and that "Neglect is a private matter of things undone, of inaction and indifference." Discusses child neglect by examining the effects of neglect on the child, characteristics of neglectful parents, what factors in a parent's life turn him into a damaged parent, the apathy-futility syndrome and infantilism, assessing the quality of child care, and rationales for intervention.

781. _____. "Isolation of the Neglectful Family." **American Journal of Orthopsychiatry**, 49(1):149–52, January 1979.

Reviews a study of child neglect conducted among families in rural Southern Appalachia. Findings indicate that these families are not usually in helping networks to the same degree as are others of similar social position. An explanation for this problem is suggested and implications for assistance by helping systems are presented.

782. _____. "Verbal Accessibility in the Treatment of Child Neglect." **The Battered Child**. Compiled by Jerome E. Leavitt. Morristown, New Jersey: General Learning Press, 1974, pp. 66–73.

Discusses a study of mothers involved in rural child neglect, with special attention to what is called "the apathy-futility syndrome." Examines the implications of the study for training and supervising the rural social worker who deals with the mother of children receiving poor care. Verbal accessibility is defined and the reactions of workers to the accessible and inaccessible client are explored. Techniques for facilitating verbal accessibility are suggested.

783. Polier, Justine Wise. "Professional Abuse of Children: Responsibility for the Delivery of Services." **American Journal of Orthopsychiatry**, 45(3):357–62, April 1975.

Examines the responsibility of professionals and social service agencies for the delivery or denial of services to children.

784. Polier, Justine Wise and Kay McDonald. "The Family Court in an Urban Setting." **Helping the Battered Child and His Family**. Edited by C. Henry Kempe and Ray E. Helfer. Philadelphia: J.B. Lippincott Company, 1972, pp. 208–24.

Examines the additional dimensions of child abuse found in big cities, and discusses the roles of the judge and the courts in child abuse cases. Topics explored include the incidence of the problem, disposition of cases, the economic status of the family as a factor in biased reporting, and long-term goals of the family court for child abuse cases.

785. Pollock, Carl and Brandt Steele. "A Therapeutic Approach to the Parents." **Helping the Battered Child and His Family**. Edited by C. Henry Kempe and Ray E. Helfer. Philadelphia: J.B. Lippincott Company, 1972, pp. 3–21.

Summarizes the psychodynamics of child abuse, and the dynamics of the abusive parent. An evaluation of the family is also presented, including patterns of response to therapy, the process of parents growing out of their patterns of living and becoming good parents, the child's return to the home, and the necessity for long-term availability.

786. Prescott, James W. "Body Pleasure and the Origins of Violence." **The Bulletin of the Atomic Scientists**, 31(9):10–20, November 1975.

Contends that the greatest threat to world peace comes from those nations which have the most depriving environments for their children, and which are most repressive of sexual affection. Recent research supports the point of view that deprivation of physical pleasure is a major ingredient in the expression of physical violence, and that until the relationship between pleasure and violence is understood, violence will escalate. Discusses a study which showed that in societies where children are given a lot of affection, violence is less. Also examines violence against sexuality and the use of sexuality for violence. Concludes by describing the reciprocal relationship between pleasure and violence, stating that when one is high, the other is low.

787. Prescott, Suzanne and Carolyn Letko. "Battered Women: A Social Psychological Perspective." **Battered Women: A Psychosociological Study of Domestic Violence**. Edited by Maria Roy. New York: Van Nostrand Reinhold Company, 1977, pp. 72–96.

Reports on a survey which showed how social stress, limitations in resources, and sex roles affect women, their children, their marriages, and subsequent help-seeking behavior.

788. Price, John and Jean Armstrong. "Battered Wives: A Controlled Study of Predisposition." **Australian and New Zealand Journal of Psychiatry**, 12:43–47, 1978.

Results of a study conducted by the authors in which they measured the hostility of the participants are presented. Cases and controls were chosen from a group of women who had recently experienced a break-up of a marriage or similar relationship. The case groups were found to be significantly more hostile than the control group, and that more than half of the case women admitted some degree of direct provocation in the assaults.

789. Prince, Russell C. "Evidence — Child Abuse — Expert Medical Testimony Concerning 'Battered Child Syndrome' Held Admissible." **Fordham Law Review**, 42:935–42, May 1974.

Discusses the admissibility of expert medical testimony on the "battered child syndrome" as circumstantial proof that a child's injuries are not accidental. Various case reports are presented to illustrate the effective use, and the potential for misuse, of this ruling.

790. Pringle, Mia Kellmer. "The Needs of Children." **The Maltreatment of Children**. Edited by Selwyn M. Smith. Baltimore: University Park Press, 1978, pp. 221–43.

Exmines the psychological consequences of child abuse, patterns of parental violence, the psychological needs of children, and ways of guaranteeing essential care to children.

791. Prinz, Lucie. "Laws That Help the Battered Spouse." **McCalls**, 106:57, May 1979.

Discusses legislation which deals with family violence as an area of concern in itself.

792. Queens Bench Foundation. Project on Sexual Assault. **Sexual Abuse of Children**. San Francisco: Queens Bench Foundation, 1976, 69 pp.

Reports on a pilot project designed to study child sexual abuse in San Francisco. The project is summarized, and literature is reviewed. Topics discussed include police response, legal processes involved in child sexual abuse cases, community and protective services, and hospital responses to the problem and its victims. Appendices summarize penal code statutes, child abuse reporting laws, and applicable welfare codes.

793. Rabkin, Brenda. "Despair that Breeds Despair." **Macleans**, 92:37–38, February 5, 1979.

Discusses young, unwed mothers and the incidence of child abuse and neglect.

794. Radbill, Samuel X. "Children in a World of Violence: A History of Child Abuse." **The Battered Child**. Edited by C. Henry Kempe and Ray E. Helfer. Chicago: University of Chicago Press, 1980, pp. 3–20.

Presents a discussion of child abuse from an historical perspective, including: child labor; mutilation; infanticide; sale of children; sexual abuse; incest; children's rights; protective services for children; and prevention and treatment.

795. _____. "A History of Child Abuse and Infanticide." **Violence in the Family**. Edited by Suzanne K. Steinmetz and Murray A. Straus. New York: Harper and Row, 1974, pp. 173–79.

Discusses physical punishment from an historical perspective and examines the establishment of the Society for the Prevention of Cruelty to Children. Laws against infanticide and child abuse throughout history, and the Battered Child Syndrome are also explored.

796. Raffalli, Henri C. "The Battered Child: An Overview of a Medical, Legal and Social Problem." **Crime and Delinquency**, 16(2):139–50, April 1970.

Defines the Battered Child Syndrome and discusses the natural and legal rights of parents. The point where discipline becomes child abuse is also explored.

797. Raisbeck, Bert L. "The Legal Framework." **Violence in the Family**. Edited by Marie Borland. Atlantic Highlands, New Jersey: Humanities Press, 1976, pp. 88–106.

Discusses violence toward children and spouses, and examines available protection and prevention for victims of physical violence.

798. Ramsey, Jerry A. and Byron J. Lawler. "The Battered Child Syndrome." **Pepperdine Law Review**, 1:372–81, 1974.

Examines the battered child syndrome, emphasizing the legal aspects of the problem. A case study is presented in order to illustrate the legal process involved in cases of child abuse in California, and the role of the physician in the identification and reporting of suspected cases of battering.

799. Ramsey, Sarah. "Child Abuse and Neglect: Against the Law." **Southern Exposure**, 8(3):76–78, Fall 1980.

Discusses the question of what standards a state should use for intruding into the privacy of a family in order to protect the children. The importance of this question in southern states is explored, stating that child abuse and neglect are tied to poverty. The California Family Protection Act is presented as the best hope for solving the privacy problem.

800. Reavley, William and Marie-Therese Gilbert. "The Behavioral Treatment Approach to Potential Child Abuse – Two Case Reports." **Social Work Today**, 7:166–68, June 10, 1976.

Two cases of child abuse are analyzed in behavioral terms. Treatment strategies and their implementation are reported in detail, with particular emphasis placed upon the educational aspects of treatment. The general applicability of the approaches outlined is also explored.

801. "Recognize Symptoms and Know Where to Get Help." **San Antonio Light**, pp. 1M–2M, June 6, 1982.

Defines the three forms of child abuse as physical, emotional, and sexual and presents signs to look for in identifying these cases. A list of agencies in the San Antonio, Texas area which provide help to victims of child abuse and neglect is provided.

802. Redeker, James R. "The Right of an Abused Child to Independent Counsel and the Role of the Child Advocate in Child Abuse Cases." **Villanova Law Review**, 23:521–46, 1977–78.

Discusses the right of an abused child to counsel, the guardian *Ad Litem* (an attorney appointed to represent the best interests of the child), and the role and responsibility of the advocate in child abuse proceedings.

803. "Refuge for Battered Wives." **Intellect**, 106:353, March 1978.

Describes La Casa de las Madres, a refuge for battered wives in San Francisco. Also discusses the characteristics of battered women, myths concerning wife beating, and characteristics of men who batter. As a possible solution to the problem, it is suggested that women be given avenues of escape, and that they be encouraged to take control of their own lives.

804. Remsberg, Bonnie and Charles Remsberg. "The Case of Patricia Gross." **Family Circle**, pp. 58+, April 24, 1979.

Examines the case of Patricia Gross, a battered wife who killed her husband, was charged with murder, and subsequently entered a plea of self-defense.

805. Remsberg, Charles and Bonnie Remsberg. "An American Scandal: Why Some Parents Abuse Teens." **Seventeen**, 36:154–55+, May 1977.

Discusses the problem of parental abuse of teenagers. Presents case studies to illustrate the incidence and nature of the problem.

806. Resnick, Mindy. **Wife Beating Counselor Training Manual#1**. Ann Arbor, Michigan: NOW Domestic Violence Project, 1976.

Designed as a guide for counselors working with wife abuse victms. Discusses the various roles of the counselor, counseling techniques, and the conflict of emotions felt by victims.

807. Resnick, Phillip J. "Child Murder by Parents: A Psychiatric View of Filicide." **American Journal of Psychiatry**, 126(3):325–34, September 1969.

Reviews 131 cases of filicide and proposes a new classification by motive.

808. Reyes, Alberto. "What Mejia Means." **Nuestro**, 3(8):19+, September 1979.

Discusses the case of Idalia Mejia, a woman who shot and killed her husband following one of many incidents of abuse against herself and her children.

809. Richards, Martin. "Parents and Children and Child Abuse." **The Challenge of Child Abuse**. Edited by Alfred White Franklin. London: Academic Press, 1977, pp. 80–95.

Suggests that child abuse should be considered as an aspect of the relationship between caretaker and child, although it is an undesirable and unusual one. Contrasts this view with one which states that child abuse is a special problem that can be considered in isolation from the usual behavior of parent toward child.

810. Ridington, Jillian. "The Transition Process: A Feminist Environment as Reconstitutive Milieu." **Victimology: An International Journal**, 2:563–75, 1977–78.

Describes the development of Vancouver Transition House, a refuge established and operated by women. Data was gathered from the residents of the house which indicates that the environment created by the women helped the victims overcome negative feelings about themselves and their role in the violent marriage, and enabled them to develop more positive self-concepts. Changes necessary to provide longer-term support and possibly prevent recurring violent behavior by husbands are suggested.

811. Roaf, Robert. "Trauma in Childhood." **The Battered Child**. Compiled by Jerome E. Leavitt. Morristown, New Jersey: General Learning Press, 1974, pp. 191–94.

Discusses physical trauma in childhood with x-rays of injuries as illustrations, and types of physical trauma are reviewed.

812. Roberts, Albert R. **Sheltering Battered Women: A National Study and Service Guide**. New York: Springer Publishing Company, 1981. 227 pp.

Reports data from the first national survey conducted on the emergency shelter programs for battered women. Offers practical assistance in the form of guidelines and recommended techniques for fostering program planning and development. Part one focuses on the nature and extent of newly emerging intervention services and shelters for abused victims and their children. Part two offers specific methods and procedures for aiding battered women, and part three addresses current and projected trends in the delivery of services.

813. Roberts, Jacquie. "Social Work and Child Abuse: The Reasons for Failure and the Way to Success." **Violence and the Family**. Edited by J.P. Martin. New York: John Wiley and Sons, 1978, pp. 255–91.

Examines the factors associated with child abuse which produce major difficulties for social workers, and discusses the reasons why social workers fail in their attempts to treat child abuse.

814. Robichaud, Jane. "How One Community Organized to Help Battered Wives." **Redbook**, 153:100, May 1979.

Discusses the establishment of a task force in the Connecticut towns of Meriden and Wallingford. The task force was organized by a group of community women for the purpose of providing assistance to battered wives. The operation of the task force's hot line and temporary shelter is examined, and the effect of this task force's work on the establishment of similar groups in other communities is highlighted.

815. Robinson, J. "Defense Strategies for Battered Women Who Assault Their Mates: *State v. Curry*." **Harvard Women's Law Journal**, 4(1):161–75, Spring 1981.

Discusses the uses of battering as a claim of self-defense in assault cases.

816. Rochester, Dean E. and others. "What Can Schools Do About Child Abuse?" **The Battered Child**. Compiled by Jerome E. Leavitt. Morristown, New Jersey: General Learning Press, 1974, pp. 213–14.

Examines the results of a questionaire sent to 45 elementary principals and counselors in representative community school districts in a midwest metropolitan area. The questionaire dealt with the role of principals and counselors in child abuse cases and the nature of typical cases they might have encountered. Concludes that school personnel have a vital role to play in breaking up the battered child syndrome.

817. Rockwood, Marcia. "Battered Wives: Help for the Victim Next Door." **MS.**, 5:95, August 1976.

Discusses the inadequacy of police response to domestic violence and efforts being made to train police to deal more effectively with the problem. Impetus for change which is coming from women's groups is explored, and the importance of domestic violence as a public rather than a private problem is emphasized.

818. _____. "Courts and Cops: Enemies of Battered Wives.?" **MS.**, 5:19, April 1977.

Examines the indifferent attitude of the New York City police and Family Court System toward battered wives. A suit files by a coalition of New York based organizations which made the above charge is also discussed.

819. _____. "How to Tell It to the Judge." **MS.**, 5:96, August 1976.

Discusses possible legal remedies available to battered women.

820. Rodeheffer, Martha and Harold P. Martin. "Special Problems in Developmental Assessment of Abused Children." **The Abused Child: A Multidisciplinary Approach to Developmental Issues and Treatment**. Edited by Harold P. Martin. Cambridge, Massachusetts: Ballinger Publishing Company, 1976, pp. 113–28.

Explores the difficulties of obtaining accurate developmental information on abused children, the behavior of abused children in a developmental testing situation, complete developmental assessment of the child, and the interpretation of developmental data.

821. Rodriguez, Alejandro. **Handbook of Child Abuse and Neglect**. Flushing, New York: Medical Examination Publishing Company, Inc., 1977. 162 pp.

Describes procedures for the management, examination, and diagnosis of child abuse.

822. Rosen, Barbara. "Interpersonal Values Among Child-Abusive Women." **Psychological Reports**, 45(3):819–22, December 1979.

Examines a study designed to compare interpersonal values of abusive and non-abusive women with children under five years of age. Results indicate that abusing women valued conformity and benevolence less, and authority over others more, than did the non-abusing women.

823. _____. "Self-Concept Disturbance Among Mothers Who Abuse Their Children." **Psychological Reports**, 43(1):323–26, August 1978.

Discusses whether self-concept disturbance significantly distinguished abusive from non-abusive mothers. Studies indicate that women who abused their children had lower and more inconsistent self-concepts than did the non-abusing women. It is concluded that self-concept disturbance leads to extreme frustration which may result in violence when socially acceptable outlets are not available.

824. Rosenbaum, Alan and K. Daniel O'Leary. "Marital Violence: Characteristics of Abusive Couples." **Journal of Consulting and Clinical Psychology**, 49(1):63–71, February 1981.

Reviews a study which compared characteristics of abusive couples with couples who had satisfactory marriages, and also with couples whose marriages were dysfunctional but non-violent. Significant differences included the presence of violence in families as children, and the likelihood that the couples were abused as children.

825. Rosenberg, Arthur H. "The Law and Child Abuse." **Child Abuse: Intervention and Treatment**. Edited by Nancy B. Ebeling and Deborah A. Hill. Acton, Massachusetts: Publishing Sciences Group, 1975, pp. 161–69.

Examines difficulties involved in dealing with child abuse from a purely legal perspective. Statutory and reporting laws concerning child abuse are also discussed.

826. Rosenblatt, Gary C. **Parental Expectations and Attitudes About Childrearing in High Risk vs. Low Risk Child Abusing Families**. Saratoga, California: R & E Publishers, 1980. 129 pp.

Discusses a possible relationship between parental attitudes toward childrearing and expectations for their children, and the incidence and severity of child abuse.

827. Rosenfeld, Alvin A. "Sexual Misuse and the Family." **Victimology: An International Journal**, 2:226–35, Summer 1977.

Traces the evolution of psychiatric ideas concerning incest. Familial attitudes toward sexuality and the expression of sexuality in the family are among the areas explored. Some general guidelines of "normal sexual life" in the family are presented.

828. Rosenfeld, Alvin A. and Eli H. Newberger. "Compassion vs. Control: Conceptual and Practical Pitfalls in the Broadened Definition of Child Abuse." **Journal of the American Medical Association**, 237:2086–88, May 9, 1977.

States that agencies which deal with child abuse are caught between feelings of compassion for the parent's need for treatment and the necessity of controlling the problem of child abuse. Examines the problems involved in the treatment and management of child abuse cases, and the need for definite standards for treatment and control of the problem.

829. Rosenheim, Margaret K., editor. **Pursuing Justice for the Child**. Chicago: University of Chicago Press, 1976. 361 pp.

Selections deal with justice for the delinquent and non-delinquent child. Although emphasis is on the juvenile justice system and juvenile deviance, but discussions of parents' and children's rights are also presented.

830. Roth, Frederick. "A Practice Regimen for Diagnosis and Treatment of Child Abuse." **Child Welfare**, 54:268–73, April 1975.

Outlines a procedure developed by the Illinois Department of Children and Family Services for the identification and treatment of child abuse. Severity of abuse characteristics of abusive parents, the child's feeling toward the abusive parent, and the needs of the child are among the topics discussed.

831. Rounsaville, Bruce J. "Battered Wives: Barriers to Identification and Treatment." **American Journal of Orthopsychiatry**, 48(3):487–94, July 1978.

Discusses the need for adequate professional treatment and aid for victims of wife beating, and examines a study which outlines the difficulties in reaching abused women and suggests treatment approaches.

832. _____. "Theories in Marital Violence: Evidence From a Study of Battered Women." **Victimology: An International Journal**, 3:11–31, 1978.

Discusses psychological and sociological explanations of wifebeating in light of the results of a study on battered women. The need for a systems analysis of the problem is also examined.

833. Rounsaville, Bruce and Myrna M. Weissman. "Battered Women: A Medical Problem Requiring Detection." **International Journal of Psychiatry in Medicine**, 8:191–202, 1977–78.

Reviews the characteristics of women treated in the emergency room of a hospital for injuries sustained as a result of abuse.

834. Rounsaville, Bruce and others. "The Natural History of a Psychotherapy Group for Battered Women." **Psychiatry**, 42(1):63–78, February 1979.

Describes the authors' experiences with evaluation and treatment of battered women.

835. Rowe, Janet. Alternative Families.'' **The Challenge of Child Abuse**. Edited by Alfred White Franklin. London: Academic Press, 1977, pp. 145-57.

Emphasizes fostering and adoption as alternatives to the biological family and discusses implications of these alternatives for social work practice.

836. Roy, Maria, editor. **The Abusive Partner: An Analysis of Domestic Battering**. New York: Van Nostrand Reinhold, 1982. 319 pp.

Discusses a variety of views concerning the causes and nature of family violence, emphasizing the batterer. Appropriate social service and criminal justice responses to battering are also examined. Articles include discussions of the psychological and social aspects of the problem, and explore the influence of alcohol and drugs on aggressive behavior. Treatment approaches are also discussed, including group counseling for men, community education and couple therapy.

837. _____. **Battered Women: A Psychological Study of Domestic Violence**. New York: Van Nostrand Reinhold Company, 1977. 334 pp.

Selections discuss battered women from an historical perspective, social aspects of the problem, neurological and psychological factors, the law and law enforcement, and methods of treatment and prevention.

838. _____. ''A Current Survey of 150 Cases.'' **Battered Women: A Psychosociological Study of Domestic Violence**. Edited by Maria Roy. New York: Van Nostrand Reinhold Company, 1977, pp. 25-44.

Presents the results of a survey which corroborates the idea that wifebeating as a social problem originates with, and is compounded by, many factors. The need for alternative solutions to the problem of wife abuse is demonstrated.

839. _____. ''A Model for Services.'' **Battered Women: A Psychosociological Study of Domestic Violence**. Edited by Maria Roy. New York: Van Nostrand Reinhold Company, 1977, pp. 287-97.

Explains how to organize a program for battered women and their families.

840. _____. ''Some Thoughts Regarding the Criminal Justice System and Wifebeating.'' **Battered Women: A Psychosociological Study of Domestic Violence**. Edited by Maria Roy. New York: Van Nostrand Reinhold Company, 1977, pp. 138-39.

Examines what is termed the criminal justice system's ''covert toleration of wifebeating'' as underlying that system's involvement in wifebeating cases.

841. Rubin, Jean. ''The Need for Intervention.'' **The Battered Child**. Compiled by Jerome E. Leavitt. Morristown, New Jersey: General Learning Press, 1974, pp. 238-43.

Explores the incidence of child abuse, characteristics of abused children, and histories of abusing parents. Methods of intervention are also reviewed.

842. Runyan, Desmond K. and others. "Determinants of Foster Care Placement for the Maltreated Child." **American Journal of Public Health**, 71(7):706–11, July 1981.

Analyzes the relationship between society, the family and the child, and discusses characteristics which are important to the placement decision. States that factors which appear to have no logical relationship to the decision to place a maltreated child in foster care are often implicated as predictors.

843. Rush, Florence. "Recommendations and Proposals for Victims of Child Abuse." **Rape: The First Sourcebook for Women**. Edited by Noreen Connell and Cassandra Wilson. New York: Plume Books, 1974, pp. 227–30.

This discussion of child abuse provides suggestions for family, parents, institutions, and women's groups for dealing with the problem. Examples of child abuse situations are presented to illustrate methods for dealing with it.

844. _____. "The Sexual Abuse of Children: A Feminist Point of View." **Rape: The First Sourcebook for Women**. Edited by Noreen Connell and Cassandra Wilson. New York: Plume Books, 1974, pp. 64–75.

Views the sexual abuse of children as an early manifestation of male power and oppression over the female. Presents statistics, statements, and conclusions of a study on sexual abuse of children, conducted by the American Humane Association, and also comments on four other studies.

845. Russell, Diana E. H. **Rape in Marriage**. New York: Macmillan, 1983. 412 pp.

Based on a representative survey of wife rape, this book examines marital rape and its relationship to other forms of violence. An appendix to the book presents a summary of the state marital rape exemption laws.

846. Sacco, Lynn A. "Wife Abuse: The Failure of Legal Remedies." **The John Marshall Journal of Practice and Procedure**, 11(3):549–77, Spring 1978.

Discusses the solutions which are possible through the legal system for wifebeating. Divorce, criminal prosecution, and tort actions are among the remedies examined.

847. Sadoff, Robert L. "Clinical Observations on Parricide." **Psychiatric Quarterly**, 45(1):65–69, 1971.

Discusses two cases of parricide, one matricide and one patricide. The cases were found to have similar psychodynamics, including cruel and unusual relationships between the child and the parent, in which the possibility of violence was high. Psychological aspects of parricide are also described.

848. Sage, Wayne. "Violence in the Children's Room." **Human Behavior**, 4:41–47, July 1975.

Child abuse is discussed as a social problem. Reasons why parents abuse their children and methods of treatment are highlighted.

849. Sanders, Lynda F. "Sweden's Unique Approach to Child Protection." **Child Abuse and Neglect Reports,** pp. 1-4, March 1979.

Describes how Uppsala, Sweden copes with cases of abuse and neglect. Discusses its mandatory reporting law, reporting follow-up by a citizen's committee, and its effectiveness. A plan proposed for the hospital handling of cases is also reviewed.

850. Sanders, R. Wyman. "Systematic Desensitization in the Treatment of Child Abuse." **American Journal of Psychiatry,** 135(4):483-84, April 1978.

Discusses the use of systematic desensitization in child abuse therapy. Presents a case report, and application of systematic desensitization to the abuser. Concludes that the desensitization process may be a major factor in the resolution of abusive behavior.

851. Sandusky, Annie Lee. "Services to Neglected Children." **The Battered Child.** Compiled by Jerome E. Leavitt. Morristown, New Jersey: General Learning Press, 1974, pp. 152-57.

Describes cases of families where children are neglected or abused, and examines available services, and blocks to services by the community.

852. Sanford, Linda Tschirhart. **The Silent Children: A Book for Parents About the Prevention of Child Sexual Abuse.** Garden City, New York: Anchor Press/Doubleday, 1980. 367 pp.

The stated purpose of this book is to examine and understand child sexual abuse. It is felt that once a parent has knowledge of the circumstances of child molestation and incest, and insight into the motivations of offenders, they can translate this information into warnings for their children. Discusses the family atmosphere, parents with special needs (single parents, parents of various ethnic groups, parents of disabled children), and ways to discuss the problem with a child. An overview of the crimes of child molestation and incest is also presented.

853. Saperstein, Avalie. "Child Rape Victims and Their Families." **Rape Victimology.** Edited by LeRoy G. Schultz. Springfield, Illinois: Charles C. Thomas, 1975, pp. 274-76.

Details the procedure developed by the counseling staff of Women Organized Against Rape in Philadelphia for treating the child victim of rape and her parents.

854. Saunders, Daniel G. "Marital Violence: Dimensions of the Problem and Modes of Intervention." **Journal of Marriage and Family Counseling,** 3:43-52, January 1977.

Reviews data concerning marital violence and recommends methods of intervention on both societal and familial levels.

855. Savino, Anne B. and R. Wyman Sanders. "Working With Abusive Parents: Group Therapy and Home Visits." **American Journal of Nursing**, 73(3):482–84, March 1973.

Describes a program conducted by the U.C.L.A. Neuropsychiatric Institute for parents deemed unfit by the court as a result of incidents of child abuse or neglect. Discusses the focus of the therapy, which includes group therapy and in-home visits, when requested by the parent.

856. Scharer, Kathleen M. "Rescue Fantasies: Professional Impediments in Working With Abused Families." **American Journal of Nursing**, 78(9):1483–84, September 1978.

Discusses possible reactions of nurses to abused family situations, and problems facing nurses in working with abused or neglected children and their parents.

857. Schatzman, Morton. **Soul Murder: Persecution in the Family**. New York: Random House, 1973. 193 pp.

Explores Dr. Schreber's methods of child rearing, which drove one son to suicide and another to madness. Schreber believed that a child should be completely submissive to his father and his strict childrearing practices reflected this. Schreber's influence on child care in Germany and other parts of the world is also discussed.

858. Schechter, Susan. "The Future of the Battered Women's Movement." **Fight Back!: Feminist Resistence to Male Violence**. Edited by Frederique Delacoste and Felice Newman. Minneapolis: Cleis Press, 1981, pp. 93–103.

Identifies two gaps in the Battered Women's Movement: no explicitly stated plan for the future of the movement, and no analysis of the external realities which may confront the movement. Discusses the strength of the movement and briefly analyzes the political and social climate in which it exists.

859. Scheurer, Susan L. and Margaret M. Bailey. "Guidelines for Placing a Child in Foster Care." **The Battered Child**. Edited by C. Henry Kempe and Ray E. Helfer. Chicago: University of Chicago Press, 1980, pp. 297–305.

Discusses involuntary placement of children in foster care, and the issue of it being temporary and not permanent removal of children from their homes. Also examines concerns about foster care and reviews one community's foster care cases in order to develop guidelines for foster care placement.

860. Schickling, Barbara H. "Relief for Victims of Intra-Family Assaults — The Pennsylvania Protection From Abuse Act." **Dickinson Law Review,** 84:815–22, Summer 1977.

The Pennsylvania Protection From Abuse Act is seen as an alternative to the problem of non-reporting of cases of abuse. This act provides access to a civil proceeding for immediate protection from abuse and makes available various forms of relief. The act is discussed in detail, including potential problems and the act's effectiveness.

861. Schmidt, Delores M. "The Challenge of Helping the 'Untreatables'." **Public Welfare,** 23(2):98–102, April 1965.

Discusses helping clients who seem to lack the motivation to improve. Uses a family to illustrate attempts to help, such as decreasing pressures, better housing, and improved education for the children.

862. Schmitt, Barton D. "The Child with Non-accidental Trauma." **The Battered Child.** Edited by C. Henry Kempe and Ray E. Helfer. Chicago: University of Chicago Press, 1980, pp. 128–46.

Explores the significance of the history of an injury for child abuse diagnoses. Discusses histories that either diagnose or suggest non-accidental trauma and discusses typical inflicted bruises, with the aid of photographs. Presents immediate actions to be taken by a physician with suspected abuse cases, and details the medical evaluation of children with physical abuse.

863. _____. "What Teachers Need to Know About Abuse and Nelgect." **Education Digest,** 41:19–21, March 1976.

Guidelines for the identification and reporting of child abuse and neglect by school personnel are outlined. Indicators of abuse and neglect are also presented.

864. Schneider, Carol and others. "Interviewing the Parents." **Helping the Battered Child and His Family.** Edited by C. Henry Kempe and Ray E. Helfer. Philadelphia: J.B. Lippincott Company, 1972, pp. 55–65.

Discusses the importance of an accurate assessment of the total situation in order to determine where therapy should be directed, how urgent the problem is, and what type of treatment is indicated. Also examines the significance of developing a rapport with the parents, and presents guidelines for doing so.

865. _____. "The Predictive Questionaire: A Preliminary Report." **Helping the Battered Child and His Family.** Philadelphia: J.B. Lippincott Company, 1972, pp. 271–82.

Examines problems with developing and administering an objective attitudes questionaire to distinguish between abusive and non-abusive parents.

866. _____. "Screening for the Potential to Abuse: A Review." **The**

Battered Child. Edited by C. Henry Kempe and Ray E. Helfer. Chicago: University of Chicago Press, 1980, pp. 420–430.

Discusses screening for the potential to abuse. Guidelines for screening, methods used, and problems confronted are also examined.

867. Schoenfield, Barbara T. and Gerry Hinkley. "It Happened to Me: The Police Said We Were Child Abusers." **Good Housekeeping**, 186:62–67, March 1978.

Relates a couple's experience of being falsely accused of child abuse.

868. Schuchter, Arnold. **Prescriptive Package: Child Abuse Intervention**. Washington, D.C.: U.S. Government Printing Office, 1976. 157 pp.

Describes a model system for child abuse intervention and discusses its development and operation. A framework and guide for child abuse decision-making, with flowcharts of the model system decision-making guide, are also presented.

869. Schultz, LeRoy G. "The Child as a Sex Victim: Socio-legal Perspectives." **Rape Victimology**. Edited by LeRoy G. Schultz. Springfield, Illinois: Charles C. Thomas, 1975, pp. 257–73.

Discusses the social and legal aspects of sexual assaults on children.

870. _____. **Rape Victimology**. Springfield, Illinois: Charles C. Thomas, 1975. 405 pp.

Examines the subject of rape, including sexual offenses against children.

871. Schuyler, Marcella. "Battered Wives: An Emerging Social Problem." **Social Work**, 21:488–91, November 1976.

Discusses the problem of the battered wife and society's failure to adequately deal with it. Suggestions are made to remedy this situation.

872. Scott, E.M. "Violence in America: Violent People and Violent Offenders." **International Journal of Offender Therapy**, 23(3): 197–209, 1979.

Presents a general discussion of violence in America, including the battered child. Also examines the rights of infants and violence in the home.

873. Scott, P.D. "Battered Wives." **British Journal of Psychiatry**, 125:433–41, November 1974.

Discusses the problem of wife battering. Areas explored include the incidence of wifebeating, the problem of definition of a battered wife, the cultural factors involved, the role of psychopathology, the aggressive personality, and the relationship between wife abuse and alcohol or drug abuse. Also examined is the possibility of a connection between wife battering and baby battering, and practical measures for dealing with the problem.

874. _____. "Fatal Battered Baby Cases." **Medicine, Science, and the Law**, 13(3):197–206, July 1973.

Presents a study of 29 cases in which a father had been charged with killing his child. Circumstances showed that the father had unrealistic interpretation of the child's activities, and viewed the child as a threat. In addition, most cases were surrounded by high environmental stress, had personality problems, and had experienced parental violence as children. Also discusses the characteristics of the parents, characteristics of the children, sentences passed on the fathers, and treatment considerations given.

875. _____. "Parents Who Kill Their Children." **Medicine, Science, and the Law**, 13(2):120–26, April 1973.

Discusses the incidence of filicide by parents in England and Wales. Examines a classification of the killers, with particular emphasis on the difficulties associated with the criteria of motive and depression. Suggests and applies a modified classification of parental filicide.

876. _____. "The Tragedy of Maria Colwell." **British Journal of Criminology**, 15:88–90, January 1975.

Examines the case of Maria Colwell, a child who was battered to death after being returned home by a social work agency. Suggestions are made for improved systems of identification for child abuse and potential abuse, and for the protection of children.

877. _____. "Victims of Violence." **Nursing Times**, 70:1036–37, July 4, 1974.

Reviews the motives behind infanticide committed by parents. Recommends awareness by nurses of the potential for violence between parent and child.

878. Scott, Peter. "Battering in Relation to Other Deviant Behavior." **The Challenge of Child Abuse**. Edited by Alfred White Franklin. London: Academic Press, 1977, pp. 38–45.

Discusses the causes of crime and delinquency, the relationship of crime to psychiatric illness, and the treatment of crime and delinquency. The possibility of child rearing as the essence of this problem is suggested.

879. _____. "The Psychiatrist's Viewpoint." **The Maltreatment of Children**. Edited by Selwyn M. Smith. Baltimore: University Park Press, 1978, pp. 175–203.

Presents the history of the battered child syndrome and discusses the degree of injury, provocation, and treatment.

880. Search, Gay. "London: Battered Wives." **MS.**, 2:24–26, June 1974.

Discusses wife beating in London using four cases of abuse as illustrations of the problem. The development of Women's Aid, a refuge for battered women, and the legal options available in Britain are also examined.

881. _____. "Scream Quietly." **MS.**, 5:96–97, August 1976.

Briefly discusses Great Britain's National Federation of Women's Aid, which operates over 50 refuges for battered women. Also discussed is the work of Erin Pizzey, founder of Chiswick Women's Aid, the pioneering group.

882. Sennet, Richard. "The Brutality of Modern Families." **Trans-action**, 7(11):29–37, 1970.

Examines the "guilt over conflict syndrome," which involves families who view a serious disruption in their lives as a moral failure. Concludes by stating that families which does not openly express anger have a higher rate of deep emotional disorders than do families which openly express their hostilities.

883. Sewell, Mabel. "Some Causes of Jealousy in Young Children." **Violence in the Family**. Edited by Suzanne K. Steinmetz and Murray A. Straus. New York: Harper and Row, 1974, pp. 82–84.

Discusses the potential for violence between siblings, emphasizing jealousy as a cause.

884. Sgroi, Suzanne M. "The Abused Child: The Physician's Obligations." **Connecticut Medicine**, 39:418, July 1975.

Examines the obligation of private physicians to report suspected cases of child abuse as is stated in Connecticut's mandatory reporting law.

885. _____. "Molestation of Children: The Last Frontier in Child Abuse." **Children Today**, May–June 1975, pp. 19–21 & 44.

Presents three case studies involving the molestation of children and discusses the incidence of the problem, ways to recognize sexual abuse, and problems involved in medical corroboration. Emphasizes that professionals must be aware of the existence of the problem, be able to recognize the danger signals, and be knowledgeable about reporting laws and sources of help.

886. Shah, D.K. and N. MacMillan. "Fatal Blunder." **Newsweek**, 93:96, March 5, 1983.

Discusses a case of child abuse in which one child died and the other was psychologically and physically damaged. The role of the welfare system in the case is highlighted.

887. Shainess, Natalie. "Psychological Aspects of Wifebattering." **Battered Women: A psychosociological Study of Domestic Violence**. Edited by Maria Roy. New York: Van Nostrand Reinhold Company, 1977, pp. 111–19.

Examines the historical background of social and psychological factors which effect violence between the sexes, the personality problems of the wife batterer and the battered, and what can be done about the problem of wife abuse.

888. Shanas, Bert. "Child Abuse: A Killer Teachers Can Help Control." **Phi Delta Kappan**, 56:479–82, March 1975.

Explores the role of teachers in the identification and management of child abuse.

889. Shay, Sharon Williams. "Community Council for Child Abuse Prevention." **The Battered Child**. Edited by C. Henry Kempe and Ray E. Helfer. Chicago: University of Chicago Press, 1980, pp. 330–46.

Summarizes basic principles for developing a community council, discusses potential problems and needed program components, and suggests models for coordinating service delivery.

890. Sheils, Merrill and others. "The Battered Children." **Newsweek**, 90:112–13, October 10, 1977.

Presents a general discussion of child abuse. Statistics concerning the nature and extent of the problem, the characteristics of abusive parents, and programs for treatment and prevention are among the areas explored.

891. Shorkey, Clayton. "A Review of Methods Used in the Treatment of Abusing Parents." **Social Casework**, 60:360–67, June 1979.

Reviews and compares methods of treatment for abusive parents. Treatment guidelines are also provided.

892. Silber, David L. and William E. Bell. "The Neurologist and the Physically Abused Child." **Neurology**, 21(10):991–97, October 1971.

The role of the neurologist in the identification and protection of abused children is discussed.

893. Silver, Larry B. and others. "Agency Action and Interaction in Cases of Child Abuse." **Social Casework**, 52(3):164–71, March 1971.

Discusses the difficulties in obtaining statistics on child abuse and examines the work of The Child Abuse Research Group of Children's Hospital of the District of Columbia. Concludes that this committee's work supports the concept that child abuse is reflective of family pathology, and that all victims of child abuse or neglect should be referred to protective services before they are released from medical care. Suggests that the only intervention successful for prevention is removal of the child by the court, although this is not considered to be the ideal solution. Recommends the collaboration and cooperation among services from all disciplines in working with child abuse cases.

894. _____. "Child Abuse Laws — Are They Enough?" **The Battered**

Child. Compiled by Jerome E. Leavitt. Morristown, New Jersey: General Learning Press, 1974, pp. 101–05.

Physicians in the Washington, D.C. area were questioned in order to assess their knowledge of the battered child syndrome, their awareness of available community resources, and their attitude toward reporting such cases under the protection of the new child abuse laws. Results suggest that methods of communication between medical and community organizations, and the physician, have not been completely effective in familiarizing the physician with the battered child syndrome or with the community procedures used for reporting suspected cases of child abuse. It is concluded that child abuse laws are not enough until the lines of communication are improved.

895. Silverman, Frederic N. "Radiologic and Special Diagnostic Procedures." **The Battered Child**. Edited by C. Henry Kempe and Ray E. Helfer. Chicago: University of Chicago Press, 1980, pp. 215–40.

Discusses contributions of diagnostic radiology to the concept of the battered child and presents functions of the radiologic examination. Concludes that radiographic signs of the battered child are very specific and serve to speak for a child who cannot speak for himself.

896. Sim, Myre. "Introduction: A Child Speaks." **The Maltreatment of Children**. Edited by Selwyn M. Smith. Baltimore: University Park Press, 1978, pp. 1–8.

Presents a view of child abuse from the victim's perspective, emphasizing the lack of a "sense of urgency" on the part of agencies involved in the management of the problem.

897. Simpson, D.W. "Non-Accidental Injury to Pre-school Children in New Zealand." **New Zealand Medical Journal**, 81:12–15, January 8, 1975.

Discusses problems of identification and treatment of child abuse in New Zealand. Suggestions for improvement in these areas are made.

898. Sims, B.G. and J.M. Cameron. "Bite Marks in the 'Battered Baby Syndrome'." **Medicine, Science, and the Law**, 13(3):207–210, July 1973.

States that since 1969, bite marks have figured significantly as a feature of the battered baby syndrome. Case reports and photographs of injuries are presented to illustrate this statement.

899. Sinofsky, Mildred Salins. "The Process of Separation." **Child Abuse: Intervention and Treatment**. Edited by Nancy B. Ebeling and Deborah A. Hill. Acton, Massachusetts: Publishing Sciences Group, 1975, pp. 109–15.

Discusses the affect of separation in childhood on the growth and development of a child, using case studies to illustrate various aspects of the separation process.

900. Smith, Clement A. "The Battered Child." **New England Journal of Medicine**, 289(6):322–23, August 9, 1973.

Presents a brief and general discussion of child abuse. Topics examined include reasons why parents abuse children, the incidence of child abuse, management of the problem, and prevention by intervention.

901. Smith, Jack L. "New York's Child Abuse Laws: Inadequacies in the Present Statutory Structure." **Cornell Law Review**, 55(2):298–305, January 1970.

Examines the statutory scheme of New York State's Child Abuse Laws and problems with the coexistence of specific articles of the family court act. Concludes by saying that many of the article 10's provisions might be valuable tools in protecting against child abuse, but until they are more effectively coordinated with those of article 3, article 10 is something less than a solution to the problem of child abuse.

902. Smith, Selwyn M. **The Battered Child Syndrome**. London: Butterworth and Company, Ltd., 1975. 292 pp.

Reviews medical, social, and legal literature on the battered child syndrome and discusses child abuse from a historical perspective. Issues examined include incidence, medical recognition of the problem, demographic characteristics of the children and their parents, treatment and management, court procedures involved in child abuse cases. A controlled study of 134 battered children and their parents, conducted in England, is discussed.

903. _____. **The Maltreatment of Children**. Baltimore: University Park Press, 1978. 452 pp.

Presents a comprehensive review of the subject from the perspectives of different fields such as law, social work, psychology, and pediatrics. A bibliography and index are included.

904. Smith, Selwyn and Ruth Hanson. "134 Battered Children: A Medical and Psychological Study." **British Medical Journal**, 3:666–70, September 14, 1974.

The results of this study show a higher risk of abuse in children under two years of age and in low birth weight children. Types of physical injuries, physical and psychological development of battered children, and the incidence of more than one victim in a family are among the topics examined.

905. Smith, Selwyn and others. "EEG and Personality Factors in Child Batterers." **Concerning Child Abuse: Papers Presented by the Tunbridge Wells Study Group on Non-Accidental Injury to Children**. Edited by Alfred White Franklin. Edinburgh: Churchill Livingstone, 1975, pp. 49–55.

Presents the results of a study which used EEGs to measure the personality factors of child batterers.

906. _____. "Parents of Battered Children: A Controlled Study." **Concerning Child Abuse: Papers Presented by the Tunbridge Wells**

Study Group on Non-Accidental Injury to Children. Edited by Alfred White Franklin. Edinburgh: Churchill Livingstone, 1975, pp. 41-55.

Discusses a study conducted by the authors which compare the age, social class, psychiatric state, criminality, and intelligence of parents of battered children and of parents in a control group.

907. _____. "Social Aspects of the Battered Baby Syndrome." **British Journal of Psychiatry**, 125:568-82, December 1974.

Discusses the familial and social characteristics of abusing families, concluding that increased social contact may help to relieve some of the stress that parents feel and thus reduce subsequent harm to their children.

908. Snedeker, Lendon. "Traumatization of Children." **New England Journal of Medicine**, 267(11):572, September 13, 1962.

Discusses one hospital's procedures for dealing with child abuse cases.

909. Snell, John E. and others. "The Wifebeater's Wife: A Study of Family Interaction." **Archives of General Psychiatry**, 11:107-12, August 1964.

Describes a family structure found to be common in violent homes. This structure is characterized by passivity, indecisiveness and sexual inadequacy on the part of the husband, and aggressiveness, frigidity and masochism on the part of the wife. Often an equilibrium is maintained within the family which is also vulnerable to specific types of stress. Recommends that additional study be done before definite conclusions can be drawn concerning the family structure in a violent home.

910. Solomon, Theo. "History and Demography of Child Abuse." **Pediatrics**, 51(4):773-76, April 1973.

Focuses on the social aspects of infanticide, stating that it has been practiced in various forms by almost every civilization throughout history. Rationales for infanticide are presented and current dimensions of the problem, and related issues, are discussed.

911. Spinetta, John J. and David Rigler. "The Child Abusing Parent: A Psychological Review." **Child Abuse: Perspectives on Diagnosis, Treatment and Prevention**. Edited by Roberta Kalmar. Dubuque, Iowa: Kendall/Hunt Publishing Company, 1977, pp. 49-62.

Reviews literature concerning parental attitudes toward child rearing in order to identify common psychological traits of abusing parents. An extensive bibliography is also included.

912. Spitzner, J.H. and D.H. McGee. "Family Crisis Intervention Training, Diversion, and the Prevention of Crimes of Violence." **Police Chief**, 42(10):252-53, October 1975.

Describes a training program for police officers dealing with family violence in Columbus, Ohio.

913. Sprey, Jetse. "The Family as a System of Conflict." **Journal of Marriage and the Family**, 31(4):699–706, 1969.

Explores the family within a consensus equilibrium framework and finds it to be inadequate. Suggests that it be reviewed as a system in conflict in order to develop a more fruitful theoretical approach to studying the family. Also attempts to clarify the analytical relationships between certain concepts within the theoretical structure of the family unit.

914. _____. "On the Management of Conflict in Families." **Journal of Marriage and the Family**, 33(4):722–30, 1971.

Presents a conflict approach to the family which views harmony within the family as problematical rather than normal. Family interaction is seen as a continual confrontation in which members have conflicting, but not necessarily opposing, views of their situations.

915. Stahly, G.B. "A Review of Select Literature of Spousal Violence." **Victimology: An International Journal**, 2:591–607, 1977–78.

Literature on marital violence is reviewed, examining social theories of violence, social-structural factors, systems analysis of family violence, descriptive and empirical studies, and in-depth interviews

916. Star, Barbara. "Comparing Battered and Non-Battered Women." **Victimology: An International Journal**, 3:32–44, 1978.

Discusses a study which compares certain psychosocial aspects of both battered and non-battered women who had sought help at a shelter in Los Angeles. Reasons why women endure abuse, the effects of education, religion, and family background on the subjects, and the need for services for abusers and the abused are among the topics explored.

917. Starbuck, George W. "The Recognition and Early Management of Child Abuse." **Pediatric Annals**, 5:27–41, March 1976.

The identification and management of child abuse cases depends to a large degree on the examining physician's knowledge of the indicators and treatment methods for such cases.

918. Stark, Evan and others. "Medicine and Patriarchal Violence: The Social Construction of a 'Private' Event." **International Journal of Health Sciences**, volume 9, number 3, 1969.

States that the medical response received by battered women contributes to the battering syndrome, and discusses a study which explored this idea.

919. Stark, Rodney and James McEvoy III. "Middle Class Violence." **Psychology Today**, 4(6):107–12, November 1970.

Examines aggression between people, and types of violence which are condoned by society. Also explores the question of using physical force to discipline children.

920. Starkweather, Cassie L. and S. Michael Turner. "Parents Anonymous: Reflections on the Development of a Self-Help Group." **Child Abuse: Intervention and Treatment**. Edited by Nancy B. Ebeling and Deborah A. Hill. Acton, Massachusetts: Publishing Sciences Group, 1975, pp. 151-57.

Discusses the development of Parents Anonymous in Boston and presents some thoughts which may be of assistance to others interested in starting similar groups.

921. Steele, Brandt F. "Child Abuse: Its Impact on Society." **Journal of the Indiana State Medical Association**, 68:191-94, March 1975.

Examines the effects of child abuse on society in general and on various social institutions.

922. _____. "Parental Abuse of Infants and Small Children." **Parenthood: Its Psychology and Psychopathology**. Edited by E. Anthony James and Therese Benedek. Boston: Little, Brown and Company, 1970, pp. 449-77.

Presents a discussion of child abuse which focuses on the abusing parent. Outlines the general pattern of child rearing by an abusive parent, including the parent's attitude that children exist in order to satisfy parental needs, and when they do not, they must be physically punished. Cultural factors, psychological aspects, the role of inadequate mothering in abusive behavior, and treatment of abusing parents are among the issues examined.

923. _____. "A Psychiatrist's View of Working With Abusive Parents." **Child Abuse: Perspectives on Diagnosis, Treatment and Prevention**. Edited by Roberta Kalmar. Dubuque, Iowa: Kendall/Hunt Publishing Company, 1977, pp. 137-43.

Discusses child abuse and the role of psychiatric consultation in treatment, characteristics and problems of abusive parents, psychological characteristics of abusing parents, and treatment methods for effective therapy.

924. _____. "Psychodynamic Factors in Child Abuse." **The Battered Child**. Chicago: University of Chicago Press, 1980, pp. 49-85.

Defines child abuse as an "extremely complex group of human behaviors characterized by maladaptive interactions between children and their caretakers," and discusses the problem with the use of case studies. Topics explored include common characteristics of abusive behavior, circumstances necessary for abuse to occur, role of children in abuse and neglect, and atypical abuse and infanticide. Concludes by stating that during the early part of the child's life, patterns are transmitted from parents to child, giving the potential for abuse to the next generation.

925. Steinmetz, Suzanne K. "The Battered Husband Syndrome." **Victimology: An International Journal**, 2:499–509, 1977–78.

Discusses the phenomenon of husband battering by referring to data from various sources. Examines the reasons why men don't report the offense and why they remain in abusive situations. Concludes by recommending that a more comprehensive approach to the problem of family violence be taken.

926. _____. **The Cycle of Violence: Assertive, Aggressive, and Abusive Family Interaction**. New York: Praeger Publishers, 1977. 191 pp.

Presents a general examination of family violence which includes myths concerning the problem, relationship between family violence and societal violence, acceptable and unacceptable levels of aggression, sources of conflict within the family, methods for resolving violence in the family, and the cycle of violence from family to the society. Also discusses a study conducted by the author which sought to obtain an accurate view of family interaction in order to resolve conflicts within the family. The study utilized conflict, resource, and social learning theories and traced patterns of conflict resolution found in 57 families. Findings indicated that each family followed a consistent pattern for resolving conflict, and that all of these patterns were passed from one generation to the next.

927. _____. "Occupation and Physical Punishment: A Response to Straus." **Journal of Marriage and the Family**, 33:664–66, November 1971.

Studies social class differences in parental use of physical punishment. Suggests that important relationships between occupational groups and socialization practices are often obscured when social class is used as an independent variable in socialization research, and that certain occupationally induced behaviors are only indirectly indexed by class.

928. _____. "Occupational Environment in Relation to Physical Punishment and Dogmatism." **Violence in the Family**. Edited by Suzanne K. Steinmetz and Murray A. Straus. New York: Harper and Row, 1974, pp. 166–72.

Examines the differences between occupational groups in the use of physical punishment to discipline children.

929. _____. "The Use of Force for Resolving Family Conflict: The Training Ground for Abuse." **The Family Coordinator**, 26:19–26, January 1977.

Discusses work conducted by the author and others concerning the use of force for resolving family disputes. This examination is based on the premise that normal families are not completely violence-free, and every family has the potential for resolving conflict with violence. In addition, violence as a problem solving device is learned within the family and reflects prevailing social attitudes toward the use of force in interaction.

930. _____. "Wifebeating, Husbandbeating — A Comparison of the Use of Physical Violence Between Spouses to Resolve Marital Fights." **Battered Women: A Psychosociological Study of Domestic Violence**. Edited by Maria Roy. New York: Van Nostrand Reinhold Company, 1977, 63-72.

Reports on a study which investigated family methods of conflict resolution. Possibilities for reducing spouse abuse based on this data are suggested.

931. Steinmetz, Suzanne K. and Murray A. Straus. "The Family as a Cradle of Violence." **Society**, 10(6):50-56, September-October 1973.

States that some form of violence occurs in almost every family, be it murder or corporal punishment. Discusses findings from a survey conducted by the National Commission on the Causes and Prevention of Violence, including statistics on the incidence of intrafamily violence, types of violence, demographic factors, and characteristics of abusers and victims.

932. _____. **Violence in the Family**. New York: Harper and Row, 1974.

Discusses violence between spouses and kin, violent parents, and the family as a training ground for violence within society. Each section is preceded by an introduction and author and subject indexes are included. An overall view of theoretical work in the field of family violence is also presented.

933. Stephens, Darrel W. "Domestic Assault: The Police Response." **Battered Women: A Psychosociological Study of Domestic Violence**. Edited by Maria Roy. New York: Van Nostrand Reinhold Company, 1977, pp. 164-72.

Discusses the traditional police response to domestic disturbances and presents an improved alternative response which emphasizes problem identification and crisis intervention.

934. Stephenson, P. and Nerissa Lo. "When Shall We Tell Kevin? A Battered Child Revisited." **Child Welfare**, 53:576-81, November 1974.

Examines the case of a battered child who had been taken from his parents and placed in a foster home. Problems faced by professionals in deciding when to tell an abused foster child why he had been taken from his parents are also explored.

935. Straus, Murray A. "A General Systems Theory of Violence Between Family Members." **Social Science Information**, 12(3):105-25, June 1973.

Make use of general systems theory to formulate a theory accounting for the presence of violence as a continuing element in the social interaction of the nuclear family. This theory views continuing violence as a systemic product rather than a product of individual behavior pathology. Also explores a propositional theory of family violence.

936. Straus, Murray A. "Leveling, Civility, and Violence in the Family." **Journal of Marriage and the Family**, 36:13–29, February 1974.

Demonstrates that the greater the amount of verbal aggression, the greater the amount of physical aggression. Also discusses therapy for marital violence.

937. _____. "Sexual Inequality, Cultural Norms, and Wife-Beating." **Victimology: An International Journal**, 1:54–70, Spring 1976.

Discusses the problem of wife beating in contemporary society by examining the social structure, the cultural norms of the society, legal issues involved in domestic disputes, the structure of the family, and the sexual and economic inequality of the sexes.

938. _____. "A Sociological Perspective on the Prevention and Treatment of Wifebeating." **Battered Women: A Psychosociological Study of Domestic Violence**. Edited by Maria Roy. New York: Van Nostrand Reinhold Company, 1977, pp. 194–239.

States that ideas about the causes of wifebeating influence the steps taken to prevent it. Explores the causes of wifebeating, cultural norms which permit wife abuse, conflict within the family, economic factors which may contribute to wife battering, and methods which exist to aid the violent family and to prevent battering.

939. _____. Some Social Antecedents of Physical Punishment: A Linkage Theory Interpretation." **Violence in the Family**. Edited by Suzanne K. Steinmetz and Murray A. Straus. New York: Harper and Row, 1974, pp. 159–66.

Discusses the way in which the use of violence in the family is influenced by the position of the family in the larger social system, particularly the economic and occupational structures.

940. _____. "Stress and Child Abuse." **The Battered Child**. Edited by C. Henry Kempe and Ray E. Helfer. Chicago: University of Chicago Press, 1980, pp. 86–103.

Examines the link between stress and violence. Defines areas of family stress, and states that a major cause of the rate of child abuse is the stress and conflict which tends to characterize families. Factors linking stress and child abuse are also discussed.

941. _____. "Wife Beating: How Common and Why?" **Victimology: An International Journal**, 2:443–58, 1977–78.

Discusses the results of a nationwide study of couples selected as being representative of all couples in the U.S. Causes of spousal abuse, the inter-relationship among various factors related to spouse abuse, and the extent of spouse battering are discussed. A "Severe Violence Index" and a "Wife Beating Index," which were constructed to aid in the study, are also presented.

942. Straus, Murray and others. **Behind Closed Doors: Violence in the American Family**. Garden City, New York: Anchor Press/Doubleday, 1980. 301 pp.

Focuses on a study conducted by the authors which examined family violence. Issues discussed include marriage as a license to batter, violence between siblings, social patterns and causes in family violence, and ways of reducing the violence. An index and bibliography are included.

943. Streshinsky, Shirley. "Help Me Before I Hurt My Child!" **Redbook**, 143:85+, June 1974.

Discusses the formation and operation of CALM (Child Abuse Listening Mediation), which was designed to prevent parents from abusing their children.

944. Stringer, Elizabeth A. "Homemaker Services in Neglect and Abuse: A Tool for Case Evaluation." **The Battered Child**. Compiled by Jerome E. Leavitt. Morristown, New Jersey: General Learning Press, 1974, pp. 157-60.

Explores the significance of the homemaker's role in enabling agencies to obtain a clear picture of family situations and presents case studies to illustrate the service of the homemaker.

945. Stroud, John. "The Social Worker's Role." **Concerning Child Abuse: Papers Presented by the Tunbridge Wells Study Group on Non-Accidental Injury in Children**. Edited by Alfred White Franklin. Edinburgh: Churchill Livingstone, 1975, pp. 95-105.

Describes the role of the local authority social worker in cases where injury to a child is believed to be non-accidental.

946. Strucker, Jan. "I Tried to Fantasize That All Fathers Had Intercourse With Their Daughters." **MS.**, 5:66-67+, April 1977.

Discusses one woman's experience as a child sexual abuse victim, how it affected her teen-aged years, and the successful program of therapy which resulted in her leading a productive life.

947. Stuart, Donald. "Mandatory Reporting of Child Abuse in Nebraska." **Creighton Law Review**, 8:791-802, June 1975.

Explores Nebraska's two mandatory and independent reporting laws that deal specifically with child abuse. Also examines another system being considered by the legislature which would eliminate the present dual system and expand the law to benefit the child's welfare.

948. Sullivan, Michael F. "Child Neglect: The Environmental Aspects." **Ohio State Law Journal**, 29(1):85–115, Winter 1968.

Criticizes the statutes pertaining to child neglect by saying that these laws are vague and allow the courts to impose differential ideas of child care and morality on parents. Suggests an alternative approach which centers on the causal relationship between a parent's behavior toward a child and subsequent harm to that child, and takes into consideration the rights of the parent.

949. Summit, Roland and JoAnn Kryso. "Sexual Abuse of Children: A Clinical Spectrum." **American Journal of Orthopsychiatry**, 48:237–51, April 1978.

Suggests that incest has been underestimated as a significant determinant of emotional disturbance, and that misuse of sexuality between parents and children can have detrimental consequences which parallel those resulting from other forms of child abuse. The spectrum of parent-child sexuality is classified into ten categories as a guide to the diagnosis, management, and prognosis of sexually abusive behavior.

950. Sussman, A. "Reporting Child Abuse: A Review of the Literature." **Family Law Quarterly**, 8:245–313, Fall 1974.

Presents a brief historical perspective, through literature, on the medical and social recognition of the problem of child abuse, and discusses early legal proposals made to encourage reporting. Also explores the literature related to reporting, statutes, and agencies that deal with child abuse cases.

951. Sussman, Alan and Stephan J. Cohen. **Reporting Child Abuse and Neglect: Guidelines for Legislation**. Cambridge, Massachusetts: Ballinger, 1975. 255 pp.

Presents a draft of a revised version of the model Child Abuse Reporting Act of the Department of Health, Education, and Welfare. Reports of additional studies and commentary of the act are also presented, and national and state reporting laws are examined. A bibliography is also included.

952. Sutton, Jo. "The Growth of the British Movement for Battered Women." **Victimology: An International Journal**, 2:576–84, 1977–78.

Examines the movement for battered women in Britain, the problems encountered by the movement in its work with battered women, and the role of the refuge as a short-term and a long-term solution to the problem.

953. Swanson, David M. "Adult Sexual Abuse of Children." **Diseases of the Nervous System**, 29:677–83, October 1968.

Discusses the problem of adult sexual abuse of children, suggesting that this type of offense occurs among persons of varying personality and cultural backgrounds. Examines a study which reviewed 25 cases of the offense and describes several types of personality disorganization which were present in offenders.

954. Swanson, Lynn D. "Role of the Police in the Protection of Children From Neglect and Abuse." **The Battered Child**. Compiled by Jerome E. Leavitt. Morristown, New Jersey: General Learning Press, 1974, pp. 112–16.

States that no agreement has been reached by either police or community agencies as to the appropriate role of the police, nor has there been effective coordination of police activities with activities of other agencies. Discusses the traditional role of the police, the police role in complaints, verifying complaints, evaluating and disposing of a case, and referral to community agencies or the court system.

955. Swartz, Herbert. "Battered Wives Battle Back." **US**, 5(25):61–64. December 8, 1981.
Examines the question of whether a battered wife has the right to kill her abusing husband by focusing on the case of Priscilla Szelog, a woman accused of murdering the husband who frequently physically abused her.

956. "Synopsis: Standards Relating to Abuse and Neglect." **Boston University Law Review**, 57:663–69, July 1977.

Presents a synopsis of the Standards for Abuse and Neglect as proposed by the Institute of Judicial Administration and the American Bar Association, Joint Commission on Juvenile Justice Standards.

957. "Team Held Best Hope in Child Abuse Intervention." **Pediatric News**, 9:76, March 1975.

Explores the use of hospital-based teams of professionals in treating cases of child abuse. The child abuse team is viewed as an effective tool in the identification, treatment and prevention of child abuse.

958. Ten Bensel, Robert W. "The Neglect and Abuse of Children: The Physician's Perspective." **Creighton Law Review**, 8:757–70, June 1975.

Defines the spectrum of child abuse in current society and the factors which interact to produce it. Various types of maltreatment are discussed and the physician's role in the identification, reporting, and follow-up of child abuse cases is examined.

959. Ten Bensel, Robert W. and Kurt J. King. "Neglect and Abuse in Children: Historical Aspects, Identification, and Management." **Journal of Dentistry for Children**, 42:348–58, September–October 1975.

Emphasizes the role of the dentist in the identification of child abuse and neglect. The historical aspects of child abuse, characteristics of abusing parents, types of physical abuse, and the incidence of child abuse in modern society are also discussed.

960. Ten Broeck, Elsa. "The Extended Family Center: 'A Home Away From Home' for Abused Children and Their Parents." **Children Today**, 3:2–6, March–April 1974.

Describes the purpose and operations of The Extended Family Center, a treatment facility for abused children and their parents. The focal point of the Center is the day care program, which eases tension that continual care of children may create for the parent. A supportive atmosphere rather than formal therapy is found to be more effective in the treatment of parents.

961. "Termination of Parental Rights — Suggested Reforms and Responses." **Journal of Family Law**, 16:239–64, 1977–78.

Discusses the present system of parental rights, the basis for state interference, and the rights of the child. Examines the responses of the courts using excerpts from applicable cases, and suggests reforms of the laws.

962. Terr, Lenore C. "A Family Study of Child Abuse." **Child Abuse: Perspectives on Diagnosis, Treatment and Prevention**. Edited by Roberta Kalmar. Dubuque, Iowa: Kendall/Hunt Publishing Company, 1977, pp. 77–87.

Examines ten cases of suspected child abuse in order to clarify the mechanisms involved in these cases. Suggestions for working with child abuse cases are also presented.

963. Thomas, Mason P., Jr. "Child Abuse and Neglect: Historical Overview, Legal Matrix, and Social Perspectives." **North Carolina Law Review**, 50(2):293–349, February 1972.

Presents a historical discussion of child abuse, including the reform movement in the U.S., founding of the New York Society for the Prevention of Cruelty to Children, the child abuse reporting movement, and the development of the state's right to intervene in child abuse cases for the good of the child. Concludes by describing the importance of the state legislatures' response to the problem, and the necessity for this to be coupled with effective protective services.

964. Thompson, Louise. "Wife Beating: What Happens When You Tell the Judge." **Majority Report**, 6:3, April 16–29, 1977.

Relates the experiences of two battered women who decided to take their cases to court.

965. Thorman, G. **Family Violence**. Springfield, Illinois: Charles C. Thomas, 1980. 190 pp.

Provides basic information on family violence, including theories of the causes of family violence, models for treatment, prevention, and sociocultural background information. Considers characteristics of victims and aggressors, and relationships between husband and wife, and the role of the family system in family violence. Concludes with a discussion which focuses on prevention, legislative reform, the development of more effective services, and advocacy for the abused child and the battered adult.

966. Thurber, Steven. "Child Abuse and the Excessive Control of Aggression." **Psychological Reports**, 44(3):994, June 1979.

Examines a possible causal link between over-controlled hostility and child abuse, and suggests a counter-intuitive approach to therapeutic intervention.

967. Tibbits, Jill. "Punishment, Retribution, and Rehabilitation." **The Challenge of Child Abuse**. Edited by Alfred White Franklin. London: Academic Press, 1977, pp. 183-91.

Discusses punishment, retribution, and rehabilitation of child abusers from the perspective of the author's own experience in the area of probation.

968. Tidmarsh, Mannes. "Violence in Marriage: The Relevance of Structural Factors." **Social Work Today**, 7(2):36-38, April 15, 1976.

Examines evidence available on marital violence in an attempt to isolate the causes of battering. Focuses on the factors within the family and the social structure which appear to have a bearing on the occurrence of family violence.

969. Till, Kenneth. "A Neurosurgeon's Viewpoint." **Concerning Child Abuse: Papers Presented by the Tunbridge Wells Study Group on Non-Accidental Injury to Children**. Edited by Alfred White Franklin. Edinburgh: Churchill Livingstone, 1975, pp. 56-62.

Discusses the neurosurgeon's role in cases of child abuse and makes recommendations for improvements in the management of problems associated with it.

970. Toby, Jackson. "Violence and the Masculine Ideal: Some Qualitative Data." **Annals of the American Academy of Political and Social Sciences**, 364:20-27, March 1966.

Attempts to explain why violence remains a central part of the masculine ideal in modern society, and is often an exaggerated way males use for distinguishing them from females when sex roles are not easily defined.

971. Tocchio, O.J. "Procedural Problems Inhibiting Effective County and Community-Wide Resolution of Battered Child Problems." **Police**, 14:16-21, 1970.

Examines legal and functional procedures presently being utilized in Fresno County, California for control and resolution of the battered child syndrome. Problems confronting the probation department, the juvenile court, police agencies, the welfare department, and the local hospital are described. Two tables are presented, one which illustrates the present approach to punitive and protective action in child abuse cases, and the other a preferred approach to protective action.

972. Tomes, N. "Torrent of Abuse — Crimes of Violence Between Working Class Men and Women in London, 1840-1875." **Journal of Social History**, 11:328-45, Spring 1978.

Discusses crimes of violence between working class men and women in nineteenth century London, and what these crimes reveal about their personal relationships. Also explores the responses of wives to beatings by their husbands and the economic situation of women during this time. The decline of violence against women is examined in relation to the changes in women's roles that were occurring around the turn of the century.

973. Tomlinson, Tom. "Interagency Collaboration: Issues and Problems." **Violence in the Family**. Edited by Marie Borland. Atlantic Highlands, New Jersey: Humanities Press, 1976, pp. 136-45.

Discusses the purposes of collaboration between agencies when dealing with family violence and emphasizes the significance of exchange and coordination in this process.

974. Tooley, Kay M. "The Young Child as Victim of Sibling Attack." **Social Casework**, 58:25-28, January 1977.

Presents a case study of a child who was the victim of sibling abuse, including treatment processes used for the child. Discusses the impact of sibling abuse on the victim and the reluctance of the parents to report the incident.

975. Torigian, John. "*Sims v. the State of Public Welfare*: Constitutional Limitations on Child Abuse Legislation." **South Texas Law Journal**, 19:491-500, 1978.

Provides a summary and analysis of the case of *Sims v. the State Department of Public Welfare*, which dealt with the removal of a suspected child abuse victim from his parents.

976. Tracy, James and Elizabeth H. Clark. "Treatment for Child Abusers." **Social Work**, 19:338-42, May 1974.

Describes a program for the treatment of abusing parents which employs the techniques of behavioral modification.

977. Tracy, James J. and others. "Child Abuse Project: A Follow-up." **Social Work**, 20:398-99, September 1975.

Discusses a follow-up program designed to identify the causes of child abuse and to provide treatment for the parents using the techniques of behavioral modification.

978. Tripp, Norman D. "Acting *In Loco Parentis* As a Defense to Assault and Battery." **Cleveland-Marshall Law Review**, 16(1):39–49, January 1967.

Examines conditions which warrant persons to be placed *In Loco Parentis*, and details the *In Loco Parentis* rule. Concludes that the idea of correction must not be confused with the constant abuse of a child. A rule that finds criminal liability only applied to cases which show permanent injuries may cause confusion. A person acting *In Loco Parentis* should not make the final decision as to what is and what is not excessive behavior. The child's welfare should be of primary concern and a conviction for assault should not be dependent upon whether a child is permanently injured.

979. Truninger, Elizabeth. "Marital Violence: The Legal Solutions." **The Hastings Law Journal**, 23(1):259–76, November 1971.

Examines the laws and procedures available for dealing with marital violence. States that the spectrum of applicable regulations extends from criminal statutes such as assault and battery to quasi-criminal procedures such as the peace bond, to civil procedures such as tort actions. The effectiveness of these laws is evaluated in terms of their possible applications as well as their actual applications. Concludes by saying that in addition to providing emergency methods to deal with marital violence, society must emphasize that marital violence will not be tolerated. Such violence has been functional because it helps to preserve a life style in which husbands play the dominant role in the relationship. Society must question this, create alternative lifestyles, and make single parent households viable institutions in the event that a marriage fails.

980. Uccella, Michaele and Melanie Kaye. "Survival Is an Act of Resistance." **Fight Back!: Feminist Resistance to Male Violence**. Edited by Frederique Delacoste and Felice Newman. Minneapolis: Cleis Press, 1981, pp. 14–25.

Summarizes letters from women who had been victims of abuse within the family structure, focusing on resistance to violence.

981. "Unforgettable Letters From Battered Wives." **MS.**, 5:97–100, December 1976.

Presents letters from battered wives which describe their experiences.

982. U.S. Commission on Civil Rights. Colorado Advisory Committee. **The Silent Victims: Denver's Battered Women**. Washington, D.C.: U.S. Government Printing Office, 1977. 22 pp.

Reviews literature on battered wives and discusses the victims of battering, incidence of assault on women, law enforcement and prosecution, alternatives to criminal action, Colorado domestic violence laws, and the incidence of domestic violence calls and arrests in Denver.

983. _____. Connecticut Advisory Committee. **Battered Women in Hartford, Connecticut**. Washington, D.C.: U.S. Government Printing Office, 1979.

Discusses wifebeating, emphasizing the incidence of the problem in Hartford. Topics examined include causes, response of the criminal justice system, and support systems such as hospitals and shelters. A table describing the disposition of cases in Hartford is also presented.

984. U.S. Commission on Civil Rights. **Under the Rule of Thumb: Battered Women and the Administration of Justice**. Washington, D.C.: U.S. Government Printing Office, 1982. 100 pp.

Describes the response of the legal system to battered women and helping programs, such as shelters, designed to aid the victims.

985. U.S. Department of Health, Education and Welfare. **Child Abuse/Neglect: A Guide for Detection, Prevention, and Treatment in BCHS Programs and Projects**.Washington, D.C.: U.S. Government Printing Office, 1977. 26 pp.

Presents a guide for professionals working in BCHS supported facilities. The purpose of the guide is to assist programs in developing more effective systems for the identification and management of child abuse and neglect. Summarizes general information concerning child abuse and discusses identification and reporting, methods of management for the problem, and possible activities for programs to initiate. A brief summary of resource material is offered.

986. _____. Office of Human Development/Child Development, Children's Bureau. Center on Child Abuse and Neglect. **Child Abuse and Neglect: The Problem and Its Management**. Washington, D.C.: U.S. Government Printing Office, 1976. 3 volumes.

Volume one presents an overview of the problem and examines factors which make child abuse and neglect a difficult problem to manage and identify. Also discusses the characteristics of parents and victims, and state reporting laws. Volume two describes the role of various professionals and agencies in the management of the problem. Volume three discusses community coordination for managing and preventing child abuse and neglect. Various resources for the identification and diagnosis of the problem are examined within the context of the "community-team approach." Suggestions for developing a coordinated community program are also presented.

987. U.S. Department of Justice. Bureau of Justice Statistics. **Intimate**

Victims: A Study of Violence Among Friends and Relatives. Washington, D.C.: U.S. Government Printing Office, January 1980. 52 pp.

Describes characteristics and identifying patterns of intimate attacks using data from the National Crime Survey. Violent crimes involving intimates were contrasted with those involving strangers or near-strangers from 1973–1976. Typical settings of attacks, the use of a weapon, employment of threats vs. actual attacks, alcohol abuse as a contributing factor, and children as catalysts to violent interactions.

988. United States Senate Committee on Human Resources. Child and Human Development. **Domestic Violence, 1978**. Washington, D.C.: U.S. Government Printing Office, 1978. 708 pp.

Reports on the hearings of this committee and includes statements and discussions by witnesses and representatives of groups such as the American Bar Association. Also reprints articles and other publications on the subject.

989. Van Dyke, Vicki. **Understanding Child Abuse**. Springfield, Illinois: Illinois State Department of Children and Family Services, 1977. 6 pp.

Briefly discusses child abuse, including the possible causes of the problem, the treatment of the abuser and the child, characteristics of the abused child, and innovative programs aimed at prevention. A bibliography is included.

990. Van Stolk, Mary. "Beaten Women, Battered Children." **Children Today**, 5(2):8–12, March–April 1976.

Compares child abuse and wife abuse. Similarities discussed include the presence of alcohol in both child and wife battering, both problems cutting across cultural and socioeconomic lines, and reliable data being difficult to obtain due to the underreporting of both crimes.

991. "Who Owns This Child?" **Childhood Education**, 50:258–65, March 1974.

Examines the perpetuation of child abuse in America as being legitimized by various historical, social, and cultural factors centering around parental rights over children.

992. Vandenbraak, S. "Limits on the Use of Defensive Force to Prevent Intramarital Assaults." **Rutgers Camden Law Journal**, 10:643–60, Spring 1979.

Discusses the limits on the use of defensive force in the prevention of intramarital assaults and the proposed self-defense standard for such cases. Suggests that a flexible necessity standard would aid spouses and juries in evaluating the reasonableness of the use of defensive force in family assault cases.

993. Varma, Margaret. "Battered Women; Battered Children." **Battered**

Women: A Psychosociological Study of Domestic Violence. Edited by Maria Roy. New York: Van Nostrand Reinhold Company, 1977, 263–77.

States that an abused wife will often express the anger she feels by turning her rage on her child. Discusses child abuse generally, presenting indicators that can be used by teachers, counselors, and nurses for identifying abuse. Ways to help parents cope with interactions between the self and a spouse or child are also examined.

994. Vasta, Ross and Phillip Copitch. "Simulating Conditions of Child Abuse in the Laboratory." **Child Development**, 52(1):164–70, March 1981.

Discusses a study which simulated a child abuse situation and examines the findings within the context of a social interactional model of child abuse.

995. Velcoff, Andrew. "Child Abuse and the Law in Massachusetts: In Search of a Proper Defendant." **New England Law Review**, 13:802–34, Spring 1978.

Child abuse and the law is explored, emphasizing the law as it is applied in Massachusetts. It is concluded that a shift in liability has occurred from the actual offender to others who deal with child abuse, as a result of the enactment of the Massachusetts law.

996. Viano, Emilio C., editor. "Spouse Abuse." **Victimology: An International Journal**, 2(3–4): 416–689, 1977–78.

Presents a collection of articles discussing various aspects of domestic violence. Book reviews, research notes, and interviews with battered women are also included.

997. Victor, Jill Blumberg. "He Beat Me: Battered Wife Tells Why She Took It For Seven Years." **Vogue**, 168:177 + , January 1978.

One woman relates her experience as a battered wife and discusses her reasons for staying in her violent home. Advice for battered women who plan to seek help is also presented.

998. "Violence to Children." **Lancet**, 1:1374, June 25, 1977.

Reviews a report from the British Select Committee on Violence in the Family which offers suggestions for the reduction of cases of battered and abused children.

999. "Violent American Home." **Science News**, 111:158, march 5, 1977.

Briefly discusses a study conducted by Richard Gelles which was later published as "Violence in the American Family."

1000. "Violent Families." **Time**, 114:55, July 9, 1979.

Discusses the incidence and types of family violence, socioeconomic factors frequently present, and ways to reduce the violence.

1001. Wald, Michael S. "State Intervention on Behalf of 'Neglected' Children: Standards for Removal of Children From Their Homes, Monitoring the Status of Children in Foster Care, and Termination of Parental Rights." **Stanford Law Review**, 28:623–706, April 1976.

Describes the existing system for state intervention and presents a proposed system which is based on intervention on behalf of the neglected child.

1002. Walker, Lenore E. **The Battered Woman**. New York: Harper and Row Publishers, 1979. 270 pp.

This comprehensive review of wife battering explores the psychology of the battered woman, ways in which men coerce women in battering relationships, and methods available to women who consider leaving their violent homes. Myths concerning the battered woman, the psychosocial theory of learned helplessness as applied to battered women, the theory of the existence of a cycle of domestic violence, sexual abuse and physical abuse, and treatment methods for victims of domestic violence are among the areas examined.

1003. _____. "The Battered Woman: What Can She Do?" **New Woman**, pp. 99–108, May–June 1979.

Examines the response of the police to incidence of wife battering and suggests ways in which the police can be more responsible in meeting the needs of the battered woman and her family. Alternatives available to the victim, including methods of treatment, are discussed.

1004. _____. "Battered Women and Learned Helplessness." **Victimology: An International Journal**, 2:525–34, 1977–78.

Discusses the psychological reasons why a battered woman becomes a victim and how this keeps her in a violent marriage. Recommendations are made for treatment of the battered wife.

1005. _____. "How Battering Happens and How to Stop It." **Battered Women**. Edited by Donna Moore. Beverly Hills, California: Sage Publications, Inc., 1979, pp. 59–78.

States that spouse abuse has been considered an acceptable resolution to marital disagreements as long as the violence remains within the home. Discusses battered women and their batterers, and presents a detailed description of the cycle of battering which emphasizes psychological aspects of the problem.

1006. _____. "The Wife-Beater: What Is He Like?" **New Woman**, pp. 99–100, May–June 1979.

Discusses the characteristics of husbands who beat their wives.

1007. _____. "Treatment Alternatives for Battered Women."

The Victimization of Women. Edited by Jane Roberts Chapman and Margaret Gates. Beverly Hills, California: Sage Publications, Inc., 1978, pp. 143–74.

Discusses the problem of battered women, emphasizing the cycle theory of battering incidents. Specific treatment alternatives are also examined.

1008. Walsh, Kathleen T. "Pennsylvania Child Protective Services Law." **Dickinson Law Review**, 81:823–36, 1977.

Explores the substance of the Pennsylvania Child Protective Services Law and potential problems associated with it, including questions concerning its constitutionality.

1009. Walters, David R. **Physical and Sexual Abuse of Children: Causes and Treatment**. Bloomington, Indiana: Indiana University Press, 1975. 192 pp.

The causes of child abuse are viewed as learned patterns of behavior derived from the culture in which the families live. The problems involved in defining child abuse, characteristics of abusive parents, treatment orientations, and suggestions for change are among the topics discussed. Distinctions between the causes and treatment of sexual abuse and of child abuse are emphasized.

1010. Warrior, Betsy. **Working on Wife Abuse**. Cambridge, Massachusetts: Betsy Warrior, 1978. 118 pp.

Focuses on the shelter movement which aids battered women. Provides a directory which lists individuals and organizations working with victims of wife abuse and discusses guidelines for the operation of shelters. Problems encountered in the establishment of shelters are outlined, and a list of resources which fund shelters and programs is presented.

1011. Wasserman, Sidney. "The Abused Parent of the Abused Child." **The Battered Child**. Compiled by Jerome E. Leavitt. Morristown, New Jersey: General Learning Press, 1967, pp. 248–52.

Discusses the abusive parent from a psychological perspective and examines treatment alternatives, including the role of the community in treatment of the parent.

1012. _____. "The Abused Child." **Today's Education**, 63(1):40–43, 1974.

Explores the problem of child abuse and concludes that the most effective preventive measure that schools can apply against child abuse is to educate children on how to be parents, and to advise parents on child care and discipline.

1013. Wayne, Julianne and others. "Differential Groupwork in a Protective Agency." **Child Welfare**, 55:581–91, September–October 1976.

Examines the differential use of groupwork therapy in the treatment of abusive families. This technique was deemed successful in meeting the treatment needs of the individuals involved.

1014. Webb, Dom Benedict. "Strengthening the Individual." **The Challenge of Child Abuse**. Edited by Alfred White Franklin. London: Academic Press, 1977, pp. 229–40.

Discusses the Christian approach to dealing with abusing families and examines the roles of the police, doctors and other professionals in the process.

1015. Webb, P.R.H. "Matrimonial Cruelty: A Lawyer's Guide for the Medical Profession." **Medicine, Science, and Law**, 7(3):110–16, July 1967.

Examines cruelty as grounds for granting divorce in Britain. Discusses the law and follow-up for cases by the medical profession, and presents examples of cases where divorce is granted and cases where it is refused.

1016. Weber, Ellen. "Sexual Abuse Begins at Home." **MS.**, 5:64–67, April 1977.

Discusses the problem of sexual abuse, particularly sexual abuse within the home, and examines the relationship between sexual abuse and later antisocial behavior. The lack of attention by society to the problem is also explored, highlighting the Santa Clara Child Sexual Abuse Treatment Program as the only one which does call attention to the problem by providing a comprehensive program designed to meet the needs of both victims and offenders.

1017. Weitzman, Jack and Karen Dreen. "Wife Beating: A View of the Marital Dyad." **Social Casework**, 63(5):259–65, May 1982.

Views both partners as active participants in the eruption of marital violence. Violence is seen as one aspect of the couple's homeostatic patterns which maintain the rules of the relationship and prevent change. Discusses the theoretical and practical implications of systems theory for the treatment of marital violence by examining the individuals and the marital system itself. Basic control themes are formulated and a variety of treatment formats are recommended.

1018. Weitzman, Lenore J. "Legal Regulation of Marriage: Tradition and Change." **California Law Review**, 62(4):1170–1288, July–September 1974.

Analyzes the terms of the present marriage contract and suggests an alternative form for the legal structure of personal relations (contracts in lieu of traditional, legal marriage). Legal challenges and alternatives are also examined. Includes an appendix which presents excerpts from personal contracts.

1019. Welner, Zila and others. "Child Abuse: A Case for a Different Approach." **Comprehensive Psychiatry**, 18:363–67, August 1977.

After examining the literature on child abuse, it is concluded that there is a lack of consensus among studies on the subject. Points of disagreement are explored and it is suggested that a definition of child abuse be developed which includes all injuries related to parental abuse or neglect.

1020. West, Lois A. and others. **Wife Abuse in the Armed Forces**. Washington, D.C.: Center for Women Policy Studies, 1981.

Discusses spouse abuse in military communities and examines the response of military officials to the problem. Details services available to abusive military families and recommends procedures for developing spouse abuse programs.

1021. Weston, James T. "The Pathology of Child Abuse and Neglect." **The Battered Child**. Edited by C. Henry Kempe and Ray E. Helfer. Chicago: University of Chicago Press, 1980, pp. 241–71.

Written by a forensic pathologist based on his experiences and directed toward other pathologists. Discusses the procedures involved in child abuse and neglect cases and patterns of maltreatment found in such cases. Concludes by emphasizing the importance of teamwork between investigating agencies and the pathologist in proving cause and manner of death. States that a perceptive clinician can help to decrease the mortality rates among battered and neglected children.

1022. "When Family Anger Turns to Violence." **Changing Times**, 35(3):66–70, March 1981.

Presents a comprehensive view of family violence by examining who gets violent and why, ways to break the cycle of violence, reporting and prevention of child abuse, and where violent families can find immediate help.

1023. "When a Wife Says No . . . Beyond the Rideout Case." **MS.**, 10(10):23, April 1982.

Examines changes which have occurred in legislation concerning the rape of a wife by her husband since the Rideout decision in 1978.

1024. White, Joyce. "Women Speak!" **Essence**, 10:121 +, June 1979.

Discusses experiences of battered wives, and lists places where battered women can get help.

1025. White, Michael Freeman. "Dependency Proceedings: What Standard of Proof? An Argument Against the Standard of 'Clear and Convincing'." **San Diego Law Review**, 14:1155–75, July 1977.

Argues against a standard of "clear and convincing" evidence in dependency hearings.

1026. White, Roger B. "Application of a Data Collection Method to Ensure Confidentiality." **American Journal of Public Health**, 67(11):1095–97, November 1977.

Discusses the double bind data collection method used in a study to estimate the incidence and prevalence of child abuse and neglect among a Native American population, and outlines the advantages of this system.

1027. Whitehurst, Robert N. "Violence Potential in Extra-Marital Sexual Responses." **Journal of Marriage and the Family**, 33(4):683–91, 1971.

Presents data from courtroom cases, surveys, and clinical cases which suggest that males are generally socialized in aggressive ways, and that violence in the family may be due, in part, to male socialization, and to female passive-aggressive input.

1028. _____. "Violently Jealous Husbands." **Sexual Behavior**, 1(4):32–41, 1977.

Examines violence within marriage, emphasizing the role of the jealous husband in violent interactions. states that violence within marriage cannot be separated from other complex factors involved in the relationship, and that men who cannot control specific situations may turn to violence against their wives as a response. Causes of jealousy are described and differences between lower and middle class violence are discussed.

1029. Whiting, Beatrice B. "Sex Identity, Conflict, and Physical Violence: A Comparative Study." **American Anthropologist**, 67(6):123–40, 1965.

Analyzes six societies which support a sex-identity conflict approach to violence, and reviews four hypotheses derived from the analysis.

1030. Whiting, Leila. "The Central Registry for Child Abuse Cases: Rethinking Basic Assumptions." **Child Welfare**, 56:761–67, January 1977.

A central registry for the reporting of child abuse cases analyzes the procedures for reporting of various agencies, evaluates statistics concerning the incidence of child abuse, maintains records of families suspected of abusing children, and receives reports of child abuse or suspected abuse. The issue of the family's right to privacy and ways to improve existing central registries are outlined.

1031. "Wife Beaters — Spotting Them Early." **U.S. News and World Report**, 81:48, September 20, 1976.

Presents a list of signals which may provide a warning to women who are potential wife abuse victims.

1032. "Wifebeating Law." **Majority Report**, 6:4, May 13, 1977.

Examines Pennsylvania's Protection From Abuse Act, effective as of December 1976, which provides for a civil procedure in cases of abuse rather than requiring a victim to file criminal charges when a legal action is desired.

170

1033. Wilcox, D.P. "Child Abuse Laws: Past, Present and Future." **Journal of Forensic Sciences**, 21:71–75, January 1976.

Surveys trends in child abuse reporting laws.

1034. Williams, A. Hyatt. "The Nature of Aggression." **The Challenge of Child Abuse**. Edited by Alfred White Franklin. London: Academic Press, 1977, pp. 161–72.

Discusses aggression and provocation to aggression, emphasizing aggression within the family.

1035. Williams, J.E. Hall. "The Neglect of Incest: A Criminologist's View." **Victimology: A New Focus**, Volume IV. Edited by Israel Drapkin and Emilio Viano. Lexington, Massachusetts: D.C. Heath, 1975, pp. 191–96.

Discusses general victim and offender characteristics in addition to drawing some conclusions concerning incest.

1036. Williams, Roger. "The Right Not to be Beaten." **Psychology Today**, p. 36, June 1977.

States that wife abuse in Appalachia is ingrained into the social system there, and that alcohol and drugs are often at the root of the abuse.

1037. Wilson, Ann L. "Promoting a Positive Parent-Baby Relationship." **The Battered Child**. Edited by C. Henry Kempe and Ray E. Helfer. Chicago: University of Chicago Press, 1980, pp. 401–19.

Reviews findings of studies which explore the relationship between parents and babies, focusing on how help can be provided to a new family in order to promote the development of a positive relationship between parent and baby. The role of time in bonding and attachment, and the role of interactional skills in developing positive relationships between parents and the baby are also explored.

1038. Winking, Cyril H. "Coping with Child Abuse: One State's Experience." **The Battered Child**. Compiled by Jerome E. Leavitt. Morristown, New Jersey: General Learning Press, 1974, pp. 243–46.

Summarizes the salient features of Illinois' Child Abuse Law, felt to be a good law because of its precise language and specific directives for implementation. Describes some problems faced by child protective agencies in providing follow-up services to the abused child and his family. Significant features of the law are summarized and the importance of follow-up procedures is discussed.

1039. Wolfgang, Marvin E. "Family Violence and Criminal Behavior." **Violence and Responsibility**. Edited by Robert L. Sadoff. New York: SP Medical and Scientific Books, 1978, pp. 87–103.

Discusses family violence by examining definitions of the problem, cultural dimensions, the extent and character of intrafamilial violence, sociopsychic dimensions, and the subculture of violence as it is applied to family violence. It is concluded that family violence is partly a reflection of violence which is expressed in the general culture, but serious crimes committed in a family setting are often related to subcultural values.

1040. Wolkenstein, Alan S. "Evolution of a Program for the Management of Child Abuse." **Social Casework**, 57:309–16, May 1976.

Outlines a program for the management of child abuse in Milwaukee, Wisconsin and makes recommendations for programs in other communities.

1041. _____. "The Fear of Committing Child Abuse: A Discussion of Eight Families." **Child Welfare**, 56:249–57, April 1977.

Examines a group of families who fear that they may injure their children.

1042. Wood, Beth. "Navajo Battered Women." **Off Our Backs**, 8:5, August/September 1978.

Domestic violence among the Navajos is attributed primarily to the conflict caused by the clash between traditional and modern life, and the breakdown of the extended family.

1043. Woodworth, Robert M. "The Physician and the Battered Child Syndrome in the United States and in Oklahoma." **Journal of the Oklahoma Medical Association**, 67:463–75, November 1974.

A detailed analysis of the battered child syndrome is presented. The topics discussed include the causes of child abuse, history and incidence of the problem, mandatory reporting, and Oklahoma's child abuse laws.

1044. Wooster, Kelly C. "The California Legislative Approach to Problems of Willful Child Abuse." **California Law Review**, 54(4):1805–31, October 1966.

Discusses the nature of the problem and considers the difficulties in discovering incidents of child abuse. The developments in California statutory law requiring the reporting of suspected cases of child abuse to public authorities are reviewed, and possible alternatives and variations are examined.

1045. Wright, Logan. "The 'Sick But Slick' Syndrome as a Personality Component of Parents of Battered Children." **Journal of Clinical Psychology**, 32:41–45, January 1976.

Convicted child abusers and matched controls were administered various personality tests. Results indicated that abusing parents attempted to appear healthy and non-abusing, but they did have personality problems.

1046. Yates, Alayne. "Narcissistic Traits in Certain Abused Children."

American Journal of Orthopsychiatry, 51(1):55–62, January 1981.

Describes three groups of severely abused, emotionally disturbed children, one of the groups being made up of "private" children who seem to possess many of the characteristics of the adult narcissistic personality. Therapy for these children is discussed.

1047. Young, Leontine. "Parents Who Hate." **Violence in the Family**. Edited by Suzanne K. Steinmetz and Murray A. Straus. New York: Harper and Row, 1974, pp. 187–89.

Presents a case of child abuse in which the father is a well-educated, middle class man.

1048. _____. **Wednesday's Children: A Study of Child Neglect and Abuse**. New York: McGraw-Hill, 1974. 195 pp.

Discusses families with neglected and abused children and profiles the neglecting family. Describes abusing parents and examines the economic and social framework for abuse, and the necessity for public support and help to manage and prevent further abuse. A study conducted by the author in which 120 cases were selected from welfare agencies is reviewed.

1049. Zahn, Margaret. "The Female Homicide Victim." **Criminology**, 13:400–15, November 1975.

Results of a study conducted by the author showed that women homicide victims were most likely killed in their own homes and the offender was most often her husband or a friend.

1050. Zalba, Serapio Richard. "The Abused Child: I. A Survey of the Problem." **Social Work**, 11(4):3–16, 1966.

Reports on studies which examined the situations and characteristics of child abuse. Findings indicate that children are often used as targets of abuse by parents who are projecting or denying hostility directed at someone or something else. Often, the child becomes the object of abuse in a family where marital conflict is present, rather than the spouse.

1051. _____. "The Abused Child: II. A Typology for Classification and Treatment." **Social Work**, 12(1):70–79, 1967.

Presents a problem and treatment typology for families in which child abuse has occurred. Also outlines treatment strategies and objectives.

1052. _____. "Battered Children." **Trans-action**, 8(9–10):58–61, 1971.

Presents statistics concerning the number of children in the U.S. who need protective services each year. Characteristics of abusive parents are described and the roles of professionals and the public in reporting and obtaining services for abused children are outlined.

1053. _____. "Treatment of Child Abuse." **Violence in the Family**. Edited by Suzanne K. Steinmetz and Murray A. Straus. New York: Harper and Row, 1974, pp. 212–22.

Summarizes specific steps which can be taken to deal with child abuse.

1054. Zauner, Phyllis. "Mothers Anonymous: The Last Resort." **The Battered Child**. Compiled by Jerome E. Leavitt. Morristown, New Jersey: General Learning Press, 1974.

Discusses the formation of Mothers Anonymous, a self-help group for abusing mothers.

1055. Zeldin, L. "Road to Hell . . . ." **Progressive**, 42:11, September 1978. Briefly discusses the recent concern of the media, law enforcement officials, and health care professionals about child abuse. It is suggested that attention be given to the causes of child abuse before professionals intrude into people's lives on the basis of "good intentions."

Indexes

Author Index

Abel, G.G. 68
Abrams, Susan 1
Ackley, Dana C. 3
Acton, William D., Jr. 4
Adelson, Lester 5, 6
Adler, Lorraine 7
Ahrens, Lois 8
Ainsworth, M.D. 75
Alexander, Helen 10, 11, 12
Alexander, Jerry 13
Allen, Letitia J. 14
Allen, Marilyn 15
Allott, Roger 16
Alvy, Kerby T. 17, 18
Andell, Eric Gordon 20
Anderson, George M. 21, 22
Anderson, William R. 23
Angel, Karen 419
Anthony, E. James 24
Appleton, Peter L. 25
Areen, Judith 26
Armstrong, Jean 788
Armstrong, Louise 27
Arnold, George L. 28
Arnold, Mildred 29
Arvanian, Ann L. 30
Asch, Stuart S. 31
Avery, Nancy C. 33
Ayoub, Catherine 34, 768
Badinter, Elisabeth 35
Baher, Edwina 36
Bailey, Margaret M. 859
Bain, Katherine 37
Bakan, David 38
Baldwin, J.A. 39

Ball, Margaret 40
Ball, Patricia G. 41
Bamford, Frank N. 42
Banagale, Raul C. 43
Bard, E. Ronald 44, 45
Bard, Morton 46, 47, 48, 49, 50, 51
Barnes, Geoffrey 52
Barnett, Ellen R. 53
Barocas, Harvey A. 54
Bass, David 55
Bean, Shirley L. 62, 63
Becerra, Rosina M. 409
Bechtold, Mary Lee 65
Beck, Connie 66
Beckelman, Laurie 67
Becker, J.V. 68
Bedard, Virginia S. 69
Beer, Sally 70
Beezley, Patricia 71, 628, 629, 630, 631
Bell, David O. 72
Bell, Joseph N. 73, 74
Bell, S.M. 75
Bell, William E. 892
Bender, Barbara 76
Bennie, E.H. 77
Bentorim, Arnon 78
Benward, Jean 79
Berdie, Jane 80
Berlin, S. 81
Bern, Elliot H. 82
Besharov, Douglas J. 83, 84, 85, 329
Beswick, Keith 86
Bevan, Hugh 88
Billingsley, Andrew 89, 410
Birrell, J.H.W. 90

Birrell, R.G. 90
Bishop, Frank 91
Bishop, J.A. 92
Black, Rebecca 93
Blager, Florence 95
Blair, Sandra 96
Blake, Phillip R. 756
Blau, M. 97
Bloch, Dorothy 98
Blount, H.R. 99
Blumberg, Marvin L. 100, 101
Blumberg, Myrna 102
Boisvert, Maurice J. 103
Bolton, F.G., Jr. 104, 105
Booth, Margaret 106
Borland, Marie 107
Boudouris, J. 108
Bourne, Richard 109, 110, 701
Bowerman, Charles E. 277
Bowley, Agatha H. 111
Boyer, Andrew 508
Brandon, Sydney 112, 113
Brant, Renee S.T. 114
Brauburger, Mary Ball 269
Breiter, Toni 115
Brenton, Myron 116
Broadhurst, Diane D. 117, 118, 119, 120
Brodeur, A.E. 358
Brody, Sylvia 122
Bross, Donald C. 123
Brown, Harold O.J. 124
Brown, John A. 125
Brown, Linda R. Insalaco 126
Brown, Rowine Hayes 127, 128, 129
Brownmiller, Susan 130
Brunnquell, Don 271
Buchanan, Ann 132
Bullard, Dexter M. 133
Burgess, Ann Wolpert 134, 135, 436
Burgess, Robert L. 136
Burke, Kathleen M. 137
Burt, Marvin 138
Burt, Robert A. 139
Bush, Malcolm 140
Bush, Sherida 141, 142, 143
Butler, Raymond V. 144

Buzawa, C.G. 145
Buzawa, E.S. 145
Bysshe, Janette 146
Caffey, J. 147
Cameron, J.M. 148, 149, 898
Campbell, James S. 150
Campbell, Ruth 151
Camps, F.E. 149
Canon, Belle 152
Cantwell, Hendrika B. 153
Carlson, Bonnie E. 154
Carmody, Francis J. 155
Carroll, Claudia A. 156
Carroll, Joseph C. 157
Carter, Jan 158, 159
Castle, Raymond L. 160
Cavenagh, Winifred 161, 162
Chadwick, David L. 163
Chaikin, Douglas A. 164
Chamberlain, Michael R. 165
Chambers, D.R. 166
Chandler, T. 99
Chang, Albert 167
Chapman, Jack 168
Chase, Naomi F. 169
Chatterton, Michael R. 170
Cherry, B.J. 171
Chester, Robert 172
Clark, Elizabeth H. 976
Clements, Theodore 179
Cohen, Harriette 180
Cohen, Melvin 181
Cohen, Morton I. 182
Cohen, Stephan J. 183, 951
Cohn, Anne Harris 184, 185
Coigney, Virginia 186
Collie, James 187
Collins, Alice H. 188
Collins, Marilyn C. 189
Collucci, N.D., Jr. 191
Conger, Rand D. 136
Cooksey, Charlotte M. 194
Cooper, Christine 195, 196, 197
Cope, Oliver 588
Copitch, Phillip 994
Corey, Eleanor J.B. 198

178

Cormier, Bruno 199
Costantino, Cathy 200
Cottom, Kris 201
Court, Joan 203, 204
Crawford, Christina 205
Crouter, Ann 367, 368
Curtis, George C. 207
D'Agostino, Paul A. 208
Danckwerth, Edward T. 209
Daniels, Robert 125
David, Charles A. 210
Davidson, Terry 211, 212
Davies, Jean M. 213, 214
Davies, Joan 215
Davis, Charles Ray 216
Davis, Gwendolyn 217
Davoren, Elizabeth 218, 219
DeCourcy, Judith 222
DeCourcy, Peter 222
DeFrancis, Vincent 223, 224, 225
Delacoste, Frederique 226
Delaney, James J. 227
De Lesseps, Suzanne 228
Dellapa, Fred 229
Delnero, Harriet 230
Delsordo, James D. 231
Del Tosto, D. 232
De Mause, Lloyd 233
Dembitz, Nanette 234
Densen-Gerber, Judianne 79, 235, 236
De Panfilis, Diane 237
Derdeyn, Andre P. 238, 239
Dickens, Bernard M. 240
Disney, Dorothy Cameron 241
Dobash, R. Emerson 242, 243, 244
Dobash, Russell P. 242, 243, 244
Doek, Jack E. 245
Doerr, Aleta E. 246
Doris, John L. 247
Dow, Mildred 248
Drake, Frances M. 249
Dreen, Karen 1017
Drews, Kay 250
Duis, Perry R. 251
Duncan, Darlene 252
Duncan, David F. 519

Duncan, Elaine 253
Duncan, Jane Watson 254
Duncan, Glen M. 254
Duncan, Lois 255
Dunstan, Gordon R. 256
Duquette, Donald N. 257
Durbin, Karen 258
Duryea, Perry 259
Earl, Howard G. 260
Earp, Joanne L. 731
Easley, Kevin O. 261
Easson, William M. 262
Eaton, Gerald M. 165
Ebeling, Nancy B. 263, 264, 265
Eber, L.P. 266
Edmiston, Susan 267
Edwards, John N. 269
Edwards, Richard L. 270
Egeland, Byron 271, 272, 273
Eisenberg, Alan D. 274
Eisenberg, Sue E. 275
Elbow, Margaret 276
Elder, Glen H. 277
Elkind, James 278
Elliott, Frank A. 279
Elmer, Elizabeth 280, 281, 282, 283, 284,
    285, 286, 287, 288
Elwell, Mary Ellen 289
English, Peter 290
Erlanger, Howard S. 291
Evans, Alan L. 292
Fairburn, A.C. 293
Faller, Kathleen Coulborn 294
Fanaroff, A.A. 296
Fanshel, David 297
Faulk, M. 298, 299
Fay, Henry J. 661
Fay, Shirl E. 300
Feinstein, Howard M. 301
Felder, Samuel 302
Feldman, Kenneth W. 303
Ferro, Frank 304
Field, Henry 305
Field, Martha H. 305
Field, Marjory D. 306, 307, 308, 309

Finkelhov, David 310
Fiora-Gormally, Nancy 311
Flammang, C.J. 312
Fleming, G.M. 313
Fleming, Jennifer Baker 314
Flynn, William R. 316
Fojtik, Kathleen M. 317
Follingstad, Diane R. 318
Follis, Peggy 319
Fonseka, S. 320
Fontana, Vincent J. 321, 322, 323, 324,
 325, 326, 327, 328, 329, 330, 331
Ford, D. 332
Forrer, Stephen E. 333
Fosson, Abe R. 334
Foster, Henry H. 335
Francke, Linda Bird 336
Franklin, Alfred White 337, 338, 339, 340,
 341
Fraser, Brian G. 342, 343, 344, 345, 346
Frazier, Claude A. 347
Freeman, M.D.A. 348
Frenzel, Rita 349
Friedman, Kathleen O. 350, 351
Friedman, Stanford B. 352, 353, 484
Frodi, Ann M. 355, 356
Fromson, Terry L. 357
Fruchtl, Gertrude 358
Gaensbauer, Theodore J. 359
Gager, Nancy 360
Gaines, Richard 361
Gaiss, Betty 121
Galdston, Richard 362, 363
Gale, Patricia 435
Gaquin, D.A. 364
Garbarino, James 365, 366, 367, 368, 369,
 370
Gardner, Leslie 371
Garinger, Gail 372
Garrett, Karen Ann 373
Gayford, J.J. 374, 375, 376, 377
Gaylin, Jody 378, 379
Geiser, Robert L. 380
Gelles, Richard J. 381, 382, 383, 384, 385,
 386, 387, 388, 389, 390, 391
Gentzler, Rie 392

George, Carol 393
George, J.E. 394
Geracimos, Ann 395
Gershenson, Charles P. 396
Gil, David G. 397, 398, 399, 400, 401, 402,
 403, 404
Gilbert, Marie T. 405, 800
Gilliam, Gwen 369
Gilmartin, Brian G. 406
Gingold, Judith 407
Giovannoni, Jeanne M. 408, 409, 410, 411
Glenn, Jean 412
Goldberg, Gale 413
Golub, Sharon 414
Gonzalez-Pardo, Lillian 415
Goode, William J. 416, 417
Goodman, Emily Jane 418
Goodpaster, Gary S. 419
Gordon, Alan H. 420
Gould, Robert W. 680
Graham-Hall, Jean 421
Gray, Jane 422, 423
Green, Arthur H. 424, 425, 426, 427, 428
Green, Frederick C. 429
Green, Nancy B. 430, 431
Gregory, Margaret 432
Griffin, Max E. 433
Griffiths, A. 434
Griggs, Shirley 435
Groth, A. Nicholas 436
Grumet, Barbara R. 437
Gulley, Kenneth G. 438
Guten, Keri 439, 440
Guthrie, Andrew D. 441
Haffner, Sarah 442
Hall, M.H. 443
Hammell, Charlotte L. 444
Hanks, Susan E. 445
Hanmer, Jalna 446
Hannan, Damian 447
Hanson, Ruth 904
Harper, Fowler V. 449
Hartman, Mary S. 450
Hass, Gerald 451
Havens, Leston L. 452
Haviland, Mary 453

Hays, Richard H. 454
Helfer, Mary Edna 455
Helfer, Ray E. 455, 456, 457, 458, 459, 460, 461, 462, 463, 464, 538, 539, 540
Helpern, Milton 465
Hendricks-Matthews, Marybeth 466
Hendrix, Melva J. 467
Henry, D.R. 468
Hepburn, John R. 469
Hepburn, Ronald W. 470
Herbruck, Christine C. 471
Herman, Bernice Jane 472
Herre, Ernest A. 473
Herrenkohl, E.C. 474
Herrenkohl, R.C. 474
Higgins, Judith 217
Hilberman, Elaine 475
Hill, Deborah A. 265, 476, 477, 478
Hindman, Margaret 479
Hinkley, Gerry 867
Hirsch, Mariam F. 480
Hoffman, Ellen 481
Hoggett, Brenda 482
Holmes, S.A. 483
Holt, Glen E. 251
Holter, Joan C. 484
Hoover, Eleanor L. 485
Horn, Jack C. 486, 487
Horn, Pat 488
Howard, Janet 489
Howell, Jackie N. 490
Hubenak, Priscilla M. 491
Hudson, R. Page 23
Hudson, Walter W. 492
Hunt, A.C. 293
Hurd, Jeanne L. 28
Hurley, John R. 654
Hurt, Maure 493
Hussey, Hugh 494
Hutchinson, F. 235
Hyde, James N. 372, 702
Hyman, Clare A. 495
Inglis, Ruth L. 499
Issacs, Jacob L. 501
Issacson, Lon B. 502
Jacobs, J. 503

Jacobson, Beverly 504
James, Howard 505
James, Jennifer 506
Jameson, Janet Corcoran 420
Jayaratne, Srinika 507
Jenkins, Richard L. 508, 509
Jensen, Rita Henley 510
Jobling, Megan 511
Johnson, Betty 512, 513
Johnson, H.R.M. 149
Johnson, Sally 515
Johnston, Pamela 516
Jones, Carolyn Okell 517
Jordan, Bill 518
Justice, Blair 519, 520, 521, 522, 523
Justice, Rita 520, 522, 523
Kaak, Ho Ho 334
Kadushin, Alfred 524
Kaiser, Gunther 525
Kaizen, Mark S. 526
Kalmar, Roberta 527
Kamerman, Sheila B. 528
Kaplan, Betty 422
Katz, Sanford N. 529
Kaufman, Irving 530
Kaul, Mohan L. 531
Kay, Melanie 980
Kaye, Loraine 532
Keller, O.J. 533
Kellum, Barbara A. 534
Kempe, C. Henry 461, 462, 463, 535, 536, 537, 538, 539, 540, 541, 542
Kempe, Ruth S. 423, 542, 543, 653
Kerr, A. 204
Kieviet, Thomas G. 544
Kinard, E. Milling 546
King, Kurt J. 959
Kohlman, Richard J. 547
Korbin, Jill E. 548
Krause, Harry D. 549
Kravetz, D. 81
Kreitman, Norman 24
Kretschman, Karen L. 550
Krieger, Ingeborg 551
Kristal, Helen F. 552
Kryso, Jo Ann 949

Kuby, A.M. 171
Kumagai, Fumie 553
Kutun, Barry 554
Lalonde, Claire 722
Lamb, Michael E. 355
Lamb, Robert L. 555
Landis, Leslie 53
Langer, William L. 556
Langley, Roger 557, 558
Larsen, Jo Ann 559
Lascari, Andre D. 560
Lauer, Brian 561
Laughlin, John 562
Laury, Gabriel V. 563
Lawler, Byron J. 798
Leavitt, Jerome E. 565, 566
Lefkowitz, Monroe M. 567
Leghorn, Lisa 568
Lehman, Elyse 309
Leistyna, J.A. 569
Lena, Hugh F. 570
Letko, Carolyn 787
Le Valley, Joseph D. 571
Levin, Marj Jackson 572
Levine, Abraham 573
Levine, Montague B. 574
Levinger, George 575
Levy, Richard C. 557, 558
Lewis, Dorothy O. 576
Lieberknecht, Kay 577
Light, Richard J. 578
Lindenthal, Jacob 579
Lion, John R. 580
Lipner, Joanne D. 581, 582
Lippi, Laura 583
Lloyd-Still, John D. 585
Lo, Nerissa 934
Lobsenz, Norman 586
Loizos, Peter 587
Long, Robert T. 588
Lord, Edith 589
Lorens, Herbert D. 590
Lourie, Ira S. 591
Lowenberg, D.A. 592
Lynch, Annette 593
Lynch, Catherine G. 594

Lynch, Margaret A. 595, 596, 597, 598
Lystad, Mary H. 599
MacCarthy, Dermod 600
MacFarlane, Kee 601
MacLeod, Celeste 604
MacMillan, N. 886
Madden, Susan 605
Maidment, Susan 607
Main, Mary 393
Malone, Charles A. 608
Mann, Andrew 609
Marcovitch, Anne 601
Marks, Alan N. 613
Marsden, Dennis 614, 615
Martin, Barbara 585
Martin, David L. 616
Martin, Del 617, 618, 619, 620
Martin, Harold P. 95, 346, 621, 622, 623
   624, 625, 626, 627, 628, 629, 630, 631
   632, 820
Martin, J.P. 633, 634, 635
Martin, Judith A. 524
Masumura, Wilfred T. 636
Maton, Andy 771
May, Margaret 637
Mayer, Joseph 93
Mazura, Adrianne C. 638
McAllister, Pam 639
McAnulty, Elizabeth H. 640
McCabe, S. 641
McCathren, Randall R. 642
McClintock, F.H. 643
McCloskey, Kenneth D. 644
McCoid, Allan H. 645
McDermott, John F., Jr. 646
McDonald, Anne E. 647
McDonald, Kay 784
McEvoy, James III 919
McGee, D.H. 912
McGeorge, John 648
McHenry, Thomas 649
McIntire, Matilda S. 43
McIntosh,Sally Rau 492
McKeel, Nancy Lynn 650
McKenna, J. James 651
McKnight, K. 671

McQuiston, Mary 652, 653
Melnick, Barry 654
Melville, Joy 655, 656, 657
Micklow, Patricia L. 275
Midlin, Rowland L. 659
Miller, Laura M. 660
Miller, Merle K. 661
Miller, Nick 662
Mills, B.G. 663
Minier, Alice 664
Mirandy, Joan 665
Mitchell, Eleanor 666
Mitchell, Marilyn Hall 667
Mitchell, Ross G. 668
Mitchell, Ruth 495
Mitchiner, Myra J. 669
Mogielnicki, R. Peter 670
Mohr, J.W. 671
Mondale, Walter F. 672
Moore, Donna M. 673, 674
Moore, Jean G. 675, 676, 677
Morgan, Dorothy 679
Morris, Marian G. 680, 681
Morse, Abraham E. 682
Morse, Carol W. 353
Morse, Harold A. 512, 513
Mounsey, Joseph 683
Mulvihill, Donald J. 684
Munson, Kit 475
Munson, P.J. 685
Mushanga, Tibamanya Mwene 686
Myers, Steven A. 687
Nagi, Saad Z. 689
Nelson, Stephen H. 693
Nelson, Susan 694
Newberger, Eli H. 110, 698, 699, 700, 701, 702, 703, 828
Newman, Charles L. 704
Newman, Felice 226
NiCarthy, Ginny 705
Nichols, Beverly B. 706
Nichols, William C. 707
Nordstrom, Jerry L. 710
Norman, Mari 712
Norris, Thomas L. 594
Nurse, Shirley M. 713

Nwako, Festus 714
Nyden, Paul V. 715
O'Brien, John E. 716
O'Brien, Shirley 717
O'Connor, Shannon P. 718
O'Doherty, N.J. 719
O'Donoghue, Gearoid 553
Oettinger, Katherine B. 720
O'Grady-Gregoire, Christine 721
Oglov, Linda 722
O'Leary, K. Daniel 824
Oliver, Jack 726
Olson, David H. 727
Olson, Robert 728
Oppe, Thomas E. 729
Orriss, Harry D. 730
Ory, Marcia G. 731
O'Shea, Ann 732
Ounsted, Christopher 733, 734
Oviatt, Boyd 736
Owens, D. 615
Owens, David 737
Ozzanna, S. Harmony 738
Packman, Jean 518
Page, Miriam O. 739
Pagelow, Mildred Daley 740
Palmer, C.H. 741
Pancost, Diane L. 188
Parker, Barbara 745
Parker, Graham E. 746
Parnas, Raymond 747, 748
Pascoe, Elizabeth Jean 749, 750
Pascoe, John M. 751
Paulsen, Monrad G. 752, 753, 754
Paulson, Morris J. 755, 756, 757, 758, 759, 760
Pavenstedt, Eleanor 761
Pedicord, Diane 762
Pelton, Leroy H. 763, 764
Pepitone-Rockwell, Fran 674
Perdue, Nancy 765
Peters, Joseph J. 766
Peterson, Karen 767
Pfeifer, Donald R. 34, 768
Pfouts, Jane H. 769
Pickett, John 770, 771

Pierron, G. Joseph 772
Piers, Maria W. 773
Pitcher, Rudolph A., Jr. 774
Pizzey, Erin 775
Plaine, Lloyd 776
Pleck, Elizabeth 777
Pogrebin, Letty Cottin 778
Polansky, Norman A. 779, 780, 781, 782
Polier, Justice Wise 783, 784
Pollock, Carl 785
Prescott, James W. 786
Prescott, Suzanne 787
Price, John 788
Prince, Russell C. 789
Pringle, Mia Kellmer 790
Prinz, Lucie 791
Rabkin, Brenda 793
Radbill, Samuel X. 794, 795
Raffalli, Henri C. 796
Raisbeck, Bert L. 797
Rako, Jules 590
Ramsey, Jerry A. 798
Ramsey, Sarah 799
Reavley, William 800
Redeker, James R. 802
Remsberg, Bonnie 804, 805
Remsberg, Charles 804, 805
Renz, Connie 769
Resnick, Mindy 806
Resnick, Phillip J. 807
Reyes, Alberto 808
Rice, Janet 55
Richards, Martin 809
Ridington, Jillian 810
Rigler, David 911
Roaf, Robert 811
Roberts, Albert R. 812
Roberts, Jacqueline 598, 813
Robichaud, Jane 814
Robinson, J. 815
Robison, Esther 330
Rochester, Dean E. 816
Rockwood, Marcia 817, 818, 819
Rodeheffer, Martha 632, 820
Rodriguez, Alejandro 821
Rosen, Barbara 822, 823

Rosenbaum, Alan 824
Rosenbaum, C. Peter 445
Rosenberg, Arthur H. 825
Rosenblatt, Gary C. 826
Rosenfeld, Alvin A. 827, 828
Rosenheim, Margaret K. 829
Rossi, Peter H. 373
Roth, Frederick 830
Rounsaville, Bruce J. 831, 832, 833, 834
Rowe, Janet 835
Roy, Maria 836, 837, 838, 839, 840
Rubin, Jean 841
Runyan, Desmond K. 842
Rush, Florence 843, 844
Russell, Diana E.H. 845
Ryder, Robert G. 727
Sacco, Lynn A. 846
Sadoff, Robert L. 847
Sage, Wayne 848
Sanders, Lynda F. 849
Sanders, R. Wyman 850, 855
Sands, Karen 359
Sandusky, Annie Lee 851
Sanford, Linda Tschirhart 852
Saperstein, Avalie 853
Saunders, Daniel G. 854
Savino, Anne B. 855
Scharer, Kathleen M. 856
Schatzman, Morton 857
Schechter, Susan 858
Scheurer, Susan L. 859
Schickling, Barbara H. 860
Schmidt, Delores M. 861
Schmitt, Barton D. 862, 863
Schneider, Carol 864, 865, 866
Schoenfield, Barbara T. 867
Schuchter, Arnold 868
Schultz, LeRoy G. 869, 870
Schumacher, Dale N. 745
Schurr, Cathleen 360
Schuyler, Marcella 871
Sclare, A.B. 77
Scott, E.M. 872
Scott, P.D. 873, 874, 875
Scott, Pena D. 876, 877

Scott, Peter D. 878, 879
Search, Gay 880, 881
Sennet, Richard 882
Sewell, Mabel 883
Seymour, E.J. 274
Sgroi, Suzanne M. 884, 885
Shah, D.K. 886
Shainess, Natalie 887
Shanas, Bert 888
Shay, Sharon Williams 889
Sheils, Merrill 890
Sherman, Deborah 370
Shorkey, Clayton 891
Silber, David L. 892
Silver, Larry B. 893, 894
Silverman, Frederic N. 895
Sim, Myre 896
Simpson, D.W. 897
Sims, B.G. 898
Sinofsky, Mildred Salins 899
Smith, C.A. 900
Smith, Jack L. 901
Smith, Selwyn M. 902, 903, 904, 905, 906,
  907
Snedeker, Lendon 908
Snell, John E. 909
Solomon, Theo 910
Spinetta, John J. 911
Spitzner, J.H. 912
Sprey, Jetse 913, 914
Sroufe, L. Alan 272
Stahly, Geraldine Butts 915
Star, Barbara 916
Starbuck, George W. 917
Stark, Evan 918
Stark, Rodney 919
Starkweather, Cassie L. 920
Steele, Brandt F. 785, 921, 922, 923, 924
Steinhilber, Richard M. 262
Steinmetz, Suzanne K. 925, 926, 927, 928,
  929, 930, 931, 932
Stephens, Darrell W. 933
Stephenson, P. Susan 934
Straus, Murray A. 391, 931, 932, 935, 936,
  937, 938, 939, 940, 941, 942
Streather, Jane 172

Streshinsky, Shirley 943
Stringer, Elizabeth A. 944
Stroud, John 945
Strucker, Jan 946
Stuart, Donald 947
Sullivan, Michael F. 948
Summit, Roland 949
Sussman, A. 950
Sussman, Alan 183, 951
Sutton, Jo 952
Swanson, Lynn D. 954
Swartz, Herbert 955
Taylor, Audrey 724
Ten Bensel, Robert W. 958, 959
Ten Broeck, Elsa 960
Terr, Lenore C. 962
Thomas, Mason P., Jr. 963
Thomas, Mary 415
Thompson, Louise 964
Thorman, G. 965
Thurber, Steven 966
Tibbits, Jill 967
Tidmarsh, Mannes 968
Till, Kenneth 969
Tisza, Veronica B. 114
Toby, Jackson 970
Tocchio, O.J. 971
Tomes, N. 972
Tomlinson, Tom 973
Tooley, Kay M. 974
Torigian, John 975
Tracy, James J. 976, 977
Tripp, Norman D. 978
Truitt, Richard B. 129
Truninger, Elizabeth 979
Tucker, Ford 552
Turner, S. Michael 920
Uccella, Michaele 980
Van Dyke, Vicki 989
Van Stolk, Mary 990, 991
Vandenbraak, S. 992
Varma, Margaret 993
Vasta, Ross 994
Vaughn, Brian 273
Velcoff, Andrew 995
Viano, Emilio C. 996

Victor, Jill Blumberg 997
Wald, Michael S. 1001
Walker, Lenore E. 1002, 1003, 1004, 1005, 1006, 1007
Walsh, Kathleen T. 1008
Walters, David R. 1009
Warkov, Seymour 570
Warrior, Betsy 1010
Wasserman, Sidney 1011, 1012
Wayne, Julianne 1013
Webb, Dom Benedict 1014
Webb, P.R.H. 1015
Weber, Ellen 1016
Weisfield, David 589
Weiss, Myra 562
Weissman, Myrna M. 833
Weitzman, Jack 1017
Weitzman, Lenore J. 1018
Welner, Zila 1019
West, Lois A. 1020
Weston, James T. 741, 1021
Wheeler, John S. 464
White, Joyce 1024
White, Michael Freeman 1025
White, Roger B. 1026
Whitehurst, Robert N. 1027, 1028
Whiting, Beatrice B. 1029
Whiting, Leila 1030
Wilcox, D.P. 1033
Williams, A. Hyatt 1034
Williams, J.E. Hall 1035
Williams, Roger 1036
Wilson, Ann L. 1037
Winkling, Cyril H. 1038
Wolfgang, Marvin E. 1039
Wolkenstein, Alan S. 1040, 1041
Wood, Beth 1042
Woodworth, Robert M. 1043
Wooster, Kelly C. 1044
Wrench, David E. 606
Wright, Logan 1045
Wyman, Elizabeth 41
Yates, Alayne 1046
Young, Leontine 1047, 1048
Zacker, Joseph 50, 51
Zahn, Margaret 1049

Zalba, Serapio Richard 1050, 1051, 1052, 1053
Zauner, Phyllis 1054
Zeldin, L. 1055

Subject Index

Abortion 124

Abused children, characteristics of 71, 225, 228, 285, 294, 394, 479, 531, 542, 565, 622, 841, 874, 986, 989, 1046

Abused Women's Aid in Crisis 515

Abusing parents, characteristics of 67, 91, 100, 101, 116, 125, 127, 143, 182, 204, 225, 234, 282, 285, 287, 313, 328, 361, 386, 394, 414, 424, 437, 461, 479, 488, 499, 512, 519, 530, 531, 537, 560, 565, 589, 604, 654, 680, 713, 717, 720, 722, 726, 757, 758, 759, 779, 780, 822, 823, 830, 841, 865, 872, 874, 890, 905, 906, 907, 911, 923, 924, 959, 986, 1009, 1011, 1044, 1047, 1048, 1052

Abusing spouses, characteristics of 374, 395, 511, 803, 824, 887, 1005, 1006

Acton Women's Aid 610

Adolescents, abuse of 80, 254, 269, 369, 591, 604, 650, 805

Adoption 238, 526, 835

Aggression 99, 150, 337, 436, 567, 636, 722, 774, 873, 875, 919, 936, 966, 1034

Alcohol 22, 43, 50, 93, 94, 407, 424, 445, 479, 511, 836, 873, 968, 987, 990, 1036

American Humane Association 19, 736, 844

American Society for the Prevention of Cruelty to Animals 247, 437

Apathy-Futility Syndrome 780, 782

Army Advocacy Program 4

Battered Child Syndrome 23, 56, 77, 90, 149, 160, 204, 210, 214, 231, 293, 325, 326, 358, 394, 396, 425, 443, 494, 537, 570, 627, 645, 659, 746, 789, 795, 796, 798, 879, 894, 898, 902, 907, 971, 1043

Battered Wife Syndrome 126, 277, 311, 745

Bibliography 24, 36, 169, 186, 189, 217, 222, 243, 284, 295, 314, 317, 381, 409, 493, 520, 537, 542, 550, 565, 606, 673, 695, 717, 773, 903, 911, 922, 942, 951, 989

Bill of Rights, U.S. Constitution 186

Binford, Jesse 251

Bonding failure 75, 272, 273, 296, 420, 474, 520, 596, 597, 598, 733, 734, 1037

Brewer, Wayne 221

La Casa de las Madres 803

Causes: child abuse 18, 91, 104, 116, 124, 197, 202, 271, 282, 293, 294, 359, 361, 386, 396, 397, 398, 401, 402, 428, 439, 454, 531, 563, 589, 604, 668, 711, 722, 848, 879, 900, 940, 966, 977, 989, 1009, 1043, 1048, 1050, 1055; family violence 112, 299, 882, 942, 965; spouse abuse 115, 154, 266, 282, 354, 357, 374, 377, 390, 391, 395, 453, 466, 568, 674, 788, 836, 838, 938, 941, 968, 983, 1042

Center for the Study of Abused and Neglected Children 456

Center for the Study of Democratic Institutions 173

Child Abuse Prevention and Treatment Act 481, 493, 672, 717

Child Abuse Reporting Act 951

Child Neglect 26, 92, 133, 136, 153, 171, 173, 182, 203, 286, 296, 341, 410, 439, 529, 549, 570, 573, 600, 659, 734, 743, 751, 753, 779, 780, 781, 782, 948, 954, 1001, 1048

Child's Bill of Rights 186

Children at Risk 34, 36, 111, 271, 355, 356, 361, 371, 454, 574, 590, 597, 598, 627, 756, 876, 904, 924

187

Children's Hospital Medical Center
(Boston) 109, 362
Children's Trust Fund (Kansas) 412
Chiswick Women's Aid 775
Colwell, Maria 611, 730, 876
Conjugal crime 211, 447
Crawford, Joan 485
Crib death 31
Crisis nurseries 10, 63, 343, 540
Cultural aspects: child abuse 17, 379, 400,
402, 403, 548, 723, 922, 990, 991, 1009,
1029, 1039; spouse abuse 8, 244, 311,
315, 348, 407, 504, 620, 686, 873, 937,
938, 990, 996, 1028, 1029, 1039, 1042
Cycle of Violence 150, 157, 178, 207, 326,
439, 471, 924, 926, 1002, 1005, 1007,
1022
Definition: child abuse 14, 17, 67, 202,
205, 260, 285, 286, 294, 322, 323, 352,
369, 373, 389, 402, 409, 411, 449, 471,
528, 531, 539, 542, 548, 586, 602, 779,
805, 816, 826, 924, 958, 1009, 1019,
1044, 1051; spouse abuse 364, 467, 480,
511, 572, 618, 656, 658, 662, 666, 740,
836, 873, 890
Demographic characteristics 108, 155, 198,
277, 284, 284, 366, 367, 370, 561, 578,
654, 674, 713, 893, 902, 911, 931, 968
Discipline of children 99, 102, 157, 201,
233, 277, 291, 389, 402, 406, 567, 795,
796, 857, 911, 919, 922, 927, 928, 931,
942, 963, 978
Drugs 43, 93, 235, 236, 836, 873, 1036
Dyscontrol Syndrome 282
Economic aspects: child abuse 43, 182, 186,
272, 283, 284, 291, 366, 367, 368, 370,
396, 403, 408, 410, 439, 441, 448, 615,
682, 763, 764, 784, 799, 927, 928, 940,
990, 1011, 1048; family violence 486,
939, 1000; spouse abuse 315, 336, 504,
575, 707, 937, 938, 968, 972, 982, 990,
1036
Education Commission of the States 175,
268
Failure to Thrive 133, 420, 543, 600, 622,
924
Family Life Center (Cornell University) 247

Family planning 679
Fields, Marjory 504
Foster care 10, 21, 29, 30, 218, 238, 29
573,629, 653, 689, 835, 842, 859, 934
Gelles, Richard J. 378, 486, 742, 999, 10(
Gilday Center (Boston) 371
Gross, Patricia 804
Health Visitor 11, 213, 214, 422, 535, 7▮
Historical perspectives 26, 38, 194, 20:
211, 212, 233, 329, 332, 369, 394, 40▮
461, 534, 538, 556, 618, 637, 673, 69:
715, 717, 723, 754, 777, 794, 795, 83▮
879, 887, 902, 911, 950, 959, 963, 97:
991, 1043
Homicide 5, 6, 24, 31, 38, 98, 108, 14▮
180, 199, 221, 232, 254, 262, 274, 27▮
301, 311, 323, 416, 417, 465, 534, 54▮
545, 605, 651, 667, 671, 687, 730, 74▮
773, 794, 795, 804, 807, 808, 847, 87▮
875, 876, 877, 886, 924, 931, 955, 102▮
1049
Identification, child abuse 34, 83, 92, 11▮
117, 119, 120, 146, 147, 148, 160, 16:
167, 174, 191, 192, 197, 209, 213, 22:
228, 265, 270, 285, 286, 287, 304, 32▮
334, 342, 352, 353, 372, 404, 409, 42▮
430, 435, 443, 457, 461, 464, 475, 47▮
484, 490, 528, 535, 543, 566, 590, 61▮
616, 628, 645, 668, 690, 697, 708, 71(
756, 768, 770, 779, 798, 801, 821, 83(
863, 876, 885, 888, 892, 897, 917, 94▮
957, 958, 985, 986, 993, 1021, 1044
Incest 79, 201, 226, 250, 310, 380, 436▮
536, 722, 794, 827, 852, 949, 1035
Incidence: child abuse 38, 43, 58, 93, 116▮
161, 183, 202, 205, 228, 234, 313, 327▮
389, 394, 414, 415, 437, 461, 497, 533▮
537, 539, 542, 543, 566, 573, 578, 616▮
668, 717, 756, 779, 793, 805, 826, 841▮
844, 872, 885, 890, 893, 900, 904, 1026▮
1030, 1043, 1052; family violence 49▮
108, 112, 931, 1000; spouse abuse 68▮
115, 305, 306, 315, 320, 336, 407, 432▮
446, 557, 658, 666, 845, 926, 982, 983
Index of Spouse Abuse 492
International Society of Family Law 722
Intervention: child abuse 10, 92, 153, 156▮
200, 215, 246, 259, 264, 342, 371, 424▮
425, 427, 444, 456, 466, 493, 517, 590▮

622, 661, 680, 681, 689, 698, 761, 768, 770, 780, 841, 900, 966; family violence 46, 47, 48, 49, 54, 270, 277, 912, 1001; spouse abuse 82, 252, 318, 557, 769, 812, 854, 933

Inventory of Marital Conflict 727

Legal aspects: child abuse 7, 9, 16, 22, 26, 28, 32, 44, 45, 72, 84, 87, 104, 106, 109, 110, 113, 115, 123, 126, 129, 137, 139, 141, 158, 161, 162, 164, 165, 168, 169, 173, 174, 179, 187, 193, 194, 196, 200, 202, 209, 212, 222, 223, 225, 227, 234, 238, 240, 246, 248, 253, 257, 261, 265, 280, 294, 300, 302, 312, 313, 323, 326, 329, 331, 332, 335, 337, 339, 343, 344, 346, 358, 394, 400, 409, 415, 419, 421, 431, 437, 438, 439, 440, 441, 449, 461, 481, 482, 490, 491, 498, 501, 506, 521, 526, 528, 529, 539, 547, 549, 555, 564, 584, 603, 638, 642, 644, 645, 651, 659, 660, 664, 683, 693, 696, 697, 701, 718, 721, 746, 752, 753, 762, 772, 774, 776, 784, 792, 795, 796, 798, 799, 802, 825, 841, 849, 860, 869, 893, 894, 901, 902, 903, 947, 948, 950, 951, 954, 956, 961, 963, 971, 975, 978, 986, 995, 1008, 1014, 1022, 1025, 1033, 1038, 1043, 1044; family, violence 46, 47, 48, 49, 50, 51, 54, 61, 107, 145, 248, 295, 378, 633, 643, 704, 732, 747, 748, 791, 912; spouse abuse 68, 74, 96, 115, 130, 172, 190, 206 216, 229, 232, 243, 244, 248, 266, 274 275, 290, 298, 305, 306, 307, 308, 309, 311, 314, 317, 336, 348, 350, 357, 376, 385, 407, 418, 432, 434, 489, 500, 504, 510, 544, 545, 554, 557, 568, 583, 607, 612, 617, 618, 620, 639, 641, 663, 667, 673, 685, 691, 694, 705, 737, 775, 804, 808, 815, 817, 818, 819, 836, 837, 840, 845, 846, 880, 933, 937, 955, 964, 979, 982, 983, 984, 992, 996, 1003, 1015, 1018, 1023, 1027, 1032

Limbo 29

Management: child abuse 2, 4, 15, 36, 67, 70, 83, 114, 160, 173, 196, 197, 202, 208, 214, 265, 270, 280, 281, 282, 294, 319, 324, 330, 337, 340, 423, 433, 536, 537, 542, 543, 552, 564, 576, 582, 585, 593, 678, 699, 700, 702, 703, 729, 755, 785, 821, 828, 843, 888, 895, 896, 900,

1040, 1053; family violence 48, 51, 108, 270, 633, 942, 973, 985, 1000, 1014; spouse abuse 68, 229, 266, 270, 351, 354, 376, 378, 381, 432, 442, 511, 559, 592, 610, 641, 803, 814, 858, 871, 873, 930, 979, 997, 1010, 1020, 1024

Maternal instinct 35

Medical aspects: child abuse 37, 42, 52, 86, 90, 107, 109, 114, 149, 158, 163, 167, 169, 195, 196, 230, 234, 245, 260, 281, 286, 294, 303, 313, 324, 328, 329, 331, 339, 352, 353, 362, 394, 414, 423, 433, 437, 449, 460, 461, 462, 464, 465, 478, 565, 585, 588, 603, 613, 623, 625, 638, 640, 649, 650, 670, 701, 708, 714, 733, 746, 765, 798, 792, 794, 811, 849, 856, 862, 898, 902, 903, 908, 917, 950, 957, 958, 959, 969, 971, 1014, 1021; spouse abuse 309, 377, 432, 467, 633, 719, 775, 833, 837, 918, 1015

Mejia, Idalia 808

Men's Aid 655

Military families, child abuse in 4, 15, 155; spouse abuse in 836, 1020

Model Child Protection Act 329

Mothers Anonymous 540, 1054

National Alliance for the Prevention and Treatment of Child Abuse and Maltreatment 259

National Center for Child Abuse and Neglect 650, 672

National Center for the Prevention and Treatment of Child Abuse and Neglect 304, 379

National Center on Women and Family Law 691

National Coalition Against Domestic Violence 152

National Commission on the Causes and Prevention of Violence 931

National Society for the Prevention of Cruelty to Children 36

New York Society for the Prevention of Cruelty to Children 247, 584, 963

Parens Patriae 963

Parent Aids 540

Parents, abuse of 58

Parents Anonymous 142, 189, 343, 471, 743, 920

The Parents Center Project 62, 363

Parents' and Children's Services Program for the Study and Prevention of Child Abuse 63

Park Slope Safe Homes Project 62, 363

Patriarchy 243, 737

Pennsylvania Coalition Against Domestic Violence 392

Pennsylvania Society to Protect Children From Cruelty 231

Physical abuse, self-inflicted 23, 450

Pizzey, Erin 881

Political aspects 8, 226, 487, 568, 617, 889

Pornography 235, 380, 836

Post Partum Depression 31

Power 68, 416, 436, 620, 634, 778, 786, 844, 852, 940, 942

Pregnancy 11, 387

Prevention: child abuse 2, 4, 3, 18, 32, 34, 36, 57, 65, 66, 67, 86, 92, 101, 116, 117, 118, 119, 120, 121, 139, 143, 147, 149, 155, 169, 195, 202, 204, 205, 208, 213, 214, 223, 227, 234, 242, 263, 281, 282, 303, 304, 321, 323, 329, 330, 331, 333, 334, 335, 338, 352, 363, 365, 379, 383, 394, 397, 398, 399, 400, 402, 412, 444, 456, 471, 482, 493, 499, 503, 505, 513, 526, 527, 531, 534, 536, 538, 542, 569, 578, 586, 590, 595, 596, 601, 604, 616, 648, 650, 659, 668, 670, 680, 681, 698, 703, 712, 715, 717, 722, 724, 728, 733, 703, 712, 715, 717, 722, 724, 728, 733, 735, 743, 752, 753, 756, 766, 774, 794, 797, 816, 876, 890, 892, 893, 900, 901, 943, 957, 986, 989, 998, 1012, 1022, 1037, 1048; family violence 51, 54, 58, 108, 417, 634, 732, 747, 965, 1000; spouse abuse 53, 60, 152, 188, 306, 357, 407, 445, 489, 504, 511, 568, 572, 592, 607, 620, 685, 707, 750, 777, 797, 803, 838, 938, 952, 980, 992, 1031

Prostitution 235, 380

Protection From Abuse Act (Pennsylvania) 1032

Protective services, child abuse 7, 9, 11, 19, 29, 40, 43, 45, 65, 67, 70, 78, 84, 89, 138, 140, 144, 156, 168, 173, 182, 196, 200, 208, 215, 219, 225, 226, 230, 231, 236, 237, 249, 263, 270, 278, 295, 300, 302, 313, 323, 335, 337, 339, 340, 400, 409, 413, 433, 439, 440, 441, 454, 473, 476, 477, 483, 484, 490, 503, 513, 518, 528, 538, 549, 562, 565, 579, 581, 585, 603, 609, 611, 626, 647, 669, 672, 690, 698, 719, 729, 736, 771, 775, 781, 782, 783, 792, 794, 801, 813, 828, 835, 841, 851, 876, 885, 886, 889, 893, 896, 944, 945, 950, 954, 963, 971, 985, 1014, 1030, 1038, 1052, 1055

Psychological aspects: child abuse 36, 62, 71, 76, 95, 101, 113, 122, 132, 149, 151, 155, 178, 195, 222, 231, 261, 265, 269, 271, 284, 285, 287, 289, 292, 294, 301, 316, 334, 337, 361, 368, 382, 393, 394, 396, 402, 426, 430, 459, 468, 382, 393, 394, 396, 402, 426, 430, 459, 468, 475, 478, 484, 488, 495, 499, 541, 546, 576, 588, 608, 613, 622, 623, 628, 630, 631, 670, 671, 676, 677, 724, 725, 734, 766, 785, 790, 801, 822, 823, 827, 875, 903, 904, 922, 923, 940, 949, 953, 994, 1011, 1044, 1045, 1046; family violence 914, 942, 1039; spouse abuse 41, 82, 199, 309, 318, 375, 391, 432, 787, 831, 832, 834, 847, 873, 887, 916, 996, 1002, 1004, 1005, 1017, 1027

Psychosocial Deprivation 551

Public services: family violence 739, 965, 973; spouse abuse 55, 81, 190, 243, 270, 277, 314, 315, 351, 378, 392, 427, 466, 511, 583, 592, 594, 617, 618, 620, 674, 692, 695, 706, 831, 836, 983, 1020

Queens Bench Foundation 792

Rainbow Retreat 619

Rape 61, 68, 130, 134, 193, 206, 290, 360, 380, 385, 489, 536, 612, 786, 845, 853, 870, 1023

Religious aspects 244, 256, 347, 358, 470, 916, 1014

Reporting: child abuse 4, 27, 37, 43, 44, 56, 84, 85, 87, 88, 119, 120, 127, 128, 167, 175, 176, 179, 191, 194, 223, 224, 225, 235, 236, 246, 250, 268, 270, 323, 342, 343, 344, 345, 368, 372, 404, 429, 437, 440, 449, 465, 502, 506, 529, 543, 547, 555, 564, 578, 593, 616, 638, 645, 689, 690, 697, 710, 752, 753, 754, 784, 792, 798, 825, 849, 860, 863, 884, 894, 947, 950, 951, 958, 963, 985, 986, 987, 1022,

1030, 1043, 1044, 1052; spouse abuse 592, 720, 925

Resources 123, 211, 222, 226, 267, 270, 314, 327, 350, 658, 691, 985, 1010

Rights of children 66, 186, 233, 253, 326, 332, 440, 542, 626, 710, 783, 794, 799, 802, 829, 872, 961

Rights of parents 238, 239, 253, 491, 529, 721, 783, 799, 829, 948, 961, 963, 991

Rights of Privacy 67

Santa Barbara County District Attorney 295

Santa Clara Child Sexual Abuse Treatment Program 1016

School, role of 19, 65, 116, 118, 119, 120, 191, 250, 304, 333, 369, 404, 435, 566, 593, 616, 697, 717, 816, 863, 888, 1012

Second International Congress on Child Abuse and Neglect 341

Select Committee on Violence in Marriage and the Family (Great Britain) 641, 737, 998

Senate Subcommittee on Children and Youth 672

Severe Violence Index 941

Sex Offender and Rape Victim Center (Philadelphia) 766

Sexual abuse of children 114, 130, 135, 224, 289, 310, 312, 380, 430, 431, 436, 505, 506, 536, 542, 601, 648, 766, 792, 794, 801, 844, 852, 853, 869, 870, 885, 946, 953, 1009, 1016

Shelters 22, 74, 190, 226, 243, 266, 308, 314, 336, 392, 442, 453, 514, 516, 571, 583, 610, 617, 618, 619, 657, 666, 694, 738, 744, 749, 775, 803, 810, 812, 814, 880, 881, 916, 952, 983, 984, 1005, 1010, 1022

Sibling abuse 5, 58, 509, 883, 942, 974

Single parents 499

Social aspects: child abuse 17, 147, 178, 181, 182, 186, 189, 222, 281, 283, 284, 285, 287, 291, 310, 329, 334, 335, 338, 358, 365, 366, 367, 368, 369, 370, 373, 382, 383, 386, 393, 394, 396, 398, 400, 402, 403, 408, 410, 439, 441, 451, 487, 499, 541, 548, 565, 567, 578, 601, 609, 624, 630, 659, 681, 682, 698, 701, 711, 736, 763, 764, 765, 774, 783, 799, 842,

848, 852, 869, 902, 903, 907, 919, 921, 927, 928, 940, 950, 963, 990, 991, 994, 1011, 1016, 1048; family violence 107, 150, 388, 416, 417, 452, 486, 614, 635, 913, 914, 929, 932, 935, 939, 942, 1000, 1039; spouse abuse 8, 41, 61, 82, 90, 96, 107, 115, 149, 155, 169, 211, 256, 275, 306, 311, 313, 315, 336, 375, 384, 407, 432, 446, 467, 471, 504, 575, 577, 583, 617, 618, 620, 686, 707, 716, 737, 778, 787, 817, 832, 837, 838, 854, 871, 887, 909, 915, 916, 926, 937, 938, 968, 972, 982, 990, 996, 1002, 1027, 1028, 1036, 1042

Society for the Prevention of Cruelty to Animals 584

Society for the Prevention of Cruelty to Children 795

Spouse Abuse Syndrome 82, 115, 232, 277

Statutes, child abuse: California 419, 799, 1044; Connecticut 44, 884; Hawaii 20, 664; Illinois 1038; Indiana 498; Kansas 772; Maryland 651; Massachusetts 564, 995; Michigan 193; Mississippi 72; New Hampshire 165; New York 247, 302, 696; Nebraska 693, 947; North Carolina 4, 261; Oklahoma 762, 1043; Oregon 246; Pennsylvania 232, 555, 860, 1008; South Dakota 718; Tennessee 87; Texas 440; 660; Washington 438; 721

Statutes, spouse abuse: California 663; Colorado 982; New Jersey 583; New York 418, 510; Pennsylvania 1032

Subculture of Violence 469; 1039

Suicide 6

Szelog, Patricia 955

Tort Actions 20, 216, 644, 846

Treatment: child abuse 3, 10, 11, 12, 21, 24, 32, 33, 45, 52, 62, 70, 71, 78, 83, 92, 93, 97, 98, 100, 101, 103, 109, 111, 125, 127, 140, 142, 146, 160, 163, 167, 169, 171, 181, 182, 184, 185, 189, 192, 204, 210, 219, 220, 230, 237, 259, 265, 278, 279, 288, 289, 294, 301, 313, 321, 323, 324, 330, 334, 337, 342, 343, 379, 383, 397, 405, 413, 422, 424, 426, 429, 431, 433, 454, 455, 456, 457, 461, 463, 472, 473, 465, 479, 483, 487, 490, 499, 503, 504, 506, 517, 518, 520, 522, 523,

527, 536, 537, 538, 539, 540, 542, 543,
552, 573, 596, 653, 659, 665, 675, 677,
678, 688, 698, 702, 703, 708, 709, 722,
726, 731, 733, 734, 760, 766, 768, 779,
785, 794, 800, 801, 813, 828, 830, 848,
850, 851, 853, 855, 856, 860, 864, 874,
879, 890, 891, 897, 902, 922, 923, 945,
946, 957, 958, 960, 966, 967, 974, 976,
977, 989, 993, 1011, 1013, 1016, 1022,
1046, 1051, 1054; family violence 58,
144, 270, 965; spouse abuse 41, 53, 55,
59, 69, 73, 74, 94, 154, 279, 306, 314,
354, 392, 466, 496, 515, 532, 558, 559,
577, 580, 620, 641, 655, 657, 666, 674,
706, 769, 775, 806, 810, 812, 831, 833,
834, 836, 837, 839, 918, 936, 952, 993,
997, 1002, 1003, 1004, 1005, 1007, 1017,
1024

United Nations Declaration of the Rights
of the Child 186

U.S. Senate Committee on Human
Resources. Child and Human
Development 988

Victim-Offender Relationship 108, 289,
298, 417, 684, 847, 864, 932, 953, 987,
1035, 1049

Victim Witness Advocate Program 592

Victims, spouse abuse 1, 59, 64, 211, 243,
364, 374, 432

Violence 22, 49, 170, 416, 417, 439, 446,
503, 533, 587, 636, 845, 872, 919, 932,
940, 970, 987, 1022, 1029, 1039

Wife Beating Index 941

Wilson, Mary Ellen 247, 437, 584

Women's Aid Crisis Refuge 375